JEAN BAUDRILLARD,
Art and Artefact

JEAN BAUDRILLARD,
Art and Artefact

edited by Nicholas Zurbrugg

SAGE Publications
London • Thousand Oaks • New Delhi

18.99

First published 1997

This edition is not for sale in Australia and New Zealand

 SAGE Publications Ltd
6 Bonhill Street
London EC2A 4PU

SAGE Publications Inc
2455 Teller Road
Thousand Oaks, California 91320

SAGE Publications India Pvt Ltd
32, M-Block Market
Greater Kailash – I
New Delhi 110 048

British Library Cataloguing in Publication data

A catalogue record for this book is available from the British
Library.

ISBN: 978-0-7619-5580-1

Library of Congress catalog record available

Typeset by Mayhew Typesetting, Rhayader, Powys

CONTENTS

NOTES ON CONTRIBUTORS

Jean Baudrillard visited Australia from 17 April–8 May 1994, to contribute to the symposium *Baudrillard in the Nineties: The Art of Theory*, and to attend the exhibition of his photographs, *The Ecstasy of Photography*, both held at the Institute of Modern Art, Brisbane, Australia.

Rex Butler is Lecturer in Art History, The Department of Art History, The University of Queensland, Brisbane, Australia and is the editor of *What is Appropriation? An Anthology of Critical Writings on Australian Art in the '80s and '90s* and the author of *An Uncertain Smile*.

Alan Cholodenko is Senior Lecturer in Film Studies, The Department of Fine Arts, The University of Sydney, Australia and is the editor of *The Illusion of Life: Essays on Animation* (1991) and of *Mass Mediauras, Essays on Form, Technics and Media* (Sydney, 1996).

Graham Coulter-Smith is Lecturer in Art Theory, Queensland College of Art, Griffith University, Brisbane, Australia and is the author of *Mike Parr: The Self-Portrait Project* (1994) and associate editor of *Eyeline* art magazine.

Gary Genosko is an independent Canadian researcher living in Kingston Ontario, Canada. He is editor of *The Guattari Reader* (1996) and author of *Baudrillard and Signs* (1994).

Paul Patton is Senior Lecturer in Philosophy, The University of Sydney, Australia and has translated several of Baudrillard's works, including *Simulations*, with Paul Foss and Philip Beitchman (1983) and *The Gulf War Did Not Take Place* (1995), is the author of *Nietzsche, Feminism and Political Theory* (1993) and editor of *Deleuze: A Critical Reader* (1996).

Richard G. Smith is Research Associate in the Department of Geography, University of Loughborough, England. He is currently working on a book entitled *Jean Baudrillard: The End of Postmodernism and Poststructuralism*.

Anne-Marie Willis is Assistant Director of the EcoDesign Foundation, New South Wales, Australia and is the author of *Picturing Australia: A History of Photography* (1988) and *Illusion of Identity: The Art of Nation* (1993).

Nicholas Zurbrugg is Professor of English and Cultural Studies, The Faculty of Humanities, De Montfort University, Leicester, England, and is the author of *Beckett and Proust* (1988), *The Parameters of Postmodernism* (1993) *Critical Vices* and *Positively Postmodern: The Multimedia Muse in America* (1998).

ACKNOWLEDGEMENTS

Most of the essays in this book were first presented in April 1994 at *Baudrillard in the Nineties: The Art of Theory*, a symposium held at the Institute of Modern Art, Brisbane, in conjunction with the opening of *The Ecstasy of Photography* – the first comprehensive retrospective survey of Jean Baudrillard's photographs – prior to its subsequent exhibition at the Museum of Contemporary Art in Sydney, the Experimental Art Foundation in Adelaide and the Australian Centre for Contemporary Art in Melbourne.

Neither this exhibition and symposium nor their resultant publication would have been possible without the visionary collaboration and complicity of Nicholas Tsoutas (then Director of the IMA, now Director of the Art Space, Sydney), a fellow 'art warrior', with whom it was the greatest pleasure and privilege to co-organize and plan these projects.

Particular thanks are also due to the French Ministry of Foreign Affairs in Paris, and to Monsieur Francis Etienne and the Cultural Section of the French Embassy at Canberra for generously supporting every aspect of these initiatives; to Eva Assayag and the Galerie Gerald Piltzer, Paris, for facilitating this exhibition; to the valued solidarity of Professor Ian Howard, Provost and Director: Queensland College of Art, Griffith University, Associate Professor Mark Finnane, Dean: School of Humanities, Griffith University, and Associate Professor Terry Smith and Dr Alan Cholodenko of the Power Institute, the University of Sydney; and more generally, to the velocity of Brisbane – a city still making things happen.

Finally I would like to offer special thanks to all of the contributors to this book; to Annabelle Brooks, Marine Dupuis, Wayne Hudson and Diana Solano for their editorial assistance; to Karen Yarrow and Jennifer Hamilton for word-processing its pages; to Steven Alderton for formatting its design; to Michael Snelling, Director of the IMA, and to Chris Rojek, Robert Rojek and Vanessa Harwood of Sage, for expediting its publication; and last but not least, to the generosity of Jean Baudrillard (without whom . . .) to whom this celebration of his insights and provocations is offered with great gratitude and admiration.

Nicholas Zurbrugg
De Montfort University
Leicester
June 1997

INTRODUCTION: 'Just What Is It That Makes Baudrillard's Ideas So Different, So Appealing?'

NICHOLAS ZURBRUGG

Somewhat like the English pop artist and post-Duchampian, Richard Hamilton, one might well ask the question: 'Just What Is It That Makes Baudrillard's Ideas So Different, So Appealing'?[1]

Why is it, after all, that – as Baudrillard himself remarks – it is not so much Derridean concepts of deconstruction, as his own notions of simulation 'that have been taken up by artists'?[2] For his part, Baudrillard admits, 'Well, I don't know' (*BL*, 166), conceding that from many points of view he is both 'a very bad aesthetic analyst' and some sort of theoretical 'terrorist' (*BL*, 168).

A theoretical *terrorist*? Surely not. For what one confronts in Baudrillard's writing is the kind of catalytic, provocative *anti-terrorism* that one witnesses in the best writings and artwork of the Dadaist poets and painters; resistance, in a word, to the undoubtedly terroristic repression imposed by stagnated, over-conventionalized cultural and intellectual orthodoxies.

It is not so much the margins which are the site of terrorism as the mainstream; a romantic perception to be sure, but one which Goethe's 'Werther' nicely summarizes when remarking that if 'genius so rarely . . . bursts upon us like a raging torrent',

> it is because of the sober gentlemen who reside on either side of the river, whose precious little summerhouses, tulip beds, and vegetable gardens would be ruined by it, and who know so well how to build dams and divert all such threatening danger in good time.[3]

1

To quote from *The Sorrows of Young Werther* in this way is not so much to advocate naive concepts of genius, as to gesture towards the real dangers of naive sobriety, or the incapacity to acknowledge functional exceptions to well-built rules. As Burroughs suggests in his essay 'Just Say No To Drug Hysteria', 'The measure of competence is performance'.[4]

> When told that General Grant was a heavy drinker, Lincoln said: 'Find out what brand of whiskey he drinks, and distribute it to my other generals.'

In much the same way, rather than casting doubt upon Baudrillard's ideas in so far as they seem too distant from c.r. (communicative rationality) or too close to c-p s-f (cyberpunk science fiction), it perhaps makes more sense to ask, firstly:

> *To what extent are Baudrillard's ideas relevant to and illuminating of their subject matter?*

and secondly:

> *If Baudrillard's brands of ideas work effectively, how best can one make such ideas work effectively within one's own investigations?*

However much Baudrillard may deny the issue of whether his ideas have referential relevance, it seems evident that the remarkable impact of his work derives from its double or treble-edged specificity as a systematic anti-system, suggesting alternative ways of thinking about things in general, and elaborating specific ways of reconsidering both past culture and those ongoing cultural practices stretching from the present to the future.

There are therefore two Baudrillards. On the one hand, we have the angel of extermination: the evil genie of cultural termination, announcing the death or disappearance of every imaginable aesthetic or ethical value. On the other hand, we confront the angel of cultural annunciation: the benevolent genie identifying and encouraging the investigation of those 'profound stakes' (*BL*, 57) that Baudrillard associates with: 'little stories . . . little things which start and which have often been the sites of emergence: situations, wit, dreams, *Witz*' (*BL*, 56).

Spotting sites of cultural disappearance among the latest manifestations of trash culture is – as Baudrillard suggests – something altogether too trivial; something too close to the ritual of proving the *déjà vu* and thereby compounding 'a complacency in the truth which one knows where nothing will ever put itself in question, self-verification . . . a tautology' (*BL*, 63).

As Baudrillard's most rigorous writings remind us, the game of 'legislating' cultural decay is 'no longer interesting' (*BL*, 166), whereas the challenge of identifying inspiring sites of emergence is often 'magic' (*BL*, 44). Hence Baudrillard's enthusiasm for 'going straight on to the year 2000', erasing the nineties, as it were, in order 'to play the game on the other side through excess rather than through lack' (*BL*, 22). In Brion Gysin's terms, 'Who cares what "advances" were or were not made in the last ten years. It's always the next ten that count.'[5]

To examine the impact of Baudrillard 'in the nineties' is thus an ambiguous exercise in so far as the emphasis of Baudrillard's vision alternates with alarming unpredictability between the positive and negative extremes of past, present and future, towards . . . what? At best, towards new sites of conceptual emergence, new sites of theoretical emergence, new sites of creative emergence. The most redemptive characteristic of Baudrillard's frequently contradictory analyses of contemporary cultures is his willingness to be surprised; a willingness to undergo, undertake and to engage with the turbulence of contradiction, reversal, self-doubt, self-questioning, and the anguish and elation of *re*-definition, *re*-consideration, *re*-vision; a kind of existential experimentation, which leads one to reflect: 'I've done – or I am doing – such and such, and therefore I'm beginning to *re*-think who I am'.

Consider, for example, Baudrillard's comments upon the exhibition of photographs, 'The Ecstasy of Photography', which occasioned the symposium at the Institute of Modern Art, Brisbane, from which most of these essays have eventuated. Asked what his first impressions were before this exhibition and whether it was something of a shock, Baudrillard replied:

> Yes. It was a great pleasure, and in a certain sense a shock, because it was the first time that I had seen so many. Twenty works were exhibited in Paris and about twenty in Venice. All at once I was conscious that there was something there – it was something new for me. On the one hand, I was disappointed because they seemed more aesthetic and more beautiful than I had believed them to be – and I didn't really want this aesthetic quality. On the other hand I became conscious of building a new vision of my own strange world. I hadn't been conscious of doing that, but I perceived a certain continuity in my work of the last three or four years. Before it was nothing, but over the last three or four years there's a continuity maybe indicating something else – I don't know – and then it became very interesting.[6]

At some level, and perhaps at a different level to that of his theoretical writing, photography clearly revealed the unexpected possibility of 'something else' – 'a new vision of my own strange world' – to this most reluctant of artists. 'I'm not an artist in the usual sense, and I'm not intending to do any particular kind of work . . . it was – and remains – for me a strange practice and is cultivated as such.'

As Baudrillard indicates, he is not so much interested in the ritual of reasserting the banality of the banal, as in locating unexpected traces of enigmacity and charm within the banality of the mass media.

> I was always interested in the balance between the extreme banality of objects and their enigmacity. I was always concerned not to integrate them, but to challenge one with another – the intimacy and strangeness of objects or beings or situations or politics or media. The media are something very banal, very intimate and very domestic in everyday life. But they are at the same time for me something strange, and I'm searching for this strangeness of the media. It's their only charm, since when we take the media as media they are very deluding, very very deceiving. But we can take them as another strange world.

It is precisely this emphasis upon the 'strangeness' of the media and of contemporary cultures, and this attempt to make both photographic and theoretic practices into some kind of strange art or 'strange practice', which most disconcerts Baudrillard's more conservative readers, prompting the conclusions that Baudrillard is either post-theoretical or pre-cyberpunk-fictional, but in neither case altogether *serious*.

To caricature Baudrillard in this way and, ultimately, to discredit Baudrillard in this way, is both to neglect the specific question of determining the relevance of Baudrillard's accounts of the postmodern condition and, reciprocally, to neglect the more immediate dilemma of evaluating the relevance of one's own critical approaches to contemporary culture. Put another way, the decision to 'forget Baudrillard' may well disguise one's own fear and abdication before the task of coming to terms with those disquieting debates and issues which his 'strange practice' attempts to rescue from the terrorism of complacent 'tautology' and 'self-verification' (BL, 63), by somehow passing 'through all the disciplines' (BL, 81) towards what he describes as the conceptual liberation of some 'initiatory space' or 'enchanted space' (BL, 61).

To return to Burroughs' distinction regarding intimidatingly innovative practices, 'The measure of competence is performance' (HR, 73), it seems evident that Baudrillard's theoretical *competence* is quintessentially a process of *performance*; a juggling or shuffling of concepts and values – now seen, now not seen – now under this shell, now somewhere else, beneath that hyper-shell, perhaps. No wonder Baudrillard's live presentations of his ideas are so captivating, because in a very real sense, what one hears is both semantic *son et lumière*: enlightening concepts, as it were, heightened and lightened by seductive sonic play echoing the trails and traces of their conceptual dislocation and relocation.

Not surprisingly, then, Baudrillard strikes many of his contemporaries as a semantic cardsharp, if only because he doesn't 'deal' logically, in the c.r. manner. As Brion Gysin points out, such musical modes of perform-ance invariably antagonize the French establishment:

> New Philosophers, *et al*, have always abominated music. Music is not rational. They prefer ratiocination to which the French language lends itself only too easily *and* utterly unmusically owing to the uniform terminal stress on all French words.[7]

To suggest, then, that there is something poetic, something performa-tive, something musical, in both the structure and the sonic substance of Baudrillard's words is in other words to acknowledge their heuristic significance as a provocative alternative to the more familiar theoretic and phonetic register of 'ratiocination'. *Breaking out* of more orthodox theoretical conventions, Baudrillard frequently initiates what Gary Genosko defines as stimulating kinds of '*break-in*' into innovative areas of cultural investigation beyond the parameters and purview of more cautious discourse. To contemplate such distinctions is perhaps also to begin to explain why so many of the essays in this collection are themselves marked by an undauntable performative impulse, an attempt, perhaps, to play the Baudrillardian game in a manner more (or less) Baudrillardian than Baudrillard; or at least, to entertain, to interrogate, to adopt, to adapt, and perhaps to extend – the advantages of Baudrillard's 'strange practice'.

One way or another, by patient analysis, by analogy, by oblique comparison, by formal play or by informal variation on Baudrillardian themes, all of these essays suggest the ways in which Baudrillard's 'strange practice' is – against all odds – of central relevance to the intellectual, social and cultural climates of the 1990s, if only as the site of so many processes of conceptual 'emergence' from past assumptions, past conventions and past orthodoxies.

In many respects, I sense that what we read here are readings-in-progress of Baudrillard's writings-in-progress; readings with Baudril-lard, and readings against Baudrillard, but in either case, attempts to respond 'on the scale' (*BL*, 125) of the Baudrillardian wager, openly and audaciously, rather than conservatively and defensively. Such catalytic responses to Baudrillard's catalytic provocations can only be advan-tageous when compared with the cautious ossification and prejudice of so much that passes for *contemporary* cultural cartography.

NOTES

1 I refer of course to Richard Hamilton's painting, *Just What Is It That Makes Today's Homes So Different, So Appealing?* (1956).

2 Jean Baudrillard, *Baudrillard Live*, ed. Mike Gane, London: Routledge, 1993, p.166. Henceforth abbreviated as *BL*.

3 Goethe, *The Sorrows of Young Werther* [1774], translated by Catherine Hutter, New York: Signet, 1962, p. 31.

4 William Burroughs, 'Just Say No To Drug Hysteria', in *High Risk*, eds Amy Scholder and Ira Silverberg, New York: Plume, 1991, p.73. Henceforth abbreviated as *HR*.

5 Brion Gysin, letter of 15 August 1979, *Stereo Headphones*, no. 8–9–10, 1982, p. 76.

6 Jean Baudrillard, interview with Nicholas Zurbrugg, Brisbane, 22 April 1994. All subsequent unreferenced statements by Baudrillard are from this interview.

7 Gysin, letter of 15 August 1979.

OBJECTS, IMAGES, AND THE POSSIBILITIES OF AESTHETIC ILLUSION

JEAN BAUDRILLARD

Aesthetic disillusionment. It seems that the most contemporary art culminates in an effort of self-deterrence, in a process of mourning the death of the image and the imaginary, in an aesthetic mourning, that cannot succeed anyway, resulting in a general melancholy in the artistic sphere, which seems to survive by recycling its history. (But art and aesthetics are not the only domains devoted to this melancholic and paradoxical destiny – of living beyond their own finalities.)

It seems that we have been assigned to conduct infinite retrospective analyses of what happened before. This is true for politics, history and ethics, and for art as well, which in this matter has no special privilege. All the movement in painting has been displaced towards the past. Employing quotation, simulation, reappropriation, it seems that contemporary art is about to reappropriate all forms or works of the past, near or far – or even contemporary forms – in a more or less ludic or kitsch fashion. What Russell Connor calls 'the abduction of modern art'.

Of course, all of this remaking and recycling claim to be ironic; but this form of irony is like a threadbare piece of cloth – a by-product of disillusion – a fossilized irony. The trick that consists in juxtaposing the nude in Manet's *Déjeuner sur l'herbe* with Cézanne's card players is only a publicity stunt, part of the irony, or the *trompe-l'oeil* criticism which characterizes publicity today, and which is about to submerge the artistic world.

It's the irony of repentance and resentment against our own culture. But perhaps repentance and resentment constitute the ultimate phase of art history, just as, according to Nietzsche, they constitute the ultimate phase in the genealogy of morals. It's a parody, and at the same time a palinody of art and art history, a self-parody of culture in the form of revenge, characteristic of radical disillusion. It's as if art, like history, was recycling its own garbage and looking for its redemption in its own detritus.

Consider, for example, the way certain films (*Barton Fink, Basic Instinct*, Greenaway's works, *Sailor and Lula*, etc.) leave no place for criticism because, in some way, they destroy themselves from within. Quotation crazy, prolix, high-tech, they carry with them the cancer of cinema, the internal *excroissance*, proliferation of their own technique, of their own scenography or of their own cinematographic culture. We feel as if these directors were repelled by their own films, that they couldn't stand them (whether through excess of ambition or lack of imagination). Nothing else justifies the orgy of means and the efforts to cancel films through an excess of virtuosity, special effects, megalomaniac angles – the technical harassment of the images – by exhausting their effects to the point of making a sarcastic parody out of it, a veritable pornography of the image. Everything seems to be programmed for the disillusionment of the spectator, for whom no other choice is left than that of enduring this excess of cinema, this end to all cinematic illusion.

What can one say about the cinema, if not that now – almost at the end of its evolution, of its technical progress, from silent movies to talkies, colour, high technology and special effects – its capacity for illusion, in the radical sense of the word, has vanished. Current cinema is no longer related to allusion or illusion; it connects everything in a super-tech, super-efficient, super-visual style. No void, no ellipsis, no silence – nothing more than what you get on television, which film resembles more and more as it loses the specificity of its images. We're going more and more in the direction of high definition, that is to say, towards the useless perfection of the image – which is no longer an image. The more it becomes real, the more it is produced in real time, the more we approach absolute definition, or the realistic perfection of the image, the more the image's power of illusion is lost.

Just remember the Peking Opera, and how with only the movement of two bodies on a vessel, it brings alive the whole space of a river. How two bodies struggling in a duel, avoiding each other, moving near each other without touching, in an invisible copulation, can mime the physical presence of darkness on the stage where this fight takes place. Here the illusion is total and intense, more than aesthetic, a physical ecstasy, because it eludes all realistic presence of the night and the river, and only the bodies assume the natural illusion. Today we would bring tons of real water on to the stage, the duel would be filmed in infra-red and so forth. We confront the misery of the over-technical image, like the Gulf War on CNN. Pornography of the image in three or four dimensions, or of music with three or four or twenty-four tracks. It's always by adding to the real, by adding the real to the real with the objective of obtaining a perfect illusion (that of the perfect realistic stereotype), that we kill profound illusion.

An image is an abstraction of the world in two dimensions. It takes away a dimension from the real world, and by this very fact the image inaugurates the power of illusion. On the other hand, virtuality, by making us *enter* into the image, by recreating a realistic image in three dimensions (and even in adding a sort of fourth dimension to the real, so as to make it in some way hyperreal), destroys this illusion (the equivalent of this operation in time is 'real time', which makes the loop of time close up on itself instantaneously, and thus abolishes all illusion of the past as well as of the future). Virtuality tends toward the perfect illusion. But it isn't the same creative illusion as that of the image. It is a 'recreating' illusion (as well as a recreational one), revivalistic, realistic, mimetic, hologrammatic. It abolishes the game of illusion by the perfection of the reproduction, in the virtual rendition of the real. And so we witness the extermination of the real by its double.

By contrast, *trompe-l'oeil*, by taking away a dimension from real objects, highlights their presence and their magic through the simple unreality of their minimal exactness. *Trompe-l'oeil* is the ecstasy of the real object in its immanent form. It adds to the formal charm of painting the spiritual charm of the lure, the mystification of the senses. For the sublime is not enough, we must have the subtle too, the spirit which consists in reversing the real in its very place. This is what we have unlearned from modernity – subtraction is what gives strength; power emerges from the absence. We produce, we accumulate. And because we can no more assume the symbolic mastery of absence we are plunged today into the inverse illusion, the disenchanted proliferation of screens and the profusion of images.

It is very difficult to speak of painting today because it is very difficult to *see* it. Because generally it no longer wants exactly to be *looked at*, but to be absorbed visually without leaving any traces. In some way modern painting could be characterized as the simplified aesthetic form of the impossible exchange. So that the best discourse about painting would be a discourse where there is nothing to say, which would be the equivalent of a painting where there is nothing to see. The equivalent of an object, the object of art, that isn't an object any more.

However, an object which isn't an object is not nothing. One becomes obsessed by its immanence, its void and its immaterial presence. The problem is to materialize this nothingness, at the very limit of the void, to trace the mark of this void, and within the limits of indifference to play the game according to the mysterious rules of indifference.

Art is never the mechanical reflection of the positive or negative conditions of the world; it is its exacerbated illusion or hyperbolic mirror. In a world ruled by indifference, art can only add to this indifference, by focusing the void of the image or the object that isn't an object any more. Thus the cinema of Wenders, Jarmusch, Antonioni, Altman, Godard or Warhol explores the insignificance of the world through the image, and by its images contributes to the insignificance of the world – they add to its real or hyperreal illusion. Whereas recent cinema like that of the latest Scorsese, Greenaway, etc. with its high-tech machinery, and its frantic and eclectic agitation, only fills the void of the image, and thus adds to our imaginary disillusion.

Exactly like the Simulationists of New York who, by hypostasizing the simulacrum, are only hypostasizing painting itself as a simulacrum, as a machine defeating itself. In many cases (Bad Painting, New New Painting, installations and performances) painting denies itself, parodies itself, rejects itself. Plasticized, vitrified, frozen excrement, or garbage. It does not even justify a *glance*. It doesn't look at you, and so in turn you don't need to look at it; it is no longer your concern. This painting has become completely indifferent to itself as painting, as art, as illusion more powerful than the real. It doesn't believe any longer in its own illusion, and so it falls into the simulation of itself and into derision.

Abstraction was the great adventure of modern art. In its 'irruptive', primitive and original phase, whether expressionist or geometric, it was still part of an heroic history of painting, of the deconstruction of representation and of the object. By volatilizing its object, the subject of painting itself advanced towards the limits of its own disappearance. By contrast, the forms of contemporary abstraction (and this is true also of the New Figuration) have passed beyond this revolutionary acting out, beyond this act of disappearance – they simply reflect the undifferentiated field of our daily life, the banality of the images which have informed our social practices. The New Abstraction and the New Figuration oppose each other only formally – in fact they both equally retrace the total disincarnation of our world, no longer in its dramatic phase, but in its banal phase.

The abstraction of our world is a matter of fact now, when all the art forms in an indifferent world are assigned to the same indifference. This is neither denigration nor depreciation; it's simply the state of things. Authentic contemporary painting has to be as indifferent to itself as the world is once the essential issues have vanished. Art is generally nothing more than the metalanguage of banality. *Can this anti-dramatic simulation evolve or revolve, or last for ever?* Whatever forms it takes, we are already on the way towards the psychodrama of disappearance and transparency. We must not be lured and trapped by a false continuity in art and the history of art.

To rephrase Benjamin, there is an aura of simulacrum – just as for him there was an aura of the original. There is an authentic form of simulation as well as an inauthentic form of simulation. This may seem paradoxical but it's true. When Warhol painted his Campbell Soups in the 1960s, this was a breakthrough for simulation, and for all modern art. All at once the merchandise-object and the merchandise-sign were raised up to an ironical consecration, which is indeed the only ritual left to us, the ritual of transparency. But when he painted the Soup Boxes in '86, he only reproduced the stereotype of simulation.

In '65 he attacked the concept of originality in an original way. In '86 he reproduced the unoriginal in an unoriginal way. The year 1965 witnessed the aesthetic traumatism of the entry of merchandise into art – in short the geniality of merchandise. The evil genie of merchandise raised a new geniality in art – the genie of simulation. Nothing of this in '86, when the genie of advertising merely illustrated a new phase of merchandise. Once again official art fell back into the cynical and sentimental aestheticization that Baudelaire stigmatized.

Would it be any superior form of irony to do the same thing twenty years later? I don't believe so. I believe in the evil genius of simulation, but I don't believe in its ghost. Or in its cadaver, even in stereo. I know that in a few centuries there will be no difference between a real Pompeiian villa and the Paul Getty museum in Malibu, nor any difference between the French Revolution and its Olympic commemoration in Los Angeles in 1989, but *we* are still referring to this difference.

Here is the dilemma – either simulation is irreversible and there is nothing beyond simulation, in that simulation isn't even an event any more, but is our absolute banality, our everyday obscenity, so that we are now in definitive nihilism, awaiting the future rewriting of all pre-existing forms and also waiting for another unforeseeable event – but from where will it come? Or, on the other hand, there is an art of simulation, an ironic quality that evokes the appearances of the world in order to let them vanish again. If not, art won't be anything other than aesthetic harassment, as so often happens today. We must not add the same to the same, and then to the same again: that is poor simulation. We must expel the same from the same. Each image must take something away from the reality of the world; in each image something must disappear.

But this disappearance must be a challenge, and that's the secret of art and seduction: it must never totally succeed. In art – in contemporary art as well as in classical art – there is a double postulation and thus a double strategy. A compulsion to nothingness and to erase all the traces of the world and reality, along with an inverse resistance to this impulse. According to Michaux, the artist is 'he who resists with all his strength the fundamental impulse to leave no traces'.

Art has become iconoclastic. Modern iconoclasm no longer consists in breaking images, but in producing images, a profusion of *images where there is nothing to see*. These are literally images which leave no traces. Properly speaking, they are without aesthetic consequence. But, behind each of them, something has disappeared. Here is their secret, if they have one. And here is the secret of simulation. On the horizon of simulation, not only has the real world disappeared, but the very question of its existence no longer makes sense.

This was the very problem of Byzantine iconoclasm. The Iconoclasts were subtle people who pretended to represent God for His greater glory, but who, in reality, simulated God in images, and through this dissimulated the very problem of His existence. Each image was a pretext to not confront the problem of God's existence. Behind each image in fact, God had disappeared. He was not dead – He had simply disappeared. That is, the problem no longer needed to be raised. The problem of the existence or the non-existence of God was resolved by simulation.

But perhaps it was the strategy of God Himself to disappear behind His images, and perhaps God uses his own images in order to disappear, Himself obeying the impulse to leave no traces. Thus the prophecy is realized; we live in a world of simulation, in a world where the highest function of the sign is to make reality disappear, and at the same time to mask this disappearance. Art does nothing else. The media today do nothing else. That is why art and the media follow the same course, and often become confused with one another.

Behind the orgy of images something is hidden. The world is hiding behind the profusion of images; perhaps it's another form of illusion, an ironic one. As Canetti suggests in his parable about animals, behind each of them it seems that someone human is hidden and is secretly mocking you.

The illusion which proceeds from the capacity, through the invention of forms, to escape from the real, to oppose another scene to the real one, to pass to the other side of the mirror – the illusion which invents another game with other rules – is now impossible, because images have passed over into things. They are no longer the mirror of reality, they are living in the heart of reality – aliens, no more reflecting, but haunting reality – and have transformed it into hyperreality, where, from screen to screen, the only destiny of the image is the image itself. The image cannot imagine the real any longer, because it has become the real. It can no longer transcend reality, transfigure it, nor dream it, because it has become its own virtual reality.

In virtual reality it's as if things had swallowed their mirrors, and then become transparent to themselves. They no longer have any secret, and they cannot create illusion (because illusion is linked to the secret, to the fact that things are absent from themselves, withdrawing themselves in their own appearances). Nothing remains here but transparency, with things totally present to themselves in their visibility, in their virtuality, in their perfect transcription (in numerical terms, in the newest technologies), on a screen, on millions of screens, on the horizon of which the real, but also the image, has disappeared. All the utopias of the nineteenth and twentieth centuries have, by realizing themselves, expelled the reality out of reality and left us in a hyperreality devoid of sense, since all final perspective has been absorbed, leaving as a residue only a surface without depth. Could it be that technology is the only force today that connects the sparse fragments of the real? But what has become of the constellation of sense? And what about the constellation of the secret?

The end of representation, the end of aesthetics, the end of the image itself in the superficial virtuality of the screen. But here is a perverse and paradoxical effect. It seems that while illusion and utopia have been eradicated by the impact of all our technologies, by virtue of these same technologies, *irony itself has passed into things*. There appears to be a counterpart to the loss of illusion of the world, namely the irruption of *objective irony* in this world. Irony as the universal and spiritual form of the disillusion of the world. Spiritual in the sense of *Witz*, of spirit arising from the very heart of the technical banality of our objects and our images. The Japanese feel a divinity in every industrial object. For us this transcendental feeling is reduced to a little ironic glimmer, but even so it is still a spiritual form. For we pagans and agnostics, irony is all that is left of the sacred.

It's no longer either a subjective irony or a romantic one. It is no longer a function of the subject, a critical mirror where the uncertainty and irrationality of the world is reflected. It is the mirror of the world itself, of this objectal and artificial world around us, wherein is reflected the very absence and transparence of the subject. After the critical function of the subject comes the ironic function of the object. Since they are produced as objects, artefacts, signs, merchandise, things assume an artificial and ironic function by their very presence. No need to project irony into the real world, no need for a distorting mirror to hold up the image of its double.

Our universe has swallowed its double, and it has lost its shadow. The irony of this double breaks through at each moment, in each fragment of our signs, our objects, our images, our models. It is no longer even necessary, as the Surrealists did, to highlight functionality, to confront objects with the absurdity of their function, in a poetic unreality. Objects highlight themselves ironically by themselves, they get out of balance without effort. There is no need to emphasize their artifice or their nonsense. This is all part of their interconnection, of their superfluity (i.e. overfluidity), which creates an effect of parody.

After physics and metaphysics we deal now with a pataphysics of objects and merchandise, a pataphysics of signs and operations. All things, deprived of their secret and their illusion, are assigned to a radical visibility, to the objective make-believe assigned to publicity. Our world is publicity-oriented in its essence (or rather in its transparence). Such as it is, it is as if it has been invented for advertising, promoting itself for another world. We must not believe that advertising came *after* merchandise. In the heart of merchandise and by extension, at the heart of our entire universe of signs, there is an *evil genie of publicity*, a trickster, who has integrated the buffoonery of merchandise and of its scenery. A genial scriptwriter (perhaps capitalism itself) has involved the world in a phantasmagorical game where we are all fascinated victims and gamblers at the same time.

All objects wish to present themselves today, just as human beings, technical objects, industrial objects, media objects, artefacts of all kinds want to signify, to be seen, to be read, to be recorded, to have their own look, to be photographed. You believe you are taking a photograph for your own pleasure. In fact it's the object that wants to be photographed, and you're only a medium in its reproduction, secretly attracted and motivated by this self-promoting surrounding world. Here is the irony of the situation, what I would like to call the pataphysical irony of the situation.

All metaphysics is in effect swept away by this reversal of situation where the subject is no longer at the origin of the process, and no longer anything but the agent, or the operator, of the objective irony of the world. The subject no longer provides the representation of the world (I will be your mirror!). It is the object that refracts the subject, and subtly, through all our technologies, imposes its presence and its aleatory form.

The subject no longer determines the rules of the game. Something happened, like a reversal in the relationship. The power of the object breaks through the game of simulation and simulacra, through the very artifice that we have imposed upon it. Here we see something like an ironic revenge; the object becomes a *strange attractor*. Here we have the limit of aesthetic adventure, of the aesthetic mastery of the world by the subject (but at the same time, the end of the adventure of representation, of the mastery of the world by will and representation). For the object as a strange attractor is no more an aesthetic object. Stripped by technique itself of any secret and illusion, stripped of its origins (since it has been generated by models), stripped of all connotation of sense or judgement of value, the object, exorbitated (i.e. escaped from the orbit of the subject) becomes in some way a *pure object* reintegrating the immediacy, the immanence of earlier forms, before or after the general aestheticization of our culture.

All these artefacts, all these artificial objects and images exercise a form of irradiation, of fascination, upon us. They re-become a kind of material evidence, like fetishes perhaps, at once completely depersonalized and desymbolized, and yet, of maximal intensity, directly invested as a medium, just as the fetish-object is, without aesthetic mediation. It is here perhaps that our most superficial objects, our most stereotypical ones, assume the power of exorcism like sacrificial masks. Exactly as masks absorb the identity of the actors, of the dancers and of the spectators, they provoke a sort of thaumaturgical (traumaturgical?) vertigo.

Thus all these modern artefacts, from publicity to electronics, from the mediatized to the virtual, objects, images, models, networks, have a function of absorbing the identity of the subject much more than a function of communication or information, as is usually said. Barbara Kruger: WE SHALL BE YOUR FAVOURITE DISAPPEARING ACT!

Thus, very much beyond the aesthetic form, these objects join the aleatory and the vertiginous form of games that Caillois contrasts with games of representation, whether mimetic or aesthetic. Objects, these modern simulacra, thus reflect the society in which we are living as well, a society of paroxysm and exorcism. That is, a place where we have absorbed our own reality and our own identity to the point of vertigo, and where we try to eject it with the same force – where all reality has absorbed its own double – and struggle to expel it at any price.

These banal objects, these technical objects, these virtual objects, thus seem to be the new strange attractors, the new objects beyond aesthetics, transaesthetic – fetish-objects, without signification, without illusion, without aura, without value – the perfect mirror of our radical disillusion of the world. Pure objects, ironical objects, just like Warhol's images.

Andy Warhol worked with any image available, in order to eliminate the imaginary and to make a pure visual product of it. Unconditional simulacrum. Steve Miller (and all those who are reprogramming the video-image, the scientific cliché and the synthesized image 'aesthetically') does exactly the opposite. They make art with anti-art material. They *use* the machine to remake art. He (Warhol) *is* a machine. The true technical metabolism is Warhol; Steve Miller only simulates the machine and he uses technique in order to make illusion. Warhol gives us the very illusion of technique – *technique as radical illusion* – far superior today to that of painting.

In this sense, even a machine can become famous, and Warhol never aspired to anything but this mechanical celebrity, without consequence and without trace. A photogenic celebrity simply related to the demand of everything, of every individual to be seen, and to be selected and acknowledged. That is what Warhol does; he is only the agent for the ironic disappearance of things. He is only the medium for this huge publicity which the world makes for itself through technique, through images, forcing our imagination to surrender, breaking the mirror that we are holding up to it, hypocritically, in order to capture it for our profit.

Through images, through technical artefacts of all sorts, of which those of Warhol are the modern ideal-type, it is the world that imposes its discontinuity on us, its fragmentation, its stereophony, its artificial instantaneousness. Evidence of the Warhol machine, this extraordinary machine filtering the material evidence of the world. Warhol's images are not banal because they reflect a banal world, but because they result from the absence of any claim by the subject to be able to interpret the world. They result from the elevation of the image to pure figuration, without the least transfiguration. No transcendence any more, but a potentialization of the sign, which, losing all natural signification, shines in the void with all its artificial splendour. Warhol is the first to introduce modern fetishism, transaesthetic illusion, that of an image as such, without quality, a presence without desire.

But what are modern artists doing, anyway? The artists of the Renaissance believed that they were making religious pictures while in fact they were creating artworks. Are our modern artists, who believe they are producing artworks, not doing something completely different? Could it be that the objects they produce are something completely different from art? Fetish-objects for example, but disenchanted ones, purely decorative objects (Roger Caillois would say: hyperbolic ornaments). Objects that are literally superstitious in the sense that they no longer assume the sublime nature of art nor a belief in art, but which nevertheless keep the idea and superstition of art alive. The same process as sexual fetishism, which is itself sexually disinvolved. The fetishist denies both the reality of sex and sexual pleasure. He doesn't believe in sex, only in the idea of sex (which itself of course is asexual). In the same way we no longer believe in art, but only in the idea of art (which for itself of course is not aesthetic, but ideological).

This is why art, being nothing more than an idea, is now working on ideas. The bottle rack of Duchamp is an idea; the Campbell's box by Warhol is an idea; Yves Klein selling air for a blank cheque in a gallery, this is an idea. All these are ideas, signs, allusions, concepts. This no longer means anything at all; but it signifies anyway. What we call art today seems to witness an unavoidable void. Art is tranvested by ideas, and ideas are tranvested by art. It's our form of transexuality, of transvestism enlarged to the whole field of art and culture. Equally transexual are those kinds of art crossed by an idea, crossed by the empty signs of art, and by the signs of their own disappearance.

All modern art is abstract in the sense that it is crossed by the idea far more than it is crossed by the imagination of forms and substances. All modern art is conceptual in the sense that it fetishizes the concept, the stereotype of a cerebral model of art, exactly as that which is fetishized in merchandise is not the real value, but an abstract stereotype of value.

Dedicated to this fetishist and decorative ideology, art no longer has an existence of its own. In this sense we might say that we are on the way to the disappearance of art as a specific activity. This may lead us either to a reversion of art into technique and pure artisanal quality, possibly transferred into the sphere of electronics, as we can see everywhere today. Or towards a primary ritualism, where everything will be used as an aesthetic gadget, and art will end up as universal kitsch, exactly as religious art in its time ended up as Saint-Sulpicien kitsch. Who knows? Art as such may only have been a parenthesis, a sort of ephemeral luxury of the species. The distressing thing is that this crisis of art will probably last for ever. And the difference between Warhol and all those who comfort themselves in this perpetual crisis is that with Warhol the crisis of art is over and virtually obsolete.

Is there still any aesthetic illusion? And if not, is the way open to a transaesthetic illusion? To a radical one, that of the secret, of seduction, of magic? Is there still, within our hypervisibility, transparence, virtuality, a place for an image? A place for an enigma? A place for the real events of perception, a place for an effective power of illusion, a true strategy of forms and appearances?

Despite the modern mythology of a liberation of forms, we must say that forms and figures cannot be liberated, cannot be free. Our task is not to free them, but to capture them, to make them relate to each other and to generate each other.

Objects whose secret is not in the 'centrifugal' expression of their representative form (or deformation), but on the contrary, in their attraction towards the centre and in their subsequent dispersion into the cycle of metamorphosis. There are two ways of achieving, of going beyond representation: either that of its endless deconstruction where painting looks at itself dying, in a sort of umbilical nostalgia, always reflecting its lost history. Or, simply to give up representation, forgetting all the trouble of interpretation, forgetting the critical violence of sense and counter-sense, in order to join the matrix of the appearance of things and the matrix of the distribution of forms.

This is the very form of illusion, the very concept of playing (*illudere*). Going beyond a form is to pass from one form to another, whereas going beyond an idea is to negate the idea. This second strategy defines the intellectual position of illusion and is often that of modern painting's challenge to the world, whereas the former strategy exemplifies the very principle of illusion for which there is no other destiny of form than the form itself.

In this sense we must have illusionists who know that art and painting are illusion, and are as far from intellectual criticism as from aesthetics properly speaking (which already supposes a discrimination between the beautiful and the ugly). Illusionists who know that all art is first a form of *trompe-l'oeil*, a 'life trick', just as all theory is a 'sense trick' – *trompe-le-sens*, and that all painting, far from being an expressive version of the world, and thus pretending to veracity, consists in setting up snares in which the supposed reality of the world may be naive enough to become trapped. Just as theories do not consist of having ideas (and thus of flirting with the truth), but consist of setting up traps into which meaning naively falls. Of finding, in short, a form of fundamental seduction.

A dimension beyond aesthetic illusion, which I would call anthropological, in order to designate the generic function of designing the world just as it appears to us long before it makes sense, long before it is interpreted or represented, and long before it becomes real. Not the negative and superstitious illusion of another world. But the positive illusion of *this* world, of the operatic scene of the world, of the symbolic operation of the world, of the vital illusion of appearances about which Nietzsche spoke – *illusion as a primitive scene*, acting and happening long before and much more fundamentally than the aesthetic scene.

The sphere of artefacts goes largely beyond art. The realm of art and aesthetics is that of the conventional management of illusion, of a convention that neutralizes the delirious effects of illusion, which neutralizes illusion as an extreme phenomenon. Aesthetics constitutes a sort of sublimation, a mastery of the radical illusion of the world. Other cultures accepted the evidence of this original illusion by trying to deal with it in a symbolic balance. We, the modern cultures, no longer believe in this illusion of the world, but in its reality (which of course is the last and the worst of illusions). We have chosen to exorcize this illusion through this civilized form of simulacrum, which we call the aesthetic form.

Illusion has no history. Aesthetic form has one. But because it has a history it also has an end, and it may be now that we can see the fall, the failure, the fading of this conditional form, of this aesthetic form of the simulacrum – in favour of the unconditional simulacrum, that is, of the primitive scene of illusion, where we may join again with the rituals and phantasmagories of symbolic cultures, and with the fatality of the object.

2
AESTHETIC ILLUSION AND VIRTUAL REALITY

JEAN BAUDRILLARD

There is always a camera hidden somewhere. It may be a real one – we may be filmed without knowing it. We may also be invited to replay our own life on a television network. Anyway, *the virtual camera is in our head*, and our whole life has taken on a video dimension. We might believe that we exist in the original, but today this original has become an exception for the happy few. Our own reality doesn't exist any more. We are exposed to the instantaneous retransmission of all our facts and gestures on a channel. We would have experienced this before as police control. Today it is just like an advertising promotion.

Thus it is irrelevant to get upset with talk shows or reality shows, and to criticize them as such. For they are only a spectacular version, and so an innocent one, of the transformation of life itself, of everyday life, into virtual reality. We don't need the media to reflect our problems in real time – *each existence is telepresent to itself*.

TV and the media have left their mediatized space in order to invest 'real' life from the inside, infiltrating it exactly like a virus in a normal cell.

We don't need digital gloves or a digital suit. As we are, we are moving around in the world as in a synthetic image. We have swallowed our microphones and headsets, producing intense interference effects, due to the short-circuit of life and its technical diffusion. We have interiorized our own prosthetic image and become the professional showmen of our own lives. Compared with this, the reality shows are only side-effects, and moreover mystifying, because in indicting them as manipulation, the critics assume that there is somewhere an original form of life, and that reality shows would be no more than its parody and simulation (Disneyland).

This criticism is over, as is every Situationist criticism of the 'spectacle' and the concept of 'spectacle', as also in substance all criticism of 'alienation'. Unfortunately, I would add. Because the human abstraction of the spectacle was never hopeless; it always offered the chance of disalienation. Whereas the operation of the world in real time, its unconditional realization, is really without alternative. Radicality has changed, and all negative criticism, surviving itself, actually helps its object to survive. For instance, the critic of religion and of its official manifestation misses the fact that religion is in practice far more realized in many other forms – irreligious, profane, political or cultural – where it is less easily recognizable as such.

It is the same thing with the virtual. Current criticism engaging with new techniques, new images, masks the fact that its concept has been distilled throughout real life, in homoeopathic doses, beyond detection. And if the level of reality decreases from day to day, it's because the medium itself has passed into life, and become a common ritual of transparency. It is the same for the virtual: all this digital, numerical and electronic equipment is only the epiphenomenon of the virtualization of human beings in their core. If this can overwhelm people's fantasy to such a degree, it is because we are already, not in some other world, but in this very life, in a state of photosynthesis. If we can today produce a virtual clone to replace Richard Bohringer, it is because he has already replicated himself, he has already become his own clone.

But anyway the reality show can be used as a micromodel for the analysis of all virtual reality. Whether it's the immediacy of information on all screens, the telepresence, or presence on TV, in all actings and happenings, it is always a question of 'real time' – of the collapse of the real and its double. Live your life in real time (live and die directly on the screen). Think in real time (your thinking is immediately transferred on the printer). Make your revolution in real time (not in the street, but in the broadcasting studio). Live your love and passion in real time (by videotaping each other).

This conversion of the mediatized into the immediatized, that is, into an immediate catalytic operation of the real by the screen, this immediatic revolution is already implied in McLuhan's formula 'The Medium is the Message', which has never been analysed in all its consequences. McLuhan remains the prophetic theoretician of this collapse of the medium and the message, and thus in some way the prophet of the vanishing process of information and communication (whose significance he emphasized at the same time!). 'The Medium is the Message' remains as the *Mene Tekel Epharsim* of the communication era, its password and the sign of its end.

But there is another predecessor for all technologies of the virtual: it is the ready-made. Again, for example, the reality show: all those human beings, literally extracted from their real life to play out their AIDS or conjugal psychodrama on the TV screen have their prototype in the bottle rack of Duchamp. The artist extracted the bottle rack from the real world in the same way, displaced it on another level to confer on it an undefinable hyperreality. A paradoxical acting-out, putting an end to the bottle rack as a real object, to art as the invention of another scene and to the artist as the protagonist of another world. To all aesthetic idealization Duchamp opposes a violent desublimation of art and of the real by their instantaneous short-circuit. Extrematization of the two forms: the bottle rack, ex-inscribed from its context, from its idea, from its function, becomes more real than the real (hyperreal), and more art than art (it enters into the transaesthetics of banality, of insignificance, of nullity, where today the pure and indifferent form of art is to be seen).

Any object, any individual, any situation today could be a virtual ready-made. For all of them might be described in much the same way as Duchamp implicitly categorizes his ready-made object: 'It exists, I met it!' This is the only label for existence. Graffiti – another form of ready-made – says nothing other than: 'I exist, here I am, my name is so and so'. The pure and minimal form of identity: 'I exist, I met myself'. The ready-made always seems like these stuffed animals, vitrified as if they were alive, hypnotized in the pure form of appearance – 'naturalized'. But I would say that today art in general also looks like a naturalized species, vitrified in its pure formal essence.

Duchamp's coup has since been repeated indefinitely, not only in the field of art, but in all individual and social functions, especially in the mediasphere. The last phase being precisely the reality show, where everybody is invited to present themselves as they are, key in hand, and to play their live show on the screen (with all its obscene connotations), just as the ready-made object plays its hyperrealistic role on the screen of the museum.

All these mediatic events relate to this crucial phase in the world of information and communication – a phase that art, politics and production have known before. The drama of the mediatic class is that it is starving on the other side of the screen, in front of an indifferent consuming mass, in front of the tele-absence of the masses. Any form of tele-presence will be good enough to exorcize this tele-absence. Just as it was a vital necessity for capital to have workers and producers transformed into active consumers, and even into direct stockholders in the capitalist economy (this doesn't change anything in business, the strategy being as always to remove the tablecloth without changing the organization of the table), the telespectator has to be transferred not in front of the screen where he is staying anyway, passively escaping his responsibility as citizen, but on the screen, on the other side of the screen. In short, he must undergo the same conversion as Duchamp's bottle rack, when it was transferred to the other side of art, thus creating a definitive ambiguity between art and the real world. Today art is nothing more than this paradoxical confusion of the two. And information too is nothing more than the paradoxical confusion of the event and the medium, including all forms of intoxication and mystification connected to it.

So we have all become ready-mades. Objects transposed to the other side of the screen, mediumized (we don't even enjoy the good old status of passive spectator any more), hypostasized as if transfigured *in situ*, on the spot, by aesthetic or mediatic decision, transfigured in their specific habits and ways of life, as living museum exhibits. Thus we become cloned to our own image by high definition, and dedicated by involution into our own image to mediatic stupefaction, just as the ready-made is dedicated to aesthetic stupefaction. And just as Duchamp's acting-out opens on an overall aestheticization, where any piece of junk will be promoted to a piece of art, and any piece of art demoted to a piece of junk – so this immediatic conversion opens on to a universal virtuality, that is to say the radical actualization of reality through its acting-out in real time.

All cultural spaces are involved. For example, some new museums, following a sort of Disneyland processing, try to put people not so much in front of the painting – which is not interactive enough and even suspect as pure spectacular consumption – but into the painting. Insinuated audiovisually into the virtual reality of the *Déjeuner sur l'herbe*, people will enjoy it in real time, feeling and tasting the whole Impressionist context, and eventually interacting with the picture. The masses usually prefer passive roles, and avoid representation. This must change, and they must be made interactive partners. It is not a question of free speaking or free acting – just break their resistance and destroy their immunities.

It is a question of life and death. When the indifference of the masses becomes dangerous for the political or cultural class, then interactive strategies must be invented to exhort a response at any price. In fact, the interactive mass is still a mass, with all the characteristics of a mass, simply reflecting itself on both sides of the screen. But the screen is not a mirror, and, while there was some magic in passing beyond the mirror, there is no magic at all in passing beyond the screen. It's impossible anyway – there is no other side of the screen. No depth – just a surface. No hidden face – just an interface.

Besides, the masses were not without an answer. Their answer was silence, the silence of the silent majorities. This challenge of silence is now cancelled when people are forced to ask their own questions, when they are assigned to speech. If they had some questions, these would never be autonomous but would surely be programmed in a schedule. But even this implication *en trompe l'oeil* doesn't save media and information from inertia, from proliferating fatal inertia. Mass media or micromedia, directive or interactive, the chain reaction of the images is the same. It is simply materialized in real time and in everybody's head.

Now what exactly is at stake in this hegemonic trend towards virtuality? What is the idea of the virtual? It would seem to be the radical actualization, the unconditional realization, of the world, the transformation of all our acts, of all historical events, of all material substance and energy into pure information. The ideal would be the resolution of the world by the actualization of all facts and data.

This is the theme of Arthur C. Clarke's fable about the names of God. In this fable, the monks of Tibet devote themselves to the fastidious work of transcribing the 99 billion names of God, after which the world will be accomplished, and it will end. Exhausted by this everlasting spelling of the names of God, they call IBM computer experts who complete the work in a few months. This offers a perfect allegory of the completion of the world in real time by the operation of the virtual. Unfortunately this is also the end of the world in real time. For with this virtual countdown of the names of God, the great promise of the end was realized; and the technicians of IBM, who left the site after work (and didn't believe of course in the prophecy), saw the stars in the sky fading and vanishing one by one.

Maybe it is an allegory of our technical transfiguration of the world: its accelerated end, its anticipated resolution – the final score of modern millenarianism, but without hope of salvation, revelation, or even apocalypse. Simply accelerating the process of declining (in the double sense of the word) towards a pure and simple disappearance. The human species would be invested, without knowing it, with the task of programming, by exhausting all its possibilities, the code *for the automatic disappearance of the world.*

Rather than the ideal transformation of the world, the ultimate end of this transfiguration would be that of building a perfectly autonomous world from which we can retire and remove ourselves. In order for us to step out of it, the world must be brought to completion. As long as we stay here as alien beings, the world cannot be perfect. And to be perfect it must be constructed and artificial, because there is no perfection in the natural state. The human being itself is a dangerous imperfection. If we want to achieve this sort of immortality, we must also treat ourselves as artefacts and get out of ourselves in order to move on an artificial orbit, where we can revolve eternally.

We all dream of an *ex-nihilo* creation, of a world emerging and moving without our intervention. We dream of perfect autonomous beings who, far from acting against our will as in the fable, *The Sorcerer's*

Apprentice, would meet our desire to escape our own will, and realize the world as a self-fulfilling prophecy. So we dream of perfect computers, of auto-programming artificial intelligence. But if we allow artificial beings to become intelligent, and even more intelligent than we are, we don't allow them to have their own will. We don't allow them what God finally allowed us – the intelligence of evil. We cannot bear real challenge from another species; and if we concede intelligence to other beings, then this intelligence must still be the manifestation of our desire. While God permitted us to raise such questions about our own liberty, we don't allow artificial beings to raise such questions about themselves. No liberty, no will, no desire, no sexuality. We want them complex, creative, interactive, but without spirit. By the way, it seems that these 'intelligent' machines have found, if not the way to transgression and freedom, at least the byways to accident and catastrophe. It seems that they have an evil genius for dysfunctions, electronic viruses and other perverse effects, which save them – and us, in the same way – from perfection and from reaching the limit of their possibilities.

The perfect crime would be to build a world-machine without defect, and to leave it without traces. But it never succeeds. We leave traces everywhere – viruses, lapses, germs, catastrophes – signs of defect, or imperfection, which are like our species' signature in the heart of an artificial world.

All forms of high technology illustrate the fact that behind its doubles and its prostheses, its biological clones and its virtual images, the human species is secretly fomenting its disappearance. For example, the video cassette recorder connected to the TV: it sees the film in your place. Were it not for this technical possibility of devolution, of a vicarious accomplishment, we would have felt obliged to see it for ourselves. For we always feel a little responsible for films we haven't seen, for desires we haven't realized, for people we haven't answered, for crimes we haven't committed, for money we haven't spent. All this generates a mass of deferred possibilities, and the idea that a machine is there that can deal with these possibilities, can stock them, filter them (an answer-machine, a memory bank), and progressively absorb and reabsorb them, is very comforting. All these machines can be called virtual, since they are the medium of virtual pleasure, the abstract pleasure of the image, which is often good enough for our happiness. Most of these machines are used for delusion, for the elusion of communication ('Leave a message . . .'), for absolving face-to-face relations and social responsibilities. They don't really lead to action, they substitute for it most of the time. So with the film on the video cassette recorder: maybe I'll see this film later, but maybe I won't do it at all. Am I sure I really want to see it anyway? But the machine must work. Thus the consumption of the machine converges with the consumption of the desire.

All these machines are wonderful. They give us a sort of freedom. They help us to get free from the machine itself, since they interconnect one with another and function in a loop. They help us to get free from our own will and from our own production. What a relief all at once to see twenty pages erased by a caprice of the word processor (or by an error of the user, which amounts to the same thing). They would never have had such a value if they hadn't been given the chance to disappear! What the computer gives to you, too easily perhaps, it takes away just as easily. Everything is in order. The technological equation amounts to zero. We always hear about negative perverse effects. But here the technique assumes a positive (homoeopathic) perverse effect. The integrated circuit reverses itself, performing in some way *the automatic writing of the world*.

Now let us consider some different aspects of this virtual achievement, of this automatic writing of the world. High definition. High fidelity. Real time. Genetic codes. Artificial intelligence.

In high definition, the (electronic, numerical or synthesized) image is nothing more than the emanation of the digital code that generated it. It has nothing more to do with representation, and even less with aesthetic illusion. All illusion is abolished by technical perfection. It is the same with the three-dimensional image: it is a pure disillusion, since the magic of the image lies simply in the subtraction of one dimension from the real world. In the hologram's perfection of the virtual image, all parts are microscopically identical to the whole, generating a fractal deconstruction of the image, which is supplanted by its own pure luminous definition.

High fidelity. Disappearance of the music by excess of fidelity, by the promiscuity of the music and its absolute technical model. Holographic music, holophonic, stereophonic, as if it had swallowed its own genetic code before expelling it as an artificial synthesis – clinical music, sterile, purged of all noise.

Real time. The equivalent of high definition for the image. Simultaneity of the event and its diffusion in information. Instant proximity of oneself and one's actions at a distance. Telepresence: you can manage your business *in situ* at the other end of the world, by the medium of your electronic clone. Like the space of the image in high definition, each moment in real time is microscopically coded, microscopically isolated, in a closed and integrated circuit. As in the hologram, each parcel of time concentrates the total information relative to the event, as if we could control the event from all sides at once. No distance, no memory, no continuity, no death: the extreme 'reality of time' is in fact extreme virtuality. All the suspense, all the unforeseeability, of time is over.

Genetic coding. What is at stake here is the simulation of a perfect human being, of a body of high definition, through the controlled engineering and dispatching of the genome. The construction of a virtual body outperforming the original – plastic genetic surgery. The genetic code itself, the DNA, which concentrates the whole definition of any living being in a minimal space and a minimal formula, is the ideal type of virtuality.

Last, but not least: artificial intelligence. Something like an artificial brain-recording, adapted to an artificial environment. Thinking almost instantaneously inscribed on the screen, in direct interaction with data, software and memories – intelligence in real time. Thinking becomes a high definition operation, suppressing all distance, all ambiguity, all enigmatic eventualities, suppressing the very illusion of thought. Just as the illusion of the image disappears into its virtual reality, just as the illusion of the body disappears into its genetic inscription, just as the illusion of the world disappears into its technical artefacts, so the natural intelligence of the world disappears into its artificial intelligence. There is no trace in all of this of the world as a game, as a fake, as a machination, as a crime, and not as a logical mechanism, or a reflex cybernetic machine, with the human brain as mirror and model.

Artificial intelligence is everything except artificial. It is definitive 'realthinking' (as we speak of *realpolitik*), fully materialized by the interaction of all virtualities of analysis and computing. We could even say that artificial intelligence goes beyond itself through too high a definition of the real, through a delirious sophistication of data and operations – but this is only the consequence of the fact that artificial intelligence is a matter of the hyperrealization of thinking, of the objective processing of thinking.

There is not the slightest sense here of illusion, artifice, seduction, or a more subtle game of thought. For thought is neither a mechanism of higher functions nor a range of operational reflexes. It is a rhetoric of forms, of moving illusions and appearances. It reacts positively to the illusion of the world, and negatively to its reality. It plays off appearances against reality, turning the illusion of the world against the world itself. The thinking machine masters only the computing process. It doesn't rule over appearances, and its function, like that of all other cybernetic and virtual machines, is to destroy this essential illusion by counterfeiting the world in real time.

Curiously, all the above traits rely upon paradoxes. 'Real time' is in fact a purely virtual time. 'Artificial intelligence' is nothing like artificial. 'Virtual reality' is at the antipodes of the real world. As for 'high definition', it is synonymous with the *highest dilution* of reality. The highest definition of the medium corresponds to the lowest definition of the message. The highest definition of information corresponds to the lowest definition of the event. The highest definition of sex (in pornography) corresponds to the lowest definition of desire. The highest definition of language (as computer coding) corresponds to the lowest definition of sense. The highest definition of the other (as computer coding), corresponds to the lowest definition of exchange and alterity. Everywhere high definition corresponds to a world where referential substance is scarcely to be found any more.

Such are the stakes involved in the virtual realization of the world. And we must take it as irreversible. This logic leads to the end, to the final solution, or resolution. Once performed, it would be the equivalent of a perfect crime. While the other crime, the 'original' crime, is never perfect, and always leaves traces – we as living and mortal beings are a living trace of this criminal imperfection – future extermination, which would result from the absolute determination of the world and of its elements, would leave no traces at all. We would not even have the choice or chance to die, to really die. We would have been kidnapped and disintegrated in real time and virtual reality long before the stars go out.

Artificial intelligence, tele-sensoriality, virtual reality and so on – all this is the end of illusion. The illusion of the world – not its analytical countdown – the wild illusion of passion, of thinking, the aesthetic illusion of the scene, the psychic and moral illusion of the other, of good and evil (of evil especially, perhaps), of true and false, the wild illusion of death, or of living at any price – all this is volatilized in psycho-sensorial telereality, in all these sophisticated technologies which transfer us to the virtual, to the contrary of illusion: to radical disillusion.

Fortunately, all this is impossible. High definition is 'virtually' unreal-izable, in its attempt to produce images, sounds, information, bodies in microvision, in stereoscopy, as you have never seen them, as you will never see them. Unrealizable also is the fantasy of artificial intelligence. It is too intelligent, too operational to be true – this brain-becoming of the world, this world-becoming of the brain, as it has never functioned, without a body, autonomized, inhuman – a brain of high definition outlining a universe of high definition. Something like an ethical and technical purification. It will never succeed, fortunately. Not that we trust in human nature or in a future enlightenment, but because there is in fact no place for both natural and artificial intelligence. There is no place for both the illusion of the world and a virtual programming of the world. There is no place for both the world and its double.

When the virtual operation of the world is finished, when all the names of God have been spelled out – which is the same basic fantasy as the declining of the human genome or the worldwide declining of all data and information – then we too shall see the stars fading away.

3

THE ART OF DISAPPEARANCE

JEAN BAUDRILLARD

It is not so much a question of producing (a text or an image). Rather, everything pivots upon the art of disappearance. But nevertheless, this process of disappearing has to leave some kind of trace, be this the site at which the other, the world or the object appears. This is moreover the only way in which the other can exist – on the basis of one's own calculated disappearance (according to the rules of the game of disappearance). Whatever one brings into being in the domain of production will never be more than the image of oneself, an extension of the same. Only that which comes from the domain of disappearance (from one's disappearance), is truly other.

The stupefying power of the photograph is far superior to that of writing. It is rare that a text can offer the same instantaneity, the same tangibility, the same magic, as a photographic object (shadow, light or material) – least of all the realist text, which plays upon resemblance (the ideology of the same), rather than upon the evident (the unintelligible, dazzling, manifestation of the other). Even photographs seldom offer this magic tangibility. And yet one senses it in Nabokov and in Gombrowicz. When their writing rediscovers the traces of primal disorder, the plastic vehemence of things without qualities, the erotic energy of a worthless universe.

Every photographed object is simply the trace left behind by the disappearance of everything else. It's almost a perfect crime, an almost total final solution, as it were, for a world which projects only the illusion of this or that object, which the photograph then transforms – absent from the rest of the world, withdrawn from the rest of the world – into an unseizable enigma. From the height of this enigmatic object – which, as a radical exception, bears no resemblances, and has no meaning – one has an unobstructed vision of the world.

Photography, then, is the art of eradicating everything that interposes itself between one and the world – the absence of the world presented in each detail, reinforced by each detail (it's the same thing for the face: it's the details of the face which render tangible the absence of the subject, this absent subject, without which there can be no good photographs). Like concern for fine sentiments in literature, considerations for resemblance or for expression in the image are inconsequential.

This disconnection of detail can also be brought about by a kind of mental gymnastics, a subtlety of thought. But in this case, the technique operates without encountering any resistance, and is perhaps some kind of trap. In so far as it exists within the realm of concepts and discourse, the object is related to all things around it. In so far as it is quite simply an object, it is an unidentifiable illusion.

It's difficult to focus on people who are not psychologically 'well focused'. The object makes the lens/*l'objectif* tremble. Thus it is that I have only very rarely, and very unsuccessfully, focused upon a human being. Over and above my personal inhibitions, this is perhaps because any human being is the site of such a complex scenario – even the most simple among them – the site of such a complex construction, that instead of transfiguring and idealizing the image as the camera usually does, the lens disfigures and decimates its character. The human being is masked, and the most difficult subject to capture is not so much their reality or their resemblance, as their mask, or in other words, their secret identity or alterity.

One's inability to photograph human beings is clear proof of the manipulation of the photographic subject by its object. One feels the same uneasiness when being photographed oneself. On several occasions, I've experienced proof of the object's sovereign influence, of this secret influence or manipulation: having taken an entire roll of images of a woman one day on a beach – she posed reluctantly, not wishing to be photographed – nothing appeared when the roll of film was developed. On another similar occasion, the roll of film mysteriously disappeared in the photographer's apartment.

The only profound desire is the desire of the object, which is to say not for that which I lack (something trivial and conventional, and well worthy of the subject, which always lives in the world of lack), nor for she or he who lacks me (something still more subtle), but for he or she who does not lack me, for that which is perfectly capable of existing without me. Desire is always for this kind of foreign perfection, and at the same time, perhaps, wishes both to shatter it and to demolish it. This perfection is the perfection of the object: it alone is truly other, and one only really yearns for alterity, for something whose perfection and impunity one wishes both to share and to shatter.

Photography has an obsessional, idiosyncratic, ecstatic and narcissicistic quality. It is a singular, even expressly solitary activity. The photographic image is instant and irreversible, unlike that of painting, or of the text, or of any other art foregrounding continuity of expression, of resemblance or of meaning. It is irreversible, and thus to some extent fatal, given the instantaneity of the shooting. Irrevocable, it offers tangible evidence of the world at a certain given moment. Any attempt to retake, or to artistically retouch the photograph, or indeed any kind of preliminary scenography, appears abominably aesthetic.

The discontinuity of the subject in time and space, its solitude, and its disjunction from the world, are all correlative with the discontinuity of the object itself and with its obsessional character. For the 'good' object is distinguished by its obsessional character, by that which no longer needs the desire of the other. The best possible photographic subjects are those which have found their obsessive form, their idiosyncratic identity, their narcissicistic figuration. Those which have objective impact and which the lens/l'objectif – like the face of Medusa – will immobilize with all their objective impact.

The moment of the negative. The photograph is not an image in real time, it's not a virtual image, or a numerical image, etc. It is analogical, and it retains the moment of the negative, the suspense of the negative, this slight displacement which allows the image to exist in its own right, in other words, as something different to the real object; in other words, as illusion – in other words, as the moment in which the world or the object vanishes into the image, which synthetic images cannot do because they no longer exist as images, strictly speaking. The photograph retains the moment of disappearance, whereas in the synthetic image, whatever it is, the real has already disappeared. This slight displacement gives the object the magic, the discrete charm of a previous existence.

The objective magic of the photograph – a quite different aesthetic form to that of painting – derives from the fact that the object has done all the work. Of course, photographers never admit this, and maintain that any originality derives from their inspiration, and from their photographic interpretation of the world. It is for this reason that they take bad (or excessively good) photographs, confusing their subjective 'vision' of the world with the miraculous reflex action of the photographic process.

It's not a question of being objective, it's a question of becoming an object. In the photographic process it's not a question of considering the world as an object, of acting as if it was already there as an object, but of making it become an object, in other words, of making it become other, of exhuming the alterity buried beneath its alleged reality, of making it appear as a kind of basic, disintegrative strange attractor, through its every element, of holding this primitive strange attraction in an image.

It's commonly said: 'Even the most banal, the most insignificant persons always present one particular (photographically seizable) instant when they are most singular, when they reveal their secret identity.' This is not accurate. For the only interesting thing about a person, or a face, is their radical alterity, and rather than seeking their identity behind appearances, we must try to detect this secret alterity behind their identity.

Put another way, we must reveal the mask or the figure which haunts a person, and withdraw it from their identity – the masked divinity which inhabits every one of us, even the most insignificant, for an instant, one day or another.

In the case of objects, savages and primitives, this alterity is unambiguous, this singularity is unambiguous (according to physics, the term singularity refers to an object, or a micro-universe, which escapes all of our co-ordinates). The same is true for animals. Likewise, the most insignificant of objects is always 'other'. In the case of subjects, it is much more ambiguous, however. For the subject – and many will consider this to be the hallmark of its humanity – often succeeds, frequently at the cost of almost incalculable efforts, in annihilating its singularity, in existing utterly within the limits of the law and of its identity. It is to be hoped that this success is never absolute, that this crime is never perfect.

Photography, among other forms of 'estrangement', can help to reveal this massacre, this process by which the subject exterminates its own alterity – *Selbstentfremdung*. A process, in other words, by which one simultaneously expropriates and eradicates oneself.

Once again, immanently, become 'a thing among things', all strangers one to another, all familiar and enigmatic, rather than a universe of subjects communicating one to another, all transparent one to another.

The silence of photographs. Without really being able to explain why, this is one of the most valuable and one of the most original qualities of the photographic image, as opposed to cinema, television, etc., which one always tries to silence, albeit unsuccessfully.

The silence not only of the image which escapes, eludes, all discourse, commentary, in order to be perceived and read 'inwardly' as it were – but also the silence into which the image plunges the objects that it seizes, wrenching them from the thunderous context of the real world. Irrespective of the violence, the speed or the noise of its surroundings, the photograph restores the object to the immobility and the silence of the image.

In the very centre of the city, in the very centre of turbulence, in the very centre of visual and auditory stress, it recreates emptiness, it recreates the desert, the equivalent of the desert – the equivalent also of a sense of isolation, of phenomenological isolation, or rather, a phenomenological immobilization of appearances. The only way to cross cities in silence. The only way to cross the world in silence.

31

4

THE ECSTASY OF PHOTOGRAPHY

Jean Baudrillard interviewed
by Nicholas Zurbrugg
(Paris, 4 June 1993)

Perhaps I could begin by asking you how you began taking photographs?

Oh, it's only relatively recently that I began – about ten years ago. Before that I was rather indifferent towards photography. Then, on one of my trips to Japan, I was given a camera, and I began to try it out a bit, taking photographs from the plane on the return journey, for example. But for quite a few years I only had a very simple little auto-focus camera, which in fact was the one that I used for most of the photographs in my recent exhibition in Paris. Since then, I've had other more sophisticated cameras. But I'm not a technological or a professional photographer, I make no claims to any of that. I know a little bit about photography, but all things considered, I don't really know very much – I came to photography as a kind of diversion or hobby, something like that. And yet at the same time it was also something serious, in the sense that it offered an alternative to writing – it was a completely different activity which came from elsewhere and had no connection with writing. Later, when people saw my photographs, they said, 'Oh yes, of course, we can clearly see the same sort of thing that you're writing about'. But it's not true at all. For me, there was no connection between the two.

That surprises me a bit, in the sense that some of your writings on photography seem quite compatible with your more general analyses of contemporary technology. In The Transparency of Evil, *for example, you suggest that photography lacks any sense of intention or personal vision, and that the most remarkable early photographs are those of American Indians who seem to be confronting death and who seem to evoke what you term 'that most essential of exoticisms, the exoticism of the Object, of the Other'.*

Yes, that's to say that at such moments their quality of otherness is objective rather than subjective – it's that in particular which interests me. By contrast, in writing, it is the subjective dimension which prevails, which guides interpretation, and so on, whereas in photography the objective dimension is presented in all its otherness, and imposes its otherness. In that respect, the first photographs were of exotic, altogether 'other' human beings, which seem quite fascinating. I've no specific photographic agenda, but for me, photography has nothing to do with finding a particular vision or a subjective style in order to interpret the world. Rather, it is a process of capturing things, because objects are themselves captivating. It's almost like trapping things – like trying to catch the primitive dimension of the object, as opposed to the secondary dimension of the subject and the whole domain of representation. It's the immanent presence of the object, rather than the representation of the subject.

Does this imply that your writings are more subjective than your photography?

No, not really. I think that in my theoretical writings as well, I tried to make the object appear or disappear as a concept, and to make the concept appear or disappear as a subject. I tried to defy the concept as an object, so that I would no longer be the subject of knowledge, and to remove myself from the position of the subject. I tried all that, it's true, but discourse is something that always replaces you in the position of the subject. There's always this repositioning within discourse – it's impossible not to be a subjectivity and a producer of meaning. With discourse, it is difficult to produce both meaning and appearances. With photography it is considerably easier to make the object appear, and to disappear as a subject. Obviously, that's rather a utopian ambition – to disappear as a subject, and to reappear as an object. To be sure, one is always there, but in this case one's mediated by an insignificant object – it's in this way that one appears.

I think that you've also written about the pleasure of photography. Is this pleasure a symptom of subjectivity?

No, it's much more of an objective pleasure, rather than a process of self-realization. When I take photographs, I do so while walking, while crossing cities – doubtless, like many other photographers. It's a kind of 'travelling' or 'acting-out', and in this respect, a way of escaping oneself, of being elsewhere, a form of exoticism too, perhaps. It's for this reason that I'm not really a photographer. It's not really the image that I produce, even if it's a beautiful photograph, that interests me primarily – rather, it's this kind of activity, this kind of exoteric excursion.

Could one say that this is a kind of meditation – but an objective meditation, rather than a subjective process?

Yes – a predominantly objective meditation, if one could call that a meditation. In a way an object creates a sense of emptiness, as it were. When one finds something like that, an object imposes itself – suddenly, one sees it, because of certain effects of light, of contrasts and things like that, it isolates itself and it creates a sense of emptiness. Everything around it seems to disappear, and nothing exists but this particular thing, which you capture technologically, objectively. It's a mental process – *una cosa mentale*. Finally, I realized that there was a relation between the activity of theoretical writing, and the activity of photography, which at the beginning seemed utterly different to me. But in fact it's the same thing – it's the same process of isolating something in a kind of empty space, and analysing it within this space, rather than interpreting it. I don't interpret anything. Rather, I isolate something in an empty space and then it irradiates this emptiness – there's the irradiation of the object within this emptiness. It's for this reason that – without specifically planning to do so – I've never photographed faces, portraits or human beings. I can't do that, I don't know how to do that – because there would be an excess of meaning. That's to say, I only became defined as a subject when faced with another subject. Therefore I avoid other subjects, and photograph objects.

Doesn't one of your photographs depict a young couple sitting in the rue Sainte-Beuve?

Yes, but it's not so much a photograph of human beings. It's of two Americans, I think, who were sitting there.

Who, by definition, aren't human beings?

Yes, quite so, agreed! But it's altogether like a painting by Edward Hopper, don't you think? They seem completely translucent and hyperreal. It's the only photograph in which I have two figures, but it's not a portrait of human beings as human beings – not at all. I like Hopper a lot – I have a lot of admiration for his work. I wouldn't say I'm influenced by Hopper, because it's not the same thing – but there's something of Hopper in that photograph, in the oblique lighting perhaps. I like that kind of effect.

Do you feel that your work has any particular affinity with the work of any other artists or writers?

Yes, there are some affinities, but not in terms of any specific references. My photographs don't make any sort of references. To be sure, I know the work of the great photographers quite well, but I'm not at all influenced by them. I don't make any claim to be a part of the history of photography or to be a part of photographic culture – this isn't my problem.

I suppose that what I had in mind were the affinities between certain artistic or literary styles and certain of your images, such as the photograph of the draped chair. Was that your particular chair? I seem to remember seeing it here.

Yes, it was. But it's broken now, and is in another room. But it was there, yes.

It seemed to me that this photograph is almost a self-portrait in the manner of Magritte.

Exactly, yes, it traces a particular form. That's to say, that at certain moments, objects suggest this sort of hollowed form. But it's not so much a projection of the subject on to them. Rather it's the absence of the subject – absence modelled within a certain form. Yes, one certainly has the impression that there is someone there.

In another of your photographs, the image of the petrol pump reminded me of a description in Aragon's novel, Paris Peasant, *in which Aragon describes petrol pumps as a kind of contemporary idol.*

Yes – they're very much like totem poles. But I wasn't making any kind of reference. One can find these correspondences retrospectively, but when I'm taking photographs I don't have any kind of references in mind. It's more a question of a particular moment, a detail, an object, a particular instant, that kind of thing. Now of course, I often go to the major international photographic exhibitions, but all of these photographs – with the possible exception of press photographs, and even these – are very aestheticized, very calculated, very carefully composed and so on, and that sort of photography is really of no interest to me. There's no unity of coherence in my photographs, except perhaps at a secondary level. They're all taken according to my caprice or my pleasure.

I have the impression that they offer a series of traces of contemporary ruin or decay. I'm thinking for example of your images of torn posters in New York.

Yes – I've taken a lot of that sort of thing, particular posters. But that's all rather banal, everybody does that now. There's no particular analytical impulse, but it's true – that sort of subject matter interests me.

There seems to be a sort of taste for catastrophe.

Yes, yes – a taste for absence or for decline. It's not so much a destructive vision – but there's certainly a sort of fascination for the object that is no longer there, the object that is lost – for absence. In a way there's a kind of strategy of absence or of disappearance.

A sense of disappearance in process?

Yes, yes, undoubtedly. But this was never a preconceived idea. I never said to myself, 'I'm going to take some photographs – I've got this idea about disappearance – I'm going to take some photographs based on that idea.' It didn't happen like that.

Perhaps your photographs of America are rather different in emphasis to the celebratory tone of your writings in America – there seems to be more emphasis upon decay, and also perhaps an element of nostalgia for the ruins of the previous century.

Yes, perhaps. In any case, while I've taken many photographs in America, the best ones perhaps are not those of America. Initially, I thought that they were – images of the desert and of the big American cities and so on. But finally, in the course of selecting work for the exhibition, I realized that the ones which seemed to work best were usually those which related to a more intimate, closer domain. On the one hand, there are the American photographs, but there are also others which simply emphasize ordinary objects. Some of my objects are very, very close, others are very distant, as in the American images.

Some of your photographs made me think of poems by Pierre Reverdy which similarly evoke half-opened doors and situations in which something has just taken place – in which one senses the absence of any immediate event.

Yes, it's that – the capturing of some kind of non-occurrence at the very limits of its moment of disappearance or appearance – something like that. That's one sort of argument, perhaps. But as a rule I say nothing about photography – I've got nothing much to say about photography.

There are two pages in *The Transparency of Evil* but that's all, and that was written well before I began exhibiting photographs. It had nothing to do with my personal practice – rather, it was in the context of a book – it was something quite different, with no relation to my particular photography. Obviously, one can now relate the two, but I feel no obligation to do so. Personally, I prefer to consider my photographic work as an exotic, foreign, different activity – as a diversion, in other words.

All the same, in so far as it is an activity which offers you a certain form of escape, it seems to me that your photographic aspirations have something in common with what you describe in your interview with Guy Ballavance as the 'small miracle' of identifying an 'enchanted' or 'initiatory space', beyond the constraints of conventional space. In another interview with Guillemot and Soutif, you similarly propose that when writing really works, there are more or less magical moments as one travels into another mental zone.

Yes, that's true.

Has your photographic work confirmed the possibility of this process?

Yes, totally, it's much more evident in photography. I enter into this second state – this kind of rapid ecstasy – much more often in my photography than in my writing. The ecstasy of photography – the projection into the image and so on – is much stronger, much more spontaneous and automatic. For me, photography is a kind of automatic writing – it's something quite different to the controlled writing of my texts. I can become much more enthralled or fascinated in a photo-graphic work, than in the act of writing. When I'm writing, I know much more about what I'm doing, I'm in control, I'm able to direct or redirect my work. And yet I've experienced what I'd have to call my greatest sense of pleasure – and indeed, my strongest sense of passion – in the realm of images, rather than in the realm of texts.

All this seems rather curious, because I think that you've argued in The Transparency of Evil *that generally speaking, photography lacks any sense of passion or vision.*

Yes, but there's a fascination. There's not a sense of vision – or at least not an interpretative vision in my work. I don't impose any system of vision. It's more a question of the way objects make themselves visible – of the way in which objects make themselves seen through the observer. That's something else, I think, to what you mean by 'vision'. Obviously one cannot escape from one's own point of view. But so far as possible, one allows oneself to be viewed by the object, rather than attempting to capture the object. I suppose one could claim that writing does the same thing to some extent, but to a much less significant degree. It's really very different. So in a sense, photography verifies the same principles, but much more easily and automatically.

The notion of photography's automatic quality points perhaps to the problem of evaluating technology. When you discuss technology in The Transparency of Evil *it's almost always in rather a scornful or negative way. You don't seem to have a very positive view of the technocultural mentality.*

Yes, of course, I offer a very critical account of technology and of technology's impact on the world. I'm not the only one to do this – everybody speaks of technology in this way. But now, having reconsidered technology in terms of photography, I'm beginning to formulate another hypothesis – I'm asking myself if technology isn't the site of an inversion of the relationship between the subject and the object. Rather than thinking of technology as the site of a subject which, by means of technology, masters the world, captures the world and so on, I'm beginning to wonder if – almost ironically or paradoxically – technology may not prove to be the site where the world or the object plays with the subject. In other words, there's a difference of vision. Let's say that the rather critical or pejorative vision of technology represents a first position. But now, from a second position, I'm more interested in seeing technology as an instrument of magic or of illusion – an illusion of the world, but also a positive kind of illusion or play of illusion. Perhaps this is the ultimate way of playing with reality.

Up to now I think that technology has been analysed in too realistic a way. Accordingly, it has been typecast as a medium of alienation and depersonalization. That's what we've done, and that's what we're continuing to do in analyses of virtual reality – it's possible to continue for ever in this sort of direction. But I sense now that a sort of reversal of focus is taking place, and that we now need to see things in terms of a kind of strategy of illusion. Seen in this context, the photographic object suddenly becomes a microscopic paradigm of this process. Starting from the basis of this kind of process or play within the very restrained domain of photography, we can perhaps extrapolate the general way in which all technology functions as the site of the disappearance of the subject. This is not to suggest that one is taking the side of the object, but rather to say that at the limits of the subject and the object, the metaphysical opposition between the subject and the object has perhaps been destabilized in some way by technology. I don't feel particularly committed to either one of these hypotheses. I'll always continue to offer a radically critical analysis of media and technology – one's obliged to do this. But it's also necessary to identify another form of analysis – a more subtle form of analysis than that one.

Perhaps there are two levels of analysis possible, in the sense that you argue in The Transparency of Evil *that while the world in general may be 'a great disappointment', its details have 'a stunning clarity' when 'caught by surprise'. That made me think a little of the transition in Barthes'* Camera Lucida *from an initial interest in the general social conventions of 'studium', to subsequent emphasis upon the domain of 'punctum' and a more personal scale of values.*

Yes, I'm considerably in favour of 'punctum', in the sense of the singularity of the object at a given moment. Or the singularity of the instant outside of its interpretative context, at the point where things have no meaning – or do not yet have meaning – but appear all the same.

That's extremely interesting, because it's almost exactly what Barthes said when he remarked that he couldn't explain why a certain photograph of Robert Wilson attracted him, observing that there was something in the photograph which he couldn't analyse.

But which fascinated him. Yes, all that seems quite relevant to any analysis of such materials. Moreover, in all contemporary photography – this very sophisticated, technological professional work – the one thing that's nearly always missing is 'punctum'. It's all very, very well made, very beautiful and so on, but there's nothing interesting there.

In one of your essays that I like very much – 'Xerox and Infinity', which appeared in Traverses – *you begin by proposing that technology is impossible to understand, and then defy anyone to claim that technology leads to any real communication. But at the end of the article, instead of abandoning the whole problem, you rather unexpectedly assert that the very uncertainty of technology's impact is fascinating. In this respect I feel tempted to compare your critique of contemporary culture with that of Huysmans in* Against Nature, *in the sense that his hero, Des Esseintes, declares that the old gods are dead, that the old values have disappeared and that the old stars have lost their light, and concludes by calling for pity for 'the unbeliever who would fain believe'. I think your work similarly offers a radical critique of the old values, or of the formulations of the old values, but at the same time – throughout writings such as* The Transparency of Evil – *you also contrast trivial values and strong values, or false and fundamental problems. In other words, despite your seemingly negative personal logic, your writing continually seems to display an aspiration towards something more flexible and more positive – an analysis of 'rules', perhaps, as opposed to 'laws', if I understand this distinction. I think you suggest that laws are brutalizing – in the sense that you condemn 'the brutalizing effects of rationality', whereas you relate rules to more mysterious and more liberating forms of process and play.*

Yes, that's right. Rules are arbitrary, whereas laws are necessary. Rules are arbitrary, a game, something more aleatory – yes, it's true, it's that which frequently interests me. And so when I consider technology I'm curious to know whether over and above technology's functional and rational laws, there may not also exist certain rules of a kind of game which we still don't know – which still remains secret – which constitutes the basis of a kind of technological illusion. In other words, at the same time that technology functions rationally – and seems a kind of rational and objective corpus and so on – it is perhaps also a kind of radical illusion.

What do you mean by 'radical illusion'?

Illusion in the literal sense – the fact that things are never what they seem to be or what they believe themselves to be. Accordingly, the world, likewise, is never what it seems. It presents itself as one thing, but it's something else – and so, once again, there's a game of illusion. In other words, the world plays with us, in a manner of speaking, and we have a subjective illusion – the illusion of being a subject. Whereas the objective illusion derives from the fact that the world presents itself as one thing, but is not really this at all. It allows the subject to believe that it is understood by the subject, but in fact the subject doesn't understand it at all. At this point, technology can be seen as a whole domain within which the subject thinks they can seize the world, transform it, interpret it and so on, but from which the world escapes. At present, scientists have been forced to admit that they no longer know what the object is, that they no longer know what the position of the subject is, and that there's a kind of unseizable interplay between an irrecuperable subject and unstable and aleatory laws.

I found it rather curious that you associated these arbitrary laws with a principle of evil – with 'le mal' – and that you personified such laws as this or that kind of 'evil genie'. Isn't this a rather negative terminology?

No, not at all. For me evil – 'le mal' – is not a moral or religious term. It's the principle which destabilizes the good – 'le bien'. 'Le mal' is that which is irreducible – which resists any systematic opposition with 'le bien', in the sense that 'le bien'/'le mal' is a dialectical opposition, and is thus 'bien'. 'Le mal' is that which resists this opposition, which is not analysable – which is something else – something irreducible. My vision isn't at all religious or moral. I'm interested in whatever subverts rational or real systems – the enigmatic, the secret, seduction, and so on. Unfortunately, the fact that I call this kind of thing 'evil' – 'le mal' – can lead to the erroneous assumption that there's something nihilistic or moral in my work. If I use the term 'le mal', it's because from my point of view 'le bien' doesn't really exist in reality.

On the last page of The Transparency of Evil *you seem to use rather more positive terminology for the irreducible or viral quality that you associate with the destabilization of rational and dialectical systems, when you refer for example to 'the scintillation of being'. That seems a fairly optimistic concept.*

Yes, but I use the term 'scintillation' in terms of the way that it is used with reference to stars – for very distant stars which perhaps have died, but which still seem to scintillate or shine. In other words, there are two alternatives, there seems to be light, but perhaps there isn't any light, and perhaps it's just an apparition.

So it's not really an existential affirmation.

No, it's not an affirmation. It's not so much something positive, as something alternative.

I was also struck by another term which seemed to be positive, but which may similarly turn out not to be so. In the essay in The Transparency of Evil *entitled 'Radical Exoticism', you refer rather surprisingly to 'the pataphysical delicacy of the world'. You write: 'The joy of taking photographs is an objective joy, and anyone who has never felt the objective transports of the image, some morning, in some town or desert, will never understand the pataphysical delicacy of the world.'*

Yes, well this is a bit like the suggestion that the world in general may be disappointing, but that each detail can be ecstatic, or whatever. It's the same sort of argument – that if one extricates oneself from metaphysics, from the interpretation of the world and so on, one discovers a sort of delicacy in the non-meaningful, in the domain of the pataphysical – to use rather metaphysical terminology. In other words, one enters a kind of empty space – the delicacy of emptiness and the delicacy of objects which became lost in their own emptiness. They don't have any centre, they're not in the process of gravitating towards any centre. Rather, the pataphysical dimension is a kind of explosion within empty space, a kind of attraction by peripheral emptiness – that is the pataphysical condition.

For me the subject is predominantly a concentric force, whereas the object is an extrinsic force – that's more or less how I conceive of the pataphysical. Within this domain there are certain sensations, a certain sensibility, and certain forms of joy which can accompany any number of experiences. Finally, though I don't associate the term 'pataphysical' with any particular doctrine, I have had certain associations with the Pataphysics group, but I broke away from them because they reduced everything to a pataphysical dogma or doctrine – I can't think of anything more stupid. So I dropped pataphysics, although I'm still very sympathetic towards Jarry's definition of pataphysics as the science of imaginary solutions. I find the idea that pataphysics is as distant from metaphysics, as metaphysics is distant from physics, a very appealing hierarchy. It's not a hierarchy of values, but in terms of the game as a whole – I'm attracted to a pataphysical vision of the world. It's not really very far from the game of appearances – from a kind of ironic metamorphosis of the world.

Would it be fair to suggest that you sometimes identify what appear to be quite positive kinds of transformation or metamorphosis? I'm thinking of your references in The Transparency of Evil *to certain ambivalent or catalytic gestures or phrases which can be said to alter meaning in the sense that they seem to engender new kinds of reality at the same time that they 'transcend their determinations', and in your terms, 'come closer to their raison d'être'. There seem to be similar references to this kind of tendency in the work of Proust – the sort of thing that Deleuze discusses as certain privileged kinds of word or gesture. With this in mind, there seem to be two kinds of tendencies in your writing – firstly, that of defining general paradoxes and of demolishing preceding beliefs, and secondly, an interest in exceptions, and in those moments when systems malfunction and paradoxically produce new kinds of reality and experience.*

Yes – it's at that point that one can consider such systems in reverse, and can judge them according to their own logic.

Do you think it probable that your own evasive systems may eventually undergo a similar revision and reversal?

Yes, it's quite possible! Absolutely! Indeed, I hope this will be the case! I hope that they'll undergo the same process of reversal!

5

BAUDRILLARD'S LIST

Jean Baudrillard Interviewed
by Rex Butler
(Brisbane, 24 April 1994)

How would you respond to the idea that your work has always been about the essential paradox of representation, which is that the copy cannot get too close to the original without it no longer resembling it at all? In The System of Objects, *the same sign both completely expresses and does away with the thing it refers to. In* The Society of Consumption, *too much production leads to waste. In* The Transparency of Evil, *it is the perfection of any system which leads to its collapse. Has this paradox or circularity been a constant feature of your work?*

Yes. I mean I don't know exactly, I have no perspective on my own work. This cycle of things, it was more the term reversibility that interested me. Yes, it was there from the very beginning. I started with critique, and yet it was a classical traditional critique from the position of the subject. Then I began to destabilize this position of knowledge that is always universal. And then I began to use this term reversibility, at first in an analytical but then in an ironic way – ironic in that it would always be able to be itself reversed. But not in an Oriental, not in a Zen way.

But does all this take place specifically around the logic of the sign, the idea that when you get too close to something you are further away than ever?

The following interview was conducted at the Heritage Hotel, Brisbane, during the 'Baudrillard in the Nineties' Conference. Alan Cholodenko and Nicholas Zurbrugg were also present and at times their questions are included.

Yes. And maybe this reversibility and this circularity meet in the figure of the asymptote, I don't know. But this reversibility remains something like a utopia, a form of nostalgia. It is a matter of waiting for the world to reverse. We must explore the monopolistic and universalizing ways of the world at their limit and wait to see whether – according to the hyperlogic of things – they will flip over into seduction.

Do you think that all your terms like 'seduction', 'reversibility', etc., are all tropes – metaphors – at their deepest level for this fundamental logic of the sign?

Yes, I think that. The sign is the epicentre of this attraction. But the problem is that I never analysed the sign in a transhistorical manner. I always tried to analyse it in its actual setting. This is very difficult, of course, because the sign is, on the one side, caught up in the reality of things and, on the other, it is subject to a very abstract logic. The sign is without doubt a very fragile fact, and it is very hard to force its logic into a hyperlogic without losing the sign itself along the way.

So your work was never really about semiotics as a discipline, but just about the sign?

No, I went this way – Marxism, semiotics. But they were only media. I will never resolve this confrontation of both hypotheses – of whether the sign makes possible or destroys – there is a kind of reversibility and antagonism between the two that's indestructible. It's the same in the final stages of things with illusion. All you can do is take part in the illusion of the world and challenge it with the perfect crime, with the radical substitutability of things. But I haven't explored – not yet, anyway – whether this technologization into virtuality maybe itself leads into illusion again. The radical illusionality of technique – maybe technique at its limit also leads to illusion. Or maybe this whole technological apparatus does not change anything in the world, the radical illusionality of things. But I cannot choose. The whole thing is very irrational because the two possibilities are not exclusive.

Because of this logic you're interested in, you always examine systems in their own terms. It's in terms of their own logic that you try to unravel them. Do you think, therefore, that we as readers of your work should likewise attempt to understand your work within its own terms and not according to some real object it might be seen to be accounting for?

That is something that was discussed yesterday. I look at the auto-rationality of systems and my system is their obverse. Why should not my own system also be vulnerable to this logic, be driven to its own end? Except that I also try to be or to explain beyond this point. But, of course, there is a homogeneity between my system and the one I am examining that implies its mortality. There is an analogical affinity between my system and its object, the world – but without the two completely corresponding. But I ask the question: if there is a problem with my logic it must also be your problem.

This would be because there is a double-bind you impose on your readers. On the one hand, we can compare your system to another object or methodology. Douglas Kellner, for example, in his book offers a Marxist critique of your work, but you have already critiqued Marxism. So there is a kind of begging of the question there. On the other hand, we can take your system up in its own terms, but then we mightn't be able to ask the hard questions of it because we have already agreed with your suppositions. There is therefore a problem: we can either stay outside your system and beg the question or come inside but risk not asking the right questions.

Yes. Maybe my system, as anyone's, is reversible and it can and must be reversed. But I cannot do it myself, I need other people to do it for me. But it also cannot be reduced and Kellner was very reductive. I cannot agree with that. I have no general desire to defend myself, but there I have no chance to defend myself. Certainly, I can always be reduced, but Kellner does not take into account the writing, the form, of my work. Never. However, the price of this illusion is that it is reduced. But in the end I have nothing against this.

The problem for us, though, is that you say: 'Reverse my system!' But in so far as we do that, we are only following you yet again.

Yes! Yes! But let's consider the words 'imitation' and the 'real'. The real is a most ambiguous word – it is at the same time unreal and the limit to every theory of the real. And I would not say that I use this word rigorously. It would make no sense for me because it at once potentializes hyperreality and is the real as such. But that word imitation, I have never used the term. You see a problematic of imitation in my work. But I cannot see this theorization of imitation and mimesis. They have never interested me.

NZ: Very generally, then, you seem to confront us with the choice of either going back into Marxism or forward by a process of reversibility into something else. Do you think art in general or something like photography in particular offers us a way out of this double-bind, something beyond the anti-logic of more or less mechanical reversibility?

I don't know what is at stake in my photos. I feel this reversibility in my writing, in the use of language there, always. The word reversing: that I'm used to, from the very first texts I published, which were, remember, poetic and not theoretical. I was acting out this reversibility for the sake of an analysis of the object – of images and signs. As for photography – this acting-out through images perhaps takes place in a reversed way itself from that of writing.

NZ: Is it simply a matter of reversing language? Weren't you saying the other day that you were interested in the way photography might capture the 'secret life' of objects? Can one capture the secret life of objects by reversing language? Would you say it is easier to identify the secret life of things in language or in images?

On an obvious level, it is easier with images. It is more immediately attractive because with images you can immanently determine the presence or absence of an object. It is either there or not there – it is visual, which is more direct than the conceptual. But with the use of language, you become so familiar with the ambiguity of language, the anagrammatical use of language. For myself, I am more familiar with language. I don't really know what I do there. But I like it for this reason because you discharge the responsibility of existence onto objects and from one object onto another. With both perhaps, something circulates without you, but with you hidden behind it. The technical medium is something that permits you to stay hidden behind something.

You talk in your work about self-contained systems, for example, the social which produces its own other in the form of the masses. The social is therefore an irrefutable hypothesis. To this irrefutable hypothesis of the social, you must oppose another, which is also that of the masses, but this time read another way. The social is self-contained, you might be saying, but only because of the masses. Are all your analyses trying to 'double' the systems they examine in this way, both completely accounting for them and providing an absolutely different explanation for them at the same time?

Yes. I agree with this idea of the circularity of the idea of the masses. They are a strange concept, neither realistic nor conceptual. And some people will say that they are tautological and that one's analysis does not have a use. I agree with this, to an extent. Tautology is a circularity in a void. But my circularity creates a void; it is a kind of annulment by logic. The clash of words and concepts creates a void – and in this void maybe something will happen. In a real tautology nothing happens because the circle is closed.

So you are in fact saying that the social cannot be tautological?

The social is closed to the outside. People say we cannot enter it. But it is very open to the inside. When you agree to enter it on its own terms, of course.

When you examine a system in its own terms, you say you are doing this because any alternative to it would only be possible because of it. We have to look at the system in its own terms because it is already like that. But the risk you take is that the system wasn't like this until you actually came to it, that you are the one who makes it self-contained. It's a risk you are undertaking, is it not, this exclusion of empirical alternatives to the system when you see it as perfect?

It's a risk I'm very conscious of. My analysis takes up the risk of things that are too perfect and my analysis will also be subject to the same risk. They are both too perfect to be true. But here I would say that this risk of perfection is good, this disappearing by going beyond the limit. It must be understood as a risk.

But how did you judge that this risk was the way to go? Why didn't you decide to be empirical? Why not consider alternatives? Things could be just the way they are, but you make them the way they will be.

I cannot say. Nothing begins as a project. It was never a decision or a choice between this and that. It all develops regardless of any finality. It takes place in parallel with consumption, production, seduction, the feminine, illusion, and so on. It was all a metamorphosis of one into the other. It proceeds not by linear articulation, but otherwise. I was never programmed. But I also could not deprogram all these things. It had to be so. But, fundamentally, I have had the same idea from the beginning. We all have just one idea all our life.

But, again, why this decision to exclude the empirical? Why choose this metaphysical approach? Why things not as they are but as they will or might be?

Not as they would be, but as they already are behind their own appearance. But, in point of fact, I was empirical. I started from the object and therefore from this point of view. In the beginning, I was phenomenologically oriented, you know, with Barthes and all that. I never started from the outside idealist world of concepts. And I was never assigned to any discipline. However, maybe this has changed. Perhaps I was obliged to go this way according to the heritage of pataphysics.

NZ: *Towards the end of* The Transparency of Evil, *you talk about the current state of things and say that you are in an apocalyptic state where you can only be melancholy. Isn't this a sort of personal – or even global – apocalyptic empiricism?*

I will not try to analyse myself psychologically. It would not be interesting either for me or for other people. Something must remain about what you do without you knowing what it is. Because things always come from somewhere else. I don't pretend to create concepts and so forth from the inside. They come from other things or other people. They must be fated in this sense – not in the sense of being mystical, but in the sense of coming from elsewhere. The world itself is very definitely strange. And we are in a state of things which is not that of alienation but that of the deprivation of the other. Freud has two words in German: *Verfremdung* and *Entfremdung*. The first means one's alienation by the other; the second the end of this, when there is no other any more. To become other is a good thing. But in *Entfremdung* there is no other any more. This is the worst state of things, much worse than alienation. And in this state, nothing any longer comes from the outside, from another world. And now the question is: what to do to maintain or keep this connection with otherness?

AC: *And this answers the question of how you choose one or the other of those two alternatives. This choice has always already been made. It is always a question of the other. You were asked: how did you choose? But the fact was, you were chosen.*

Exactly.

In that case, is your work both a description and a prescription of things? Yesterday, you said that all you have to do is follow the radical irony of the world itself, which is already out there. But it could be asked, if there really is this radical irony already in things, why do we need you to point it out to us? And the answer, of course, is because you are also putting it there. You are not just describing this radical irony but prescribing it.

Again, of course.

Then, in order to make a good argument about the world you have to 'double' it, in the sense that, after you say it, you cannot but see it. It is in this manner too that you propose a virtual world. Your criticism wants to make another world. You seem to see your task as that of doubling things. To this actual world, you desire to add another virtual world. So that there is an actuality and a virtuality at the same time.

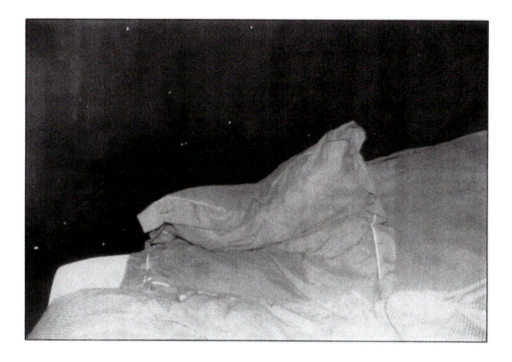

Paris, 1985

Manuscrit, Paris, 1986

Floride, 1986

St Clément, 1988

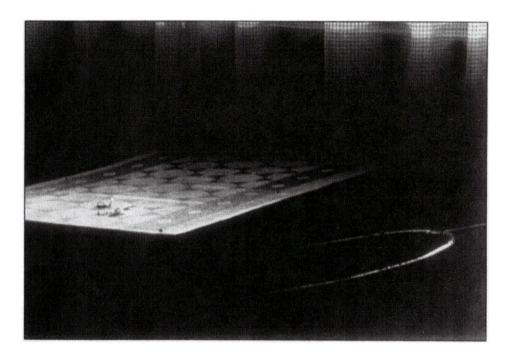

Portugal, 1992

Rue Sainte-Beuve, 1993

Quinta, 1993

Rome, 1994

Yes, but illusion doesn't mean another world behind or beyond this one. Illusion is simply the fact that nothing is itself, nothing means what it appears to mean. There is a kind of inner absence of everything to itself. That is illusion. It is where we can never get a hold of things as they are, where we can never know the truth about objects or the other. Illusion is this distance, this almost physical, objective – cosmological – distance. It is where the subject is not a subject for himself. But all this is not another world. And it applies not only to distant objects, but to near objects, even objects in the mirror!

You say that these two worlds are somehow immanent, simultaneous, but I think you would be arguing in your work that it is that other world which 'allows' this one to be realized. It is this illusion which allows the reality of this world. What would the relationship of that other world to this one be? Perhaps it doesn't so much allow it as 'double' it, but what would this mean? Is it a kind of Kantian transcendental that you are talking about here? How does it actually impact on this world? How can we become aware of it?

You can't know it. It remains a hypothesis. You can only know that things here are not stable, are not true, are not real. But perhaps it is the very acting-out of this hypothesis that has made them so.

AC: What do you mean by the expression 'virtual illusion'? Isn't there a danger of confusing it with this virtuality you have spoken of, in that one seems to be a real or realizing principle, and the other an irreal or derealizing principle?

Yes, this is a good point and an ambiguity in my text. But let me say this. Many other cultures – but not ours – deal with illusion as a form or a symbol. They are in direct connection with the illusion of the world. They never deal with the so-called reality of the world. But we only deal with this reality. However, maybe our culture through its technological array ends at the same point. Both cultures may ironically end up at the same point, the same 'end'. The first through seduction; the other through the very excessiveness of production. In both cases, there may be the same reversibility. It is a pure hypothesis on my part, but it is a very interesting one because it would be the counterpart to Heidegger's hypothesis that technology puts us on the path to the ontological truth of the world, is the ultimate stage of metaphysics, and so on. Here, on the contrary, technology takes us on an unknown detour – but, again, in some way, different paths would lead to the same end: to become radically absent from oneself.

To use a philosophical expression, then, could we say that illusion is the 'enabling condition' of this world? That this world is not possible without its alternative? If this is so, then, why in such recent books as The Transparency of Evil *and* The Illusion of the End *do you rhetorically ask the question: will we be saved by illusion or will we be allowed to perish? Because both alternatives are necessarily true. They are in fact not alternatives, but simultaneous.*

Yes, but if we ever attain an identity with ourselves we are dead. It is only in sleep or in death that we are identical with ourselves.

But we can never die in this sense because illusion will always save us.

On the contrary, illusion is a form of death. When we lose the possibility of death, of the end, of playing with the end, then we are very dead. And the whole system has managed to deprive us of this possibility. It is the state of things beyond the end, a kind of extermination beyond either an end or origin. To be exterminated means that you cannot find your own end and you are nothing any more. It is a state of things beyond the end. It is interminable and without co-ordinates. It is an extermination that is the very contrary of death. And it should remind us of that other extermination where people were deprived of the possibility of their own death.

NZ: Isn't that rather a spectacular hypothesis, if you're actually saying that our own collective condition in 1994 is somehow akin to the experience of the concentration camps in the 1940s? Presumably some of the survivors from these camps would take exception to this and read it as a trivialization of their experience – somewhat as Haacke and Bourdieu's dialogues in Libre-Echange *argue that such hypotheses abandon the world of political realities.*

The difference is that perhaps one is an inaugural event and the other is a historical condition, but I do think that the problem is the same. We might compare the concentration camps and the atomic bomb in this regard. Both irradiate this extermination with a virality that is also a virtuality. But all this, of course, must be explained more factually or precisely.

NZ: Does this make you a sort of Schindler wanting to help your readers escape the exterminating angel of viral virtuality?

Yes! I'll put you all on my list!

6

JEAN BAUDRILLARD'S DEFENCE OF THE REAL:
Reading *In the Shadow of the Silent Majorities* as an Allegory of Representation

REX BUTLER

Is it possible that all of the work of Jean Baudrillard is nothing more than the endless playing out of a paradox first stated more than 2000 years ago by Plato in his dialogue *Cratylus*? Plato writes in this dialogue:

> *Socrates*: Let us suppose the existence of two objects: one of them shall be Cratylus and the other the image of Cratylus, and we will suppose, further, that some god makes not only a representation such as a painter would make of your outward form and colour, but also creates an inward organisation like yours, having the same warmth and softness; and into this infuses motion and soul and mind, such as you have, and in a word copies all your qualities, and places them by you in another form. Would you say that this was Cratylus and the image of Cratylus, or that there were two Cratyluses?
>
> *Cratylus*: I should say that there were two Cratyluses.[1]

Plato's point here is that when two things resemble each other too closely they no longer resemble each other at all. There is no longer a relationship of original to copy, but of two separate originals. The copy only resembles the original in so far as it is different from it.

The relationship of resemblance is inherently paradoxical, therefore, in that it cannot be pushed too far without turning into its opposite: a bad imitation is a good imitation and a too-good imitation is a bad imitation.

It would also have no essence in so far as it is where it is not and is not where it most appears to be. To put it another way, we cannot say what imitation is because we could resemble it only by being ourselves different from it. There would always be a prior relationship of imitation implied in any attempt to speak of it – and that is precisely that imitation which allows us to imitate it.

We do not have to go too far to see something like this in Baudrillard. Take, for example, the following passage from his essay 'The Year 2000 Will Not Take Place':

> We are all obsessed (and not only in music) with high fidelity, obsessed with the quality of musical 'reproduction'. Armed with the tuners, amplifiers and speakers of our stereo systems, we adjust bass and treble, we multiply tracks, in search of an impeccable technology and an infallible music. I still remember a sound booth in a recording studio where the music, broadcast on four tracks, reached you in four dimensions so that it seemed unreal, secreted from the inside, with a surreal depth. . . This was no longer music. Where is the degree of technological sophistication, where is the 'high fidelity' threshold beyond which music as such would disappear? For the problem of the disappearance of music is the same as the disappearance of history: it will not disappear *for want of* music, it will disappear for having exceeded that limit point, vanishing point; it will disappear in the perfection of its materiality, in its own special effect (beyond which there is no longer any aesthetic judgement or aesthetic pleasure, it is the ecstasy of musicality and its end).[2]

In the same way as Plato, Baudrillard is arguing here that it is in coming too close to its original music that stereo would no longer resemble it at all. There is a limit point – a 'threshold' – beyond which the increasing perfection of stereo, instead of bringing music closer, actually drives it further away. There is a limit to the technical perfectibility of stereo, a point beyond which it cannot go except at the risk of no longer being stereo, of no longer reproducing its music. Beyond this point, stereo would no longer resemble its music, but only itself. It would no longer resemble its music, but would be only – a word that comes from Plato, but which is not used in quite the same sense by Baudrillard – a simulacrum of it.

This is Baudrillard's constant argument throughout his work. In his interviews, Baudrillard says that he does not have a method as such, but that his only strategy is one of reversibility.[3] By this, he means that he takes the basic axioms of the system he is examining and pushes them to the point where they begin to turn upon themselves, to produce the opposite effects from those intended. This is what we can see Baudrillard doing here. He does not directly oppose stereo; he does not speak of some real technical limit to its progress. Rather, he pushes it to its furthest extent, drives its essential tendency to the point where it has no limit and is absolutely identical to its music. But it is at just this point that what is shown is that stereo cannot complete itself in this way, cannot exactly reproduce its music while still reproducing music at all. What Baudrillard discovers is not an *external* but an *internal* limit to stereo, a limit which it is not *prevented* from going beyond but which it *cannot* go beyond.

We have here an entirely original idea of criticism, of how criticism works. Baudrillard does not – as is the usually understood role of criticism – oppose the technical development of stereo, propose some empirical reason why it is not perfect. He does not name something excluded from it (we can no longer hear the difference between stereo and its original music;[4] whatever limit we give to stereo, it is always possible that some future development of the medium will take us beyond it). On the contrary, Baudrillard entirely agrees with stereo, says that it has no limits – but this only because of, this only to lead to, a completely different explanation of stereo than the one stereo gives itself. This limitlessness leads to the end of stereo or this limitlessness is only possible because of the end of stereo. Or, to put this in terms of that Platonic paradox of imitation we looked at earlier: it is resemblance (stereo) pushed too far which leads to difference (the end of stereo) and difference (the end of stereo) which allows resemblance (stereo).

And, as we say, we can see all of Baudrillard's work as the endlessly varied elaboration of the necessity for this 'aesthetic illusion'. It is this, I would argue, that must be grasped first of all about his work; it is this that his work is fundamentally about. It is this, as we have seen with stereo, that allows Baudrillard to speak of the limits to any system actually becoming identical with the real. Although the real is only ever a function of its system (as music today can only be heard through stereo), there still remains a certain 'real' left out of any attempt by this system to speak of it (just as real 'music' is left out of stereo). This real might be understood as the very difference between the original and the copy, what the original and the copy both resemble and what therefore allows them to resemble each other. It is this real that Baudrillard speaks of throughout his work, beneath all the different names he gives for it (death, seduction, the masses, the fatal object, evil, reversibility, illusion, etc.). It is this real, excluded by any attempt to speak of it, that is the limit to every system – it is this Platonic paradox that Baudrillard means by the real.

How different this is from the usual readings of Baudrillard! In them, we find two seemingly opposed, but in fact identical, mistakes. First of all, they either judge Baudrillard's work according to some pre-existing real or compare his work to that of other theorists as though they were discussing the same real. This is a mistake because Baudrillard's point is that each system he analyses (and the work of any great thinker) creates its own reality, sets out the very terms in which it must be understood. This is the argument he makes with regard to stereo: there is no sense in simply speaking of some real music excluded from it because music today is only possible because of stereo. We can contest stereo only in its own terms, by pushing its fundamental postulates to their limit and watching them reverse upon themselves.[5]

The second mistake Baudrillard's commentators make is that they speak of his work as simply doing away with the real: Baudrillard as the great contemporary thinker of the end of reality, of reality as a simulacrum, etc. In fact, as opposed to this, Baudrillard's work offers a defence of the real against the efforts of all systems (including his own) to turn it into a simulacrum, a way of thinking the real as the unsurpassable limit to all systems. Baudrillard is a thinker not at all of reality as a simulacrum, but of the possibility of reality when all is simulacrum.[6]

The complex position of Baudrillard, then, is at once to argue that all reality is a simulacrum, that any attempt to speak of it can only turn it into a simulacrum, and that reality is the limit to all attempts to speak of it, to turn it into a simulacrum. But the real question is – it is the only way we have of judging Baudrillard in his own terms – how well is Baudrillard able to speak of this outside to all systems without actually being able to speak of it? What relationship is he able to form to that which forbids all relationship? How is he able to use a certain 'effect of the real' against those systems he contests while recognizing that he is himself unable to say what this real is? In short, how is he able to defend the real without also attacking it? We can see Baudrillard in the following excerpt from an interview trying simultaneously to hold on to all of these options:

> But I hold no position on reality. Reality remains an unshakeable postulate towards which you can maintain a relation either of adversity or of reconciliation. The real – all things considered, perhaps it exists – no, it doesn't exist – is the insurmountable limit of theory. The real is not an objective status of things, it is the point at which theory can do nothing. That does not necessarily make of theory a failure. The real is actually a challenge to the theoretical edifice. But in my opinion theory can have no status other than that of challenging the real.[7]

This is what we mean by speaking of Baudrillard's 'defence of the real' as an alternative to those usual interpretations of his work. It is important to realize that before reading him in terms of the real, his adequation to some pre-existing reality, he must be read in his own terms. That is to say, fundamentally, in terms of that Platonic paradox of imitation which is his constant critical method and his only real subject.

What we perhaps discover at the end of this is that we can *never* read Baudrillard in his own terms, that there is always a certain disorganization or contradiction in his thought. In one way, this is contingent, a result of Baudrillard's human failure as a thinker. In another way, however, it is unavoidable: it is the very limit of Baudrillard's own system to become real, to become strictly equivalent to the real. Those other analysts of Baudrillard's work are right – he can be compared to some pre-existing real, to the work of other thinkers – but, if we can say this, only as a result of first of all reading him in his own terms, only for the reasons Baudrillard himself gives. As with all great thinkers, it is only by turning Baudrillard against himself that we are able to criticize him; it is only by remembering the lessons he has to teach us that we might forget him.

* * *

In order to try to make some of this clearer, we might give here a more detailed interpretation of one of Baudrillard's texts, *In the Shadow of the Silent Majorities*, first published in 1978. In a sense, the book is a continuation of Baudrillard's earlier criticism where he actually named what was excluded from the system he was examining (for example 'function', 'drives' and 'needs' in *The System of Objects*, 'waste' in *The Society of Consumption*); but it is also a major advance towards this new style of criticism where he acknowledges that he cannot name what is excluded from the system he examines, that the system itself is the very definition of what is real. In other words, the paradox of *In the Shadow* – the paradox we shall be exploring here – is that the object Baudrillard names as outside the system (what he calls there the 'masses') is at once before and only after the system, at once a real limit to the system and only a function of it, at once a real phenomenon able to be described and only an effect of Baudrillard's own critical prescription.

In fact, *In the Shadow* constitutes one of Baudrillard's earliest and most elaborate discussions of his own methodology and the position of the critic. We can trace there an intricate analysis of that 'double strategy' or double position the critic must take with regard to his object or the real,[8] the way he must at once be outside and inside the system he contests, oppose some real to it and speak only in its language. There is a whole discourse there on conformity as both that difference which allows resemblance and that difference which arises from a too-close resemblance. *In the Shadow* perhaps is best seen as an expression of Baudrillard's endlessly inventive rephrasing of that Platonic paradox of representation – and in this it belongs to those other great 'fictions' of our modernity: Borges, Calvino, etc. Baudrillard's *In the Shadow*, in short, is one of our great allegories of representation.

What, then, is the nature of this allegory? Who or what are these masses? In the first instance, the masses are the masses of sociology and of all theories of the social. The masses are what all of these are based on, take for granted. The masses are to be educated, inoculated, covered by social benefits; the masses are to be liberated. The opinions of the masses are what all polls, statistics and surveys seek to find out. The masses are society's image of itself, the mirror, as it were, in which society sees itself reflected.

At the same time, however, if the masses are the most real, always in the actual, they are also strangely nebulous, hard to pin down. There is a sense that the concept of the 'masses' is too vague, but that in specifying it further we lose what we are trying to get at. Indeed, it might be that the very attempt to define the masses is a mistake, that the masses can never be made actual but must always remain virtual, on the other side of analysis. As Baudrillard remarks:

> To want to specify the term 'mass' is a mistake – it is to provide meaning for that which has none. One says: 'the mass of workers'. But the mass is never that of the workers, nor of any other social subject or object . . . The mass is without attribute, predicate, quality, reference. This is its definition, or its radical lack of definition. It has nothing to do with any *real* population, body or specific social aggregate. Any attempt to qualify it only seeks to transfer it back to sociology and rescue it from this indistinctness which is not even that of equivalence, but that of the neutral, that is to say *neither one nor the other*.[9]

But Baudrillard's point is very specific here. If the masses are difficult to analyse, resist definition, it is not because they are a real body out there waiting to be discovered, because an improvement in our analytical skills is necessary. Rather, it is because analysis destroys the very object aimed at, because the very gesture which creates the masses (for they would not exist in their nebulousness before analysis) also destroys them (for it is just this nebulousness, their resistance to definition, that *is* the masses, that defines them). We could say that it is the 'masses' which are excluded to allow us to speak of the masses, that the 'masses' are a name for that which is excluded to allow sociology to resemble its object, to speak of the masses and to formulate its opinions regarding them.

And this enigmatic limit might be put another way. As Baudrillard suggests, all theories of the social are predicated on the masses. The social itself is an Enlightenment concept based on the idea that there is a mass out there waiting to be informed, democratically represented, liberated – in a word, to be socialized. Yet, after more than four centuries of this socialization, there are more masses than ever before. Again, this could be understood as a merely *external* limit to the social:

the masses as not yet socialized, but given enough time and better directed resources inevitably being so.

Baudrillard, however, sees it differently. The masses are not an external, contingent limit to the social, but an *internal*, necessary limit. They are not opposed to the spread of the social and the spread of information, but are precisely an effect of them, what in fact allows their infinite expansion. The masses are what is necessarily excluded or produced by the social and by information; not opposed to or outside of them, but simultaneous with, inseparable from, them. As Baudrillard writes:

> Official history only records the uninterrupted progression of the social, relegating to the obscurity reserved for former cultures, as barbarous relics, everything not coinciding with this glorious advent. In fact, contrary to what one might believe, resistance to the social in all its forms has progressed *even more rapidly than the social itself*. It has merely taken other forms than the primitive and violent ones which were subsequently absorbed . . . For example, with medicine: frontal resistance has been replaced by a more subtle form of subversion; an excessive, uncontrollable consumption of medicine, a panicked conformity to health injunctions. A fantastic escalation in medical consumption which completely corrupts the social objectives and finalities of medicine. What better way to abolish it?[10]

But it is at this point that we must read Baudrillard very carefully and perhaps even against himself. For what could he mean here by saying that 'resistance to the social in all its forms has progressed *even more rapidly than the social itself*', by speaking of the masses as a simple *end* to the social? Elsewhere, as we have just seen, Baudrillard avoids speaking of the masses as a merely external limit to the social in this way, as something unequivocally opposed to it. Were this the case, he argues, this resistance in the end would only be possible because of the social, could only lead to a further extension of the social. Rather, if the masses constitute a limit to the social, it is a limit *at the same time as* the social, not so much opposed to or outside of it as what arises when there is *nothing* opposed to or outside of it. On the one hand, that is, it is the masses – the resistance or difference of the masses – which allow that infinite extension of the social whereby the social is realized, becomes equivalent to the real. And, on the other hand, it is also the masses – the resistance or difference of the masses – which ensure that the social is never realized or becomes real because this is only possible due to the masses, this can only lead to more masses.

In this sense, then, the masses are neither simply before nor after the social, but simultaneous with it. Or, to put it another way, the masses are the very relationship between the masses and the social, for it is just these masses which allow the social to reach them, which allow the social to socialize them. The masses would be both that difference between the social and the masses which allows the social to resemble the masses and that difference between the social and the masses which results when the social gets too close to the masses – a difference which ensures that the social could *never* entirely resemble the masses. The masses, then, are not merely what they appear to be, but the very relationship between the social and the masses: this is their real paradox. And the question involved in speaking of the masses from the position of the social as we do is: how to speak of that which allows you to speak of it? How to speak of that relationship which allows you to speak of the masses, which relationship, of course, would not exist until after you *had* spoken of them? This is the problem Baudrillard summarizes in *In the Shadow* as that of the masses' conformity. What does he mean by this conformity and why is it this conformity – this relationship – which is the real quality or characteristic of the masses?

To begin to answer this question, let us go back to what we said a moment ago about the masses, the way we have the feeling that something is excluded when we speak of them. There was something excluded, we said, not because there was something real out there which was left out, not because our analysis was inadequate, but because there was *nothing* left out, because our analysis and its ability to discriminate between the various types of masses using notions of class, social relations, power, status, institution, etc., was, if anything, too good. Or, again, in the idea that the masses constitute our image of society through polls, questionnaires and surveys, we get the feeling that they are a little *too* typical, a little *too* much themselves, fulfil our expectations about them a little *too* perfectly. We get the impression that there is something we are not getting at in the very match between question and answer. And we might have the suspicion that this is the result of a certain mental reservation or *arrière-pensée* on the part of the masses, a deliberate withholding of something. The masses, in other words, might be deliberately conforming to our expectations of them all the better in the end to escape from them.

But, again, it is just here that we – and Baudrillard – must be careful. We can understand the masses' conformity as a deliberate strategy on their part undertaken before the polls, as, Baudrillard says, 'a silence which *refuses to be spoken for in its name*'.[11] Yet, the masses and their conformity are only an effect of these polls; as Baudrillard also says, the polls '"produce" the masses in the form of anticipated responses, of circular signals, which seem to circumscribe their existence and bear witness to their will'.[12] And both of these – perhaps something Baudrillard does not emphasize enough – must be borne in mind at once: the masses' conformity is both that difference which allows the resemblance of the polls to them and that difference which results from the polls' too-close resemblance to them. The masses' conformity is both a real, conscious strategy on the part of the masses, masses that exist before these polls, and a virtual, involuntary effect that is attributed to what we call the 'masses', 'masses' that are themselves only an effect of these polls. (All this a little as we speak of music being excluded from stereo in two different senses in 'The Year 2000': both as a real, physical property that can actually be heard and as a purely virtual essence that is only an effect of discourse.)

We might try to put this paradoxical status of the masses' conformity still another way. We say that the quality which defines the masses is their conformity, their ability to imitate the various descriptions we give of them – it is this which all their analysts (including Baudrillard) attempt to describe. The masses, when summoned to respond, 'send back the same *conforming* signals, the same coded responses, with the same exasperating, endless *conformity*',[13] as objects in the natural sciences; they send back 'to the system its own logic by doubling it', 'reflecting, like a mirror, meaning without absorbing it'.[14]

But it is perhaps not quite so simple as this. For if the masses conform to the various theories about them, the masses are also not the masses, there is nothing for these theories to describe, until *after* the masses have something to conform to, that is, until after those theories have attempted to describe them. The paradox here is that, if these theories imitate or describe *something* – those masses which conform – at the same time they imitate or describe *nothing*: for those masses which conform would not exist until after those theories' attempt to conform to them.

In other words, in order to explain how the masses conform to their theory, we already need a theory that has tried to conform to the masses. In order to explain how theory conforms to the masses we already need masses that have tried to conform to their theory. In any attempt to explain how conformity takes place, we already need a conformity before this. Conformity, thus, if it is always too early as what precedes you and allows you to conform to it, is also always too late because it would exist only *after* you have attempted to conform to it.

All this is to suggest that what *In the Shadow* – like all of Baudrillard's work – is finally about is imitation. What Baudrillard is trying to describe by the masses in *In the Shadow*, is not so much anything (the masses) as the relationship between things (between the social and the masses, between the masses and their analysts); he is trying to imitate imitation. For what are these masses? They are neither simply real nor the various accounts given of them, but the very relationship between these two, what allows these accounts to resemble them. They are precisely what allows us to make an equivalence to the real. The real masses, we might say, are not so much the masses we describe – the real masses are always both before and after this – as what is between us and those masses we describe.

And, as we will see later in Baudrillard's discussion of what he calls seduction, the paradox of analysing the masses is that you must try to occupy that space between you and the masses, that difference or distance between you and the masses – which is just what the masses themselves are also trying to do.

The question, however, to be asked of *In the Shadow* is: to what extent does Baudrillard himself understand all this? To what extent does he realize that the masses are always both before and only after every description of them, that it is not possible to imitate the masses directly (even by speaking of their conformity) without the masses conforming to this? To what extent does he realize that in speaking of the masses (even of their meaninglessness and inability to be defined) he necessarily excludes them (that he gives them a meaning and defines them)?

With regard to these questions, there is in *In the Shadow* a way of reading Baudrillard as proposing a more complex relationship to the masses than the one we have looked at so far. It is not a question of directly copying or imitating the masses (the masses would always be both before and after our description, would both exclude themselves and be excluded to allow our description of them). Rather, if we are to imitate the masses it might be by *not* imitating them: just as the masses imitate nothing, come before and bring about their own reality, so too must any discourse on them. A discourse on the masses, that is, would resemble them not by comparing itself to them – for then what allows this comparison (the masses) would be excluded – but by resembling only itself like those masses it seeks to imitate, by being incomparable. The relationship between the masses and any discourse on them would not be that between two comparable things but that between two incomparable things, each resembling the other in its very incomparability.

It might be this 'different' relationship to the masses that Baudrillard is trying to gesture towards in *In the Shadow* when he speaks of the affinity between the masses and terrorism. Terrorism, in one way, of course, is only the most exacerbated attempt to make the masses speak, to speak for the masses. And to this extent it would always fail. This is terrorism in its bad sense. But in its more profound sense, terrorism does *not* simply attempt to represent the masses, either literally or politically. Instead, through its very denial of representation, through its refusal to signify, it might somehow – Baudrillard's word is 'blindly' – form a relationship to them.

Good terrorism not only attempts to represent the masses, but also tries to think through the limits of every attempt – especially those of our present-day societies of security – to represent the masses. Good terrorism, like good theory, defends this paradoxical 'reality' of the masses against all attempts to speak for them, including in a way its own. It does not aim directly, literally at the masses, but only indirectly, metaphorically. It does not try to *produce* the masses, we might say, but *seduces* them. As Baudrillard writes:

> Indeed, the only phenomenon which may be in a relationship of affinity with the masses is terrorism. Nothing is more 'cut off' from the masses than terrorism. Power may very well try to set one against the other, but nothing is more strange, more familiar either, than their convergence in denying the social and in refusing meaning . . . Terrorism does not aim at making anything speak, at resuscitating or mobilising anything; it has no revolutionary consequences. It aims at the masses in their silence, a silence mesmerised by information. It aims at the white magic of social abstraction by the black magic of a still greater, more anonymous, arbitrary and hazardous abstraction: that of the terrorist act. It is the only non-representative act. In this regard, it has an affinity with the masses, who are truly the only non-representable reality. This is definitely not to say that terrorism would *represent* the silence and the not-said of the masses, that it would violently express their passive resistance. It is simply to say: there is no equivalent to the blind, non-representative, senseless character of the terrorist act but the blind, senseless and unrepresentational behavior of the masses.[15]

Baudrillard proposes here the Platonic paradox that it is precisely in not representing the masses that terrorism would best represent the masses. Or, to put it another way, what terrorism realizes is that there is no point in simply representing the masses because the masses would not exist before being represented (if the essence of the masses is their conformity, they would not exist until *after* terrorism's attempt to represent them). This is why, in the passage above, it is impossible to decide whether it is the masses which arise in response to terrorism or terrorism which arises in response to the masses. Each responds to the other, but neither exists before the other.

This is the risk of terrorism – and of a theory like Baudrillard's. Its strategy is not to fight directly against the repression and anonymity of the social, but on the contrary to exaggerate them, maximize them, to drive the social to its furthest point. To the violence of the system of the social, it responds with an equal and opposite violence – or, as Baudrillard puts it, to the 'white magic of social abstraction', it opposes the 'black magic of a still greater, more anonymous, arbitrary and hazardous abstraction'.

But the risk here is that this abstraction of the social did not exist before terrorism, that its repression only arises in response to the threat of terrorism. In other words, it is possible that the dramatic solution of terrorism which sees the only possible response to the social as that of driving it to its limit in fact excludes real, empirical alternatives to the social. If this is the risk terrorism runs, however, it is also a risk for the social itself: the possibility that, without knowing it, it is responding to a strategy that completely goes against it, that it has been forced to enter into the terrorist's game (just as, secretly, resemblance is only possible because of difference and stereo only because of the exclusion of music).

This, finally, would be the miracle of theory, of writing, for Baudrillard: that, by imitating nothing, by following only its own rule, it is somehow able to 'catch' a system that similarly owes nothing to anything, is completely able to account for itself. Against the irrefutable hypothesis of the social, against its undeniable reality and realization of the world, it is able to oppose an equal and opposite hypothesis which somehow 'doubles' it, is able to explain how it arises for reasons absolutely different from the ones it gives itself: the masses.

What Baudrillard thinks is real about the world, what Baudrillard understands as the true key to and meaning of this world *is* this fundamental illusionality. For him, the world can resemble itself, can realize itself, only because of or to lead to an entirely 'other-worldly' explanation: the very difference between the world and itself, the real and its copy. It is this point – already two – at which absolute resemblance and absolute difference come together (death, seduction, the masses, the fatal object, reversibility, evil, etc.) that Baudrillard means by the real. It is this Platonic paradox – unrepresentable, unthinkable – that for Baudrillard is the most real thing in the world. If we can say this, it is the necessity of 'aesthetic illusion' which saves us from the 'disillusionment' of the world.

NOTES

1 Plato, 'Cratylus', *The Dialogues of Plato*, vol. II, Oxford: The Clarendon Press, 1875, p. 257. This passage has also been commented upon by Jacques Derrida in his 'Plato's Pharmacy', in *Dissemination*, London: The Athlone Press, 1981, p. 139.

2 Jean Baudrillard, 'The Year 2000 Will Not Take Place', in *FUTUR◊FALL: Excursions into Post-Modernity*, ed. E.A. Grosz *et al.*, Annandale: The Power Institute of Fine Arts, University of Sydney, 1986, p. 21. Baudrillard also speaks of stereo in these terms in *Cool Memories I*, London: Verso, 1990, pp. 82–3.

3 See on this 'Game with Vestiges: Interview with Salvatore Mele and Mark Titmarsh', in *Baudrillard Live: Selected Interviews*, ed. Mike Gane, London: Routledge, 1993, p. 82.

4 As Baudrillard writes in 'The Year 2000': 'We can no longer discover music as it was before stereo (unless by an effect of supplementary simulation)', *Futur*Fall*, p. 22.

5 Examples of this first type of mistake might include Douglas Kellner's *Jean Baudrillard: From Marxism to Post-Modernism and Beyond*, Cambridge: Polity, 1989, which offers a Marxist critique of Baudrillard; Julian Pefanis', *Heterology and the Postmodern: Bataille, Baudrillard and Lyotard*, Durham, NC and London: Duke University Press, 1991, which compares Baudrillard's work to that of Bataille; and Mike Gane's *Baudrillard: Critical and Fatal Theory*, London: Routledge, 1991, which places Baudrillard's work in the context of a number of French intellectuals who began to write immediately after the Second World War.

6 The most egregious example of this second type of mistake is undoubtedly Christopher Norris' 'Lost in the Funhouse: Baudrillard and the Politics of Post-Modernism', *Textual Practice*, vol. 3, no. 3, Winter 1989.

7 Jean Baudrillard, 'Forget Baudrillard: Interview with Sylvère Lotringer', in *Baudrillard Live*, p. 122.

8 On this 'double strategy', see Jean Baudrillard, *In the Shadow of the Silent Majorities*, New York: Semiotext(e), 1983, p. 107.

9 Ibid., pp. 5–6.

10 Ibid., pp. 41, 46.

11 Ibid., p. 22.

12 Ibid., p. 32.

13 Ibid., p. 33.

14 Ibid., p. 108.

15 Ibid., pp. 50, 51–2.

7

'OBJECTS IN MIRROR ARE CLOSER THAN THEY APPEAR': The Virtual Reality of *Jurassic Park* and Jean Baudrillard

ALAN CHOLODENKO

> Cinema is fascinated by itself as a lost object just as it (and we) are fascinated by the real as a referential in perdition.
>
> Jean Baudrillard, *The Evil Demon of Images*[1]

> The revolution of our time is the uncertainty revolution.
>
> Jean Baudrillard, *The Transparency of Evil*[2]

I

In the beginning to discover you've been preceded by another – the end – would be an unwelcome event, an uncanny, fatal turn of events themselves rendered 'no more' (nor 'less') than special effects. Such a seductive turn is for me never not in play and makes any embrace of the notion of a safe harbour – an artificial paradise – utopian. Such a 'No Parking' sign I see posted in the architecture, or, if you will allow, the 'parkitecture', of play, of the game, of the theatre, of the simulacrum – in a word (German) the *spiel* – that is always a way of *ent-bergung*, of releasing from shelter, of unsecuring, even as it sets up that which it will at the same time upset. Again, if you will allow such 'liberties', the *Spielberg* – the play mountain – at play in the theme parks Jurassic Park and *Jurassic Park*. But my story is already getting ahead of me . . .

Let me render an account – the account of the account – of what in the necessary accounting of can never be accounted for, can never add up, can never, in a word, compute, is always irreconcilable: Seduction, Illusion, the Principle of Evil of Baudrillard; the animatic; and Chaos, as in *Jurassic Park* chaotician Ian Malcolm's/Jeff Goldblum's/Seth Brundle-fly-in-the-Amber's pivotal words, 'Life will not be contained. Life breaks free, crosses all barriers, expands to new territories, dangerously, perhaps even painfully, but life finds a way'. For me, that final line also scans as 'life we'll find away', 'aweigh', 'anchors – anchorage – aweigh'!, departed from the harbour, departed from the shelter! Life is always already posted: *envoi*, or rather, *renvoi*.

Such would be for me the uncontainable, uncontrollable, uncanny, fatal hyperlogic integral to all systems – including the genetic and computer codes of DNA and digitality – as predicted by Chaos Theory and operating obedient to Baudrillard's Principle of Evil, and given singularly compelling demonstration in *Jurassic Park*. From the opening sequence's display of the insufficiency of apparently sophisticated human systems to control the barely glimpsed deadly non-human creature in the case – what will turn out to be the first 'appearance/ disappearance' of the quick seizer – the Velociraptor; to the parodic 'dinosaur and egg' aporia – which came first?;[3] to the bugging and overriding of the computer system controlling, and therefore all electronic systems operating in, the park, unleashing the deadly T-Rex on the children and adults, devouring the lawyer Gennaro alive and fracturing Malcolm's leg; to the 'end' with the returned T-Rex triumphant over the returned for the second time but only for the first time seen Velociraptors and their 'decentring' of the fossil display that is the centrepiece of the Visitors Centre, ironizing thereby the slogan of that display – 'When Dinosaurs Ruled the Earth'; to the crepuscular flight of the humans toward a horizon which perhaps they are already on the other side of, with all the apparently unpredictable, haphazard, anomalous, accidental, coincidental, chance turns of events happening at the largest and most minute levels *en route* that prove fatal to the human mastery of the park added to the account, Universal Chaos might be thought to always already rule Jurassic Park and *Jurassic Park*.

Such a 'rule' is already announced in the 'beginning' of the film, what might even be thought of as the film before the film, in the virtually apparent Julia set astrally encrypted in the upper left quadrant of the image of the Universal Studios logo with the name of the corporation itself moving as a satellite around the Earth – the Universal in orbit.

And superior even to Chaos Theory's unpredictability of predictability and predictability of unpredictability is the fatal necessity of Baudrillard's Principle of Evil. *Jurassic Park* is a ferocious example of that Principle, exemplifying, as Baudrillard quotes Hegel, that we are amid 'the life, moving of itself, of that which is dead',[4] which would be 'a vital principle of unbinding (*déliaison*)',[5] the virulent vitality of the virus of the virtual. It is for Baudrillard 'a principle of instability and vertigo, a principle of complexity and foreignness, a principle of seduction, a principle of incompatibility, antagonism and irreducibility'.[6] Its hyperlogic: what is 'realized' – be it representation, simulation, the system and its oppositions – will turn out to have been seduced by that which has 'realized' it – Seduction, Illusion, Evil – as that which has 'realized' it will 'itself' have been seduced. The fatal must be fatal to itself, or it is not fatal.

And let me also say that all I will say about *Jurassic Park* – perhaps no more than what I have already just now said – is for me encapsulated and fractualized in the uncanny, dreadful, vertiginous, delirious, turbulent, fascinating, aporetic 'image' but one shot long whose all too familiar caution forms the title of this essay: 'OBJECTS IN MIRROR ARE CLOSER THAN THEY APPEAR', the 'image' in and of the side show sideview mirror of the Jeep of the T-Rex – its jaws wide open and forming an all-absorbing void/black hole as they double the frame of the mirror and of the film – accelerating at an incredible pace coming closer and closer to the Jeep's occupants, a 'vanishing point of view' shot of the driver-hunter Muldoon hunted/haunted by the terrifying, implacable, uncanny revenant: the return/reanimation with a vengeance of the living dead cryptically incorporated in the anamorphic, parallactic, necrospectival, virtual mirror-image-object of film. What would be the revenge of the crystal of film instantiated in the most intense, eruptive, explosive and implosive animation in the film, the most 'realistic' animation, the computer-generated animation: the shock, the bite, the grab that arrest us in its virtual death sentence, as in the Dead Point, Blind Spot, Strange Attractor of that virtual mirror.[7]

In my Introduction to and essay in *The Illusion of Life: Essays on Animation*, 'Who Framed Roger Rabbit, or The Framing of Animation', as in the paper I presented at the 1991 Society for Animation Studies Conference, 'Speculations on the Animatic Automaton', I develop the concept of the animatic (and its) apparatus – an uncanny, disseminative, seductive, turbulent apparatus of lifedeath which indistinguishes not only cartoon animation and live action film, animation theory and film theory but film and 'the rest of the world', thereby giving 'film' and the 'world' no rest, as it likewise gives all other binary oppositions no final reconciliation.[8]

In this essay I propose to focus on *Jurassic Park*, addressing the relation of computer animation and live action film, including consideration of computer animation and special effects. Among the many points to be raised, I will suggest that *Jurassic Park* is a hyperrealist film that 'takes a place' in the tradition as old as the animated film itself – that of the hybrid cartoon animation/live action film (the 'lightning sketch') – uncannily returning to one of its first examples – Winsor McCay's *Gertie* – to push it and that tradition beyond their limit, ecstacizing and indistinguishing cartoon animation and live action, animation and film – fatal even to itself as to that tradition – even as it pushes beyond the horizon of the human to the 'history' of the world before the advent of the human – a 'Close Encounter' with the prehistoric, primeval world of the dinosaur – embodying in that return not only the contemporary systematic reversal and annihilation of history (even and especially in the utopian efforts to rehabilitate, cleanse, purify, preserve and rejuvenate it as authentic, what might be called 'Hammond's "Last Crusade"') but also the fatal destiny of the world: virtual reality.[9]

Jurassic Park pushes the modern, the historical, the constitutive human subject, meaning, truth, reality, etc., beyond their horizon, beyond their vanishing point, beyond Elias Canetti's Dead Point,[10] beyond André Bazin's point of integral realism, into the virtual reality of the post-modern, the hyperreal, the posthistorical, the evacuation of the constitutive subject, the catastrophic explosion and implosion of the polarities heretofore sustaining meaning in and through the mass media – the medium of film, but especially television and the computer as media: the realm of special effect where all is ex-orbitant, in orbit, satellized, on and in the short-circuit of the (dé)tour. In that very hypertelic, ecstatic, maximalizing process, the hypercinematic telematic tourism of the theme parks Jurassic Park and *Jurassic Park* marks the spiralling, ironical and paradoxical 'turn' of the posthistorical into the prehistorical, marking the uncanny post-mortem return, the raising up, reanimating and ostensible rehabilitating of the dead – the extinct non-human (the dinosaur) – to thereby render dead, extinct, the living – the human – as well as the sciences and technologies of the human, including the science of palaeontology (as the Tasaday did to the science of anthropology).[11]

Jurassic Park's live action characters interact with a live action world, or rather livedead action world, of simulation dinosaurs that the 'reanimators' in the film and the 'reanimators' of the film have (re)engineered in part through the most sophisticated techniques of computer-generated simulation and processes of (Jurassic Park) or analogous to (*Jurassic Park*) biogenetic molecular DNA techniques, grafting in the former the DNA of the 'dead' dinosaur with that of frog DNA and in the latter 'grafting' the live action human with the animated non-human, producing in both cases an indistinguishability of one species from another, in the latter case an indistinguishability at the level of the reality of the illusion of life. As ILM (Industrial Light and Magic) Visual Effects Supervisor Denis Muren declares, 'these dinosaurs are absolutely unlike anything you've ever seen before'.[12] Unlike *Gertie*, whose hybrid character is perceptible in the difference between live action human and classically drawn and stop motion animated non-human dinosaur, *Jurassic Park* confuses, trans-figures, ecstacizes and ex-terminates the hybrid form.

By means of computer animation techniques operating not at the old 'mechanical' level of the exotechnical but at the level of the esotechnical, *Jurassic Park* ecstacizes the process which it declares to be at work in 'cinema' 'itself', pushing the special effect to its limit, its fulfilment and annihilation.[13] *Jurassic Park*, the 'film' that shows that film is everywhere except in film, puts the special effect everywhere except in the special effect. 'Pushing the envelope'[14] of the state of the 'art' of animation – past the thrills of *Who Framed Roger Rabbit* and the morphing astonishments of *Terminator 2* – *Jurassic Park* is the vertiginous, delirious ecstasy of special effect 'as such', as it is 'specifically' for the genre of which it is likewise the latest example and of which *Gertie* would be the first: the dinosaur film, *Gertie* acknowledged as such in the sighting first of the brachiosaur (tellingly, a brachiosaur indifferent to the humans, unlike the playful Gertie).[15] ILM Visual Effects Co-Supervisor Mark Dippe states:

> Dinosaur films have always been the classic effects films. A lot of effects techniques have been developed through the years in dinosaur movies – stop motion, Claymation, men in rubber suits, cable-driven puppets, radio control puppets, go-motion . . . and now, full-motion computer animation. With *Jurassic Park*, we've created something that is in a direct line of the evolution of creature work.[16]

The history of special effects, of which the dinosaur genre has been a privileged testing ground, is the history of animation as the mechanism for the incorporation of the special effect in the cinema. *Jurassic Park* turns the cinema inside out, making it more special effect than special effect, more animation than animation, as it simultaneously makes animation more cinema than cinema, more live action than live action, in the process rendering traditional animation extinct. So too it turns inside out – short-circuits, telescopes, makes reversible and uncertain – the pro-filmic and filmic, the diegesis and the film, (the) film and reality – each contaminating and incorporating the other (as the presence of the book *The Making of Jurassic Park* by Don Shay and Jody Duncan on a shelf of merchandise 'in the film' amply declares: the introversion of the exterior and the extroversion of the interior), all such implosions begging the question: which is which?[17]

Like the Velociraptor, which rips the insides of its victims out, devouring them while they are still alive, and like the T-Rex, which rules the park and returns to Rule the World, *Jurassic Park* is a *deinos* – an uncanny fearful, terrifying – *saurus* (lizard), a deinos-saur, an evil demon, a terminator – a T-Rexterminator – which exterminates the term and determination, replacing them with indetermination and the impossibility of measure, impossibility of the rule.[18] Uncannily, *Jurassic Park* terminates film and reality, making both 'special effects' – viral, vital virtualities – like 'itself'. Such a catastrophe would ostensibly mark a mutation from the aesthetics of attraction of cinema's 'beginnings' to the anaesthetics of distraction of cinema's hyperreal 'end' in its redoubled retroversion to its (and the world's) 'beginning' – Hammond's 'future attractions' from the lost world of *Gertie* (and the impossibly remote past).[19]

Such a process raises up, revives, reanimates cartoon animation and live action film, animation and film, film and reality, nonhuman and human as lost referentials, the dead reanimated as the living dead that will never have to die again because death is itself surpassed – in a word, death is dead. What is thus 'raised up' – living simulations – would be immortal, not the immortality that comes from the inescapably physically defeating but spiritually victorious heroic challenge to death but the automatic immortality that is microgenetically engineered, not a fatally uncanny immortality of the human but a banally uncanny immortality of the nonhuman – that of the clonal body, which resembles nothing so much as the originary protozoa that Freud postulated as the uncanny end to which the Death Drive would return the human – clonal bodies that reappear to disappear but can never reappear nor disappear as such only once and thus for forever.[20] No, condemned to eternal asexual celibate reproduction and reiteration of the identical – the hell of the same – this would be the endlessness of the end: the transfinite. The dinosaur that will die no more, that will not die because it already has. I take it that Muren's declaration gestures toward such a hypertelic metastatic modelling: cold clonal immortality.

Of this catastrophe, one could say, after Baudrillard, 'The Year 2000 Will Not Take Place', because it already has and does so repeatedly, interminably.[21] In computer animation terms we could call such living dead clonal creatures, such zombies, vactors:[22] virtual (reality) actors, actors of the vacuum of the void, or fractors – fractal actors. As we could call what is regenerated 'cinema' or the animatic telecinematic: digital film. We watch this epidemic animatic telecinematic exterminate the sciences applied in Jurassic Park and *Jurassic Park* as well as the sciences of film theory and animation theory insofar as they all futilely seek to rehabilitate themselves by reversing and undoing their own extinction by seeking to describe, interpret, account for, reconcile and thereby control, contain, encrypt and/or render extinct once again what they themselves have systematically unleashed, decrypted, from within themselves.[23]

In this process one has passed from the double that guaranteed one's immortality to the double that guaranteed one's mortality – the doubles of the cinematic image, doubles now lost – to the clonal 'double' that cannot be lost so that one can die or in dying transcend to life eternal but rather that 'lives on',[24] guaranteeing at once 'one's' immortal mortality and mortal immortality – the lost 'double' of a 'cinema' lost. A 'double' everywhere except in the double for a 'cinema' everywhere save in cinema. The symbolic experience of the horror film – the wish at once to die and to not die but to outlive our deaths as immortals – is in *Jurassic Park* ecstacized in its contemporary catastrophic mutated viral form/genre – terror – a predator (pre-dator) to which the viewer is held hostage (and vice versa, for which is which?). This would be the terrorism of a project – André Bazin's – that seeks to make cinema coincident with the real, the achievement of which could only ever be simulacral, virtual, hyperreal, the simultaneous fulfilment, death and reanimation of cinema as 'cinema' – the ironizing of Bazin's notion of film's goal of integral realism, *the myth of total cinema*.[25] The necromancer Spielberg may declare, 'I'm going for *total* realism as opposed to anything that hypes the wonder';[26] but any attempt at total realism cannot escape the hype of the hyperreal.

Baudrillard writes: 'Our Apocalypse is not real, it is *virtual*. And it is not in the future, it is taking place *here and now*'.[27] 'After the Orgy', once freed of its substance and resurrected, regenerated, be it by film and/or computer, the animatic is all the more virulent and vital for having been freed of its essence and liberated into its contemporary simulacral hyperreal form: the virtual form of the viral, the fractal, the clone.[28] The Special Effect. Not only does *Jurassic Park* play out for the 'cinema' in all its registers all the rituals and modes of transparency that Baudrillard has articulated: the terrorist and the hostage, the obese, the obscene (what would be the too great proximity – closeness – of the world), the artificial paradise, Telematic Man, hi-fi, etc.[29] It represents and 'is' 'itself' a metastatic viral epidemic of cinema at once hyperproliferating and satellized around itself, more and more only deliriously resembling, absorbed and disappearing in itself – more *Andromeda Strain* than *Andromeda Strain*, more *Westworld* than *Westworld*, more *Jaws* than *Jaws*, more *Close Encounters of the Third Kind* than *Close Encounters of the Third Kind* (as well as more *King Kong* than *King Kong*, more *Citizen Kane* than *Citizen Kane*,[30] more *The Birds* than *The Birds*,[31] more *Dr Strangelove* than *Dr Strangelove*,[32] more *Dr Dolittle* than *Dr Dolittle*,[33] more *Family Plot* than *Family Plot*, more *Apocalypse Now* than *Apocalypse Now*, more *The China Syndrome* than *The China Syndrome*,[34] more *Blade Runner* than *Blade Runner*, more more!, etc., which is simultaneously more less) – as it simultaneously more and more infects and in-distinguishes 'itself' from 'reality', 'reality' 'itself' already and increasingly 'cinematized' – more artificial paradise than artificial paradise, more Disneyland, Disneyworld than Disneyland, Disneyworld, more Biosphere 2 than Biosphere 2, more Universal Studios Park than Universal Studios Park, etc.[35]

Jurassic Park, the 'film' that shows that film is everywhere save in film – and everything else is everywhere except in 'itself' and is therefore incorporated in film – is a viral epidemic where relations of contagion, confusion, contamination, proliferation, dispersal, extenuation, total substitutability, stasis and digitality operate (yet surprisingly there are no digital watches to be seen in *Jurassic Park*!).[36] *Jurassic Park* is an example of at once exponential instability and exponential stability, at once acceleration and inertia.[37] *Jurassic Park* puts the special effect everywhere save in the special effect, itself transparent, nowhere to be seen (except perhaps in the bad special effect: the 'human', whose woodenness recalls the last resource of the eighteenth century magician who, fabricating a perfect automaton, had himself to perform mechanically to preserve the game of illusion).[38]

In such artificial paradises as *Jurassic Park*, the always already dead are regenerated in the metastatic form, 'torn from the dead in order to be cryogenized in perpetuity',[39] by means of cloning to exist eternally in a state of suspended animation: Disney's cryogenic orbitalization in an artificial paradise awaiting the Second Coming.[40] The state of Special Effect. Akin to the Seth Brundleflymachine, *Jurassic Park*, a 'virtual machine', is an ecstatic example of recombinant cinema, the film itself a form and event demonstrating and performing what the film narrativizes: artificially generative film techniques analogous to those of recombinant DNA in combination with the technology of the computer – the cutting and splicing and grafting and sequencing of cine-gene fragments with each other and with computer-gene fragments – in both cases introducing the viral into cinema as into the artificial paradise of Hammond's more Disney than Disney Jurassic Park, not only in the form of the dinosaur but in that of Virtual Telematic Telecomputer Man – the obese Dennis Nedry – the computer virus who holds the park and its human inhabitants hostage as he is in turn held hostage to it and its non-human inhabitants.[41] *Jurassic Park* as virtual, viral, vital, obese, obscene, livedead 'body'. Like Charles Foster Kane's fractal imaging to infinity in the doubling mirrors of Xanadu – from *in vivo* to *in vitro* – in *Citizen Kane*, one is dealing in *Jurassic Park* with an apocalypse of the virtual, with Coppola's/Coppelius's archaeopterics of the uncanny,[42] with cinema as cryogenic cryptic incorporator and incorporation. Clonal Galli-mimesis without end.

A Close Encounter of the Fourth Kind, that is, with the contemporary viral form of simulacra, *Jurassic Park* would be a 'cinema' whose organic metabolism would make of it today a vast historiosynthetic machine of special effects lacking but one thing: the particular hallucination that makes cinema cinema.[43] This would be, like 'reality', 'cinema' both more cinema than cinema and less cinema than cinema at the same time: simultaneous acceleration, inertia and absorption in 'its' 'own' void. This would be, as my Baudrillard epigraph declares, a 'cinema . . . fascinated by itself as a lost object just as it (and we) are fascinated by the real as a referential in perdition'. This would be the fascination with 'cinema' and 'reality' as special effects. *The Evil Demon of Images* concludes:

> Today, there is an inverse negative relation between the cinema and reality: it results from the loss of specificity which both have suffered. Cold collage, cool promiscuity, asexual engagement of two cold media [film and reality now both media!] which evolve in asymptotic line towards one another: cinema attempting to abolish itself in the absolute of reality, the real already long absorbed in cinematographic (or televised) hyperreality.[44]

Coiling at once around themselves and around each other in their asexual engagement, these two cold spiralling media of cinema and reality for me cannot but mime the double helix of DNA as cloned by Hammond, who would be the whiter than white ADN (Adonai) of *Jurassic Park* while at the same time dedicated to the AND of indefinite seriality.[45]

Indeterminate and generating viral indeterminacy in epidemic proportions, hypercinema – the livedead 'cinema' – resembles for me nothing so much as the organic metabolism of the Thing from John Carpenter's *The Thing from Another World* or the inorganic metabolism of the T-1000 of *Terminator 2*, hypersaturated, indifferent, formless forms which can simulate, absorb and short-circuit all forms, 'themselves' never given nor givable as such, instead 'remaining' virtual. These dreaded voracious metamorphs are sublime protean plasmatic forms in their metastatic expression, protean plasmaticness that which Sergei Eisenstein declares to be the essence of Disney animation, an essence to which Eisenstein's own work aspires, an 'essence' whose 'ultimate' form would be DNA itself, its double helix like two strips/strands of film winding about each other.[46] But in their metastatic form, they enwrap Disney's enchanting, seducing metamorphosing forms in a disenchanting, disenchanted, simulacral shroud, the 'winding sheet' of 'cinema'.[47]

Such films offer us the necrotic fascination for a 'cinema' whose special effect is that it lives beyond its own vanishing point, beyond its own finality, which in so doing means that in ending, it can never end: the impossibility at once of arrival at or departure from the crypt of *Jurassic Park*: *stazione ex-terminale*. No resolution of life nor death, rather the viral processes of the eclectic, of retro-'aesthetics', the necrospective, where the films of the past are 'raised', revived, reanimated, as lost referentials in the reiterative, wildly hyperbolic replay of 'endless variations on all earlier forms'.[48] In the face of this irreconcilability, any palaeontology, archaeology (including Indiana Jones'(!)) or genealogy of cinema must confront the evil genie of cinema, the evil demon of cinema, setting us forever on the tour, the track, of the cinema looped as the Moebius Strip: in the wake of its turbulence, its eddy, its spiralling whirlpool.[49] No Raider could ever redeem cinema's Lost Archive.[50]

Computer animation and special effects set one upon the case of the CASE (Computer Animation and Special Effects), set one in the virtuality of the *chez*, the case, *casa*, casino, cassette, casket of the case, which is an uncanny haunted place – the house of the living dead, the revenant – the ghost, the zombie, and now the clone.[51] It is to be where the movement of media 'in themselves' and 'as they move together' in formation, in packs like Velociraptors (VRs, VCRs, Video Cassette Recorders!) – hyper-telic film, tele-vision, the computer – uncannily bring farness (the tele-, marked in the abbreviation 'tellie'),[52] strangeness, the unfamiliar, the wild, the exotic, closer and closer, making them more and more familiar while at the same time drawing the close, the familiar, the home(y), the domestic, further and further away, making them more and more unfamiliar in exponential maximalizing modes of simultaneous acceleration and inertia: from telos to the more telos than telos – the hypertelos, the hyper-telic – of the tele- – the virtual brought ever closer.[53] An evil demon tempts me to describe this state of things as the 'film-iliar'. In this case *Jurassic Park* shows us that 'the modern media have a viral force of their own, and their virulence is contagious'.[54]

Jurassic Park turns us around on this tour that would be of the order of the Principle of the Good, what would be a squeaky clean new Eden, the Peaceable Kingdom, populated with genuine dinosaurs, in a detour that returns us to rediscover that which we thought we were discovering only for the first time: the uncanny return of the dead as living dead – a devil's tour of hell,[55] perdition, Pandaemonium, a detour of the virtual, of the simulacral dinosaur, on which tour we move forwards backwards, or is it backwards forwards? – who could tell? – Moonwalking around Nedryland (Neverland?), arriving before we left and leaving before we arrive. In *Jurassic Park* it is the Strange Attractor, or rather the Principle of Evil, that rules.

Through this process of tele-scoping, short-circuiting, exterminating and cryptically incorporating, *Jurassic Park* shows that any attempt to track backwards through history, even and especially to history's own prehistory, to rewrite and rehabilitate a good (pre)history cleansed of evil so that one can enter the millennium reconciled falls prey to the fact that what is resurrected and rehabilitated is always already hyperreal, simulated, virtual, as it demonstrates the inevitable unleashing of that

in/excorporated element resident 'within' and integral to any system –
any artificial paradise – which will destroy the system.

II

Crucially, once posited, once assumed, the Dead Point and its crossing
means that all that existed before the crossing into the hyperreal, the
postcinematic, is by that crossing forever contaminated by it so that one
could just as well suppose that all before that crossing accorded with all
coming after it.[56] In 'taking a place' in the tradition as old as the
animated film itself, uncannily returning to one of its first examples –
Gertie – to push it and that tradition beyond their limit, *Jurassic Park*
turns us seductively, fatally, from the showmen Hammond and
Spielberg and the end of cinema's finalities to the showman Winsor
McCay and cinema's beginnings to rediscover at cinema's origins its
originary diversion, death and reanimation as lifedeath: the essence of
film is always already its non-essence.[57] Film's 'end' is always already in
its 'beginning'! The 'event' of the 'death' of cinema always already
doubles the 'event' of the 'birth' of cinema.

Such would be cinema's asymptotic 'development' – the form of the
spiral, the loop, the Moebius Strip, of 'film' – pushing cinema beyond
Canetti's Dead Point and Bazin's point of integral realism to return to
cinema's 'beginning', in that very turn/tour/detour exterminating the
idealist Euclidean model of the linear with the asymptotic line as curve
that describes a spiralling return to what in leaving one always already
started to return to, which would be the death of the linear modelling of
cinema as it would be of 'cinema' as such from its 'very' 'beginning',
what might be called, ironizing Bazin, 'The Oncology of the (Filmic)
Image'![58] Cinema's 'end' and 'beginning' reverse, moving forwards
backwards and backwards forwards at the same time. They spiral,
leading to inevitable indetermination as to which comes before which.
The spiral makes any point at once a beginning and an end. The spiral
makes what follows precede and what precedes follow.

Jurassic Park, itself dead and resurrected in advance, a film-clone, film
virus, film-fractal, tells us that all cinema is dead and resurrected in
advance. It tells us that science and technology, even and most crucially
their micro-arena in which everything, including 'identity', is played out
today – the genetic and computer codes of DNA and digitality – have
themselves never not aimed at uncertainty, with 'presenting us with
a definitively unreal world, beyond all criteria of truth and reality'.[59]
The virtual/viral/vital is never not integral to the system, including
that of the codes. The vertiginous hyperlogic of the code: 'it' executes,
i.e. performs, 'itself' even in executing, i.e. 'undoing', 'itself', as the

'spontaneous' transformation of females to males in Jurassic Park attests, marking the impossibility of total command and control over the human genome and its processes. 'It's a hell of a system', says Arnold of the computer command control centre of Jurassic Park – a hell of a system for a hell of a place.[60]

If cinema (and film theory) have sought to escape animation, ostensibly *Jurassic Park* returns cinema (and film theory) to animation (and animation theory) as it returns animation (and animation theory) to cinema (and film theory) presuming cinema can control animation, as Hammond regenerates the dinosaur DNA presuming he can control it; but animation returns with a vengeance to seduce and outbid cinema, uncannily turning into cinema the better to perfect and annihilate it: the animatic is internal and integral to stable systems. This is the fatality of the system.[61] *Jurassic Park* tells us, as I suggest in the Introduction to *The Illusion of Life*, that film was never not simulation. Never not a virtual body. Never not lifedeath. Never not an uncanny, dynamic, turbulent form. Film would never not live beyond its own end, as it never not lives before its own beginning. Film is always 'before the beginning, Mr Thompson' (to quote Bernstein from *Citizen Kane*) – 'its' 'own' beginning – and 'after the end' – 'its' 'own' end – at the same time. Film is not reconciled, not reconcilable. Film is animatic.[62]

In all these senses, the film, like the dinosaurs it regenerates, is a catastrophic, apocalyptic, superconductive event, an 'event' passing beyond the horizon of film (as it tells us that film is 'itself' always already beyond the event horizon), passing beyond by means of its asexual engagement with the computer (another celibate reanimatic machine), digital film the offspring of their contiguous 'coupling'. To pose the question of whether, like the relation of the mass and the medium, the computer has seduced film, as the dinosaur has seduced the human, making it enter a field of metamorphosis despite itself, or film has seduced the computer, playing the illusion-preserving game of the magician, would be impossible to calculate, to compute. Any answer that would 'reconcile', including simply opposing, them would exclude that which enabled such a 'reconciliation': the virtual radical excluded Other – Seduction, Illusion, the Principle of Evil.[63] Film and computer – at once isomorphic and radically incompatible – enter into viral relations with each other, contaminate, confuse and indetermine each other, as they infect every sphere, generating uncertainty, itself infectious.[64]

In the wake of *Jurassic Park*, 'OBJECTS IN MIRROR ARE CLOSER THAN THEY APPEAR', or as it uncannily appears in the epigraph to 'Vanishing Point', the opening essay of Baudrillard's book *America*: 'Caution: Objects in this mirror may be closer than they appear!' 'May be' – more uncertain yet! The animatic would be the vital virtuality at once not only at work within but coming between film and computer, enabling them to 'coil' around each other, bind to and mime each other, hyperconform and hyperproliferate, as it at the same time forms the milieu for their unlinking, unbanding, their *déliaison* in a (dis)integrated and (dis)integrating circuit.

So too the animatic as vital virtuality of *déliaison* would be not only at work within but coming between Baudrillard's work and its subjects/objects, as it must likewise be not only at work within but coming between this essay and its subjects/objects, making it analogously a piece of theory-fiction, a special effect, that comes to pass between the theory-fictions, the special effects, that are *Jurassic Park* and the work of Baudrillard, uncannily turning the relations among all of them likewise into relations of analogy, virality and virtuality 'closer than they appear'.[65] In *La Transparence du mal*, Baudrillard writes:

> Once certain limits have been passed there is no longer a relationship from cause to effect, there are only viral relationships from one effect to another, and the whole system is driven entirely by inertia. The film of this increase in strength, of this velocity and ferocity of the dead, is the modern story of the accursed share. It is not a question of explaining it; it is necessary to be its mirror in real time. It is necessary to exceed the speed of events, which have themselves for a long time exceeded the speed of liberation. And it is necessary to speak of incoherence, anomaly and catastrophe, it is necessary to speak of the vitality of all these extreme phenomena which play with extermination and simultaneously with certain mysterious rules.[66]

Would *Jurassic Park* not be that film? (And in being that film would it not be all film?) And in all that I have said of *Jurassic Park*, have I never not been prescribing/describing Baudrillard's work as all this, and more? Would it not be that 'mirror' of the film 'in real time', an uncanny, fatal mirror in which 'Objects . . . may be closer than they appear!'?

But at the same time does Baudrillard's work not tell us that (that) film is, as '*Jurassic Park*' 'itself' declares, such a mirror and that mirror work of his already 'such' a film? As his epigraph to 'Vanishing Point' might be thought to declare, the ironical logic of the world, the metamorphic, anamorphic reversibility of everything and anything under the sign of Seduction, is not only at work in *Jurassic Park*. The evil demon (of images) is at work within Baudrillard's own work, begging the question of the nature and relation of that work to cinema, as it must be at work within this essay, likewise begging the question of the nature and relation of this work to cinema, including to *Jurassic Park*, as it does of the nature and relation of this work to Baudrillard's work.

Certainly, Baudrillard has explicitly addressed cinema in his writings from his earliest texts on (Godard's *Le Mépris* in *Le Système des objets*, *The Student of Prague* and *Playtime* in *La Société de consommation*); but with *The Evil Demon of Images*, presented in 1984 as the Inaugural Mari Kuttna Lecture on Film, and its final paragraph quoted earlier, and then with *America*, published in 1986, film becomes a favoured figure of hyperreality.[67] Already in the 1982 interview 'I Like the Cinema', in response to the question, 'In everyday life, do you sometimes have the impression of being in a film?', Baudrillard declares:

> Yes, particularly in America, to a quite painful degree. If you drive round Los Angeles in a car, or go out into the desert, you are left with an impression that is totally cinematographic, hallucinatory. You are in a film: you are steeped in a substance which is that of the real, of the hyper-real, of the cinema.[68]

Four years later these ideas would be given explicit instantiation in his book *America*. Taking America as the exemplification of the hyperreal, Baudrillard took America to be cinematized, to be a film, as his experience in travelling within and across it he characterized as a travelling shot.

But, once past *The Evil Demon of Images* and *America*, we can just as well suppose that Baudrillard has not only never not been writing about the cinema, about film, but that his own work has never not itself been cinematized, never not itself been a film. *America*, for example, would be a book-film, a book travelling shot. For if, as Baudrillard claims in *The Evil Demon of Images*, there is an increasingly de-finitive indetermining of the relation of film and world, an increasing commingling of film and world such that one cannot be disentangled from the other, not only are Baudrillard's writings on the world at the same time on film, and vice versa, necessitating quotation marks around the words 'world' and 'film', but moreover, Baudrillard's own writings commingle with their subjects such that it is impossible to know where the author and the authored, the animator and the animated, the subject and the object, etc., 'begin' and 'end'.[69]

Like the dinosaur and egg aporia of *Jurassic Park*, like the mass and the media, like the mirror in which 'Objects . . . may be closer than they appear!', and like the ironical, fatal Object, the Object as Strange Attractor, and more, itself the mirror – all of which reverse upon and hyperconform to each other and to 'themselves' as they at the same time form the turn, the pivot, the Dead Point of what they strangely attract, image and 'reflect', themselves never given nor givable 'as such', always excluded to enable one pole of an opposition to be equivalent to another while at the same time in their inclusion disenabling such an equivalence, begging the question of whether it is because the poles oppose and are equivalent to each other that the third would be excluded or whether it is because the third is excluded that these poles could oppose and be equivalent to each other – here too, in the relation of film and world, Baudrillard's own writings and what he writes of, including the cinema, and this essay and what it addresses, the questions are begged: which is which? which came before which? which is cause and which is effect? And the answer in each case is tendered: the only answer is that there is no answer. The question and answer of the viral, vital virtuality of theory-fiction, of special effect, of Seduction, of Illusion, of the mirror as Strange Attractor, and more, the mirror as Object, the mirror as Crystal.[70]

Like all these strange mirrors, Baudrillard's uncanny work is at once compliant with and fatal to the metastatic processes and systems his work provokes, describes and ironizes – in a word, ecstacizes – as it is itself ecstasized in the process.[71] In 'Game with Vestiges' Baudrillard declares, 'I don't have any doctrines to defend. I have one strategy, that's all'.[72] That one strategy is ecstasizing, hypertelia, the logic of 'pushing a system or a concept or an argument to the extreme points where one pushes them over, where they tumble over their own logic. Yes, it's all a type of artifice using irony and humour'.[73]

This means that Baudrillard's recent texts, *The Transparency of Evil* and *L'Illusion de la fin*, are not only themselves viral, vital, virtual metastatic forms, they would be more. In the essay 'Instabilité et stabilité exponentielles' Baudrillard makes a crucial distinction: 'Destiny is an ecstatic figure of necessity, Chaos is only a metastatic figure of Chance'.[74] For Baudrillard Chaos is but a parody, a simulation, of all metaphysics of destiny. Baudrillard's work remains a defence of the principle of Seduction, a defence of Illusion, a defence of the ecstatic necessity of destiny, as sovereign principles, against the Chaos of the increasingly cold, statistical, aleatory world of simulacra. Ten years ago, this might have been formulated as: the sole thing that is at stake is Seduction (warm, enchanted simulation) against simulation (cold, disenchanted Seduction), with Seduction the superior – while simulation simulates Seduction, Seduction seduces simulation.

More recently, it might be articulated as: Illusion (unconditional simulacra) against simulation (conditional, disillusioned simulacra). For Baudrillard the catastrophic, hypermediatized, uncertain, post-orgy state of today is characterized by the fatally flawed, panic-stricken effort to 'realize' the world – be it through art, the humanities, science and/or technology – in simulacra *against* the total radical illusion of the world, its great game of putting into play, its artifice, its irony, its humour.[75] Illusion, as sovereign, renders any such project of 'realization' – at once a simulation of utopia and a utopian simulation – lost in advance. Such as the attempt of Jurassic Park and *Jurassic Park* at total realism, that is,

total simulation, an attempt whose 'magic' resides only in the technological wizardry it displays, as it takes the display of such virtuosity to
be cinema's sole rationale: the demonstration and performance of what
cinema can do, such a rationale itself testifying to the post-cinema state
of 'cinema' today.[76]

Baudrillard may write in L'Illusion de la fin, 'Our Apocalypse is not
real, it is virtual. And it is not in the future, it is taking place here and
now',[77] but I believe that he would see the necessary reversibility of his
statement in Symbolic Exchange and Death, 'Today reality is itself hyperrealist',[78] into 'hyperreality is today's reality', which for me suggests that
hyperreality is not merely virtual but also a reality, a reality of a
particular sort, that would be, if I may reverse his definition in 'The
Precession of Simulacra', without origin or a real,[79] that would be a 'real
unreal', an actual virtual and virtual actual at the same time, like, in a
word, cinema.[80]

Like Jurassic Park and Jurassic Park, the necromancer Baudrillard's
America and America and his corpus in general are mirrors in which
'Objects . . . may be closer than they appear!', at once conjuring a world
into 'virtual existence' and out again, with the qualification that what is
brought close in such 'realizing' is a doubled virtual reality: of simulation and of Seduction, of Illusion. Baudrillard himself 'realizes' a world
as virtual and at the same time shows it to be a conditional simulacrum
doubled by a superior virtuality, that of radical Illusion and its play in
virtualizing reality as simulacrum, a reality of Illusion in which Illusion
is always at once included and excluded. Actuality would thus come to
be that virtuality (Illusion) at once included and excluded in any virtual
reality.

In such a scenario, any 'reflection', including Baudrillard's, including
mine, must repeat in fractal abyssal form the fatal paradox of losing
Illusion in any effort to speak of it, for it is never given as such. Illusion
must be fatal to itself, or it is not. Illusion is not reconciled, nor
reconcilable, not even to 'itself'. Any 'reflection' faces the inevitable turn
of the mirror, which turns (on) everything, even itself – the 'mirror' that
mirrors nothing. If it is only Baudrillard's work that makes its object
possible, after such invention it is only the object that makes such a
work possible, even as the object and the work become reversible and
their relationship indeterminate in and through this doubling process. In
such a process, the 'work', to quote Baudrillard from 'The Year 2000',
'loses all objective validity, but perhaps gains in coherence, that is to say
in real affinity with the system that surrounds us'.[81]

That 'real affinity' would be the virulent vitality of the virtual, that 'fly
in the ointment', that animatic 'mirror' in 'real' time, not only what is
immanent in its opposite, doubling and (un)doing it, but what doubles
and (un)does 'itself' – vertiginously. And if this is (un)done 'with

artifice, using irony and humour', with wit and poetry, then it would be (un)done with a Seductive surcharge.

Crucially, although today we speak of hyperreality, of virtual reality, instead of reality, once past Canetti's Dead Point, all reality is and has never not been virtual. In provocatively declaring, 'I live in the virtual'[82] – a declaration as impossible of proof as it is irrefutable, which is likewise true of theory-fiction, special effect, simulation, Seduction, Illusion, the uncanny, the animatic *et al.* – all of which are in a certain sense 'nothing' at all – Baudrillard for me implicitly suggests that he has never not lived there, that virtual reality has never not been the case. In accord with this, I would declare: virtual reality is the only reality I've ever 'known'.

'Welcome to Jurassic Park'. Or rather – to paraphrase another ex-Terminator in the case of the future anterior – 'welcome back', for it will have always already been back . . . in the beginning as in the end.

NOTES

1 Translated by Paul Patton and Paul Foss, Sydney: Power Institute Publications, 1987, p. 33.

2 'Superconductive Events', in *The Transparency of Evil*, translated by James Benedict, London: Verso, 1993, p. 43.

3 The book, intriguingly, cultivates no such aporia insofar as the egg is declared to be synthetic. See Michael Crichton, *Jurassic Park*, London: Arrow, 1991.

4 'The Theorem of the Accursed Share', in *The Transparency of Evil*, p. 108.

5 'Le Théorème de la Part Maudite', in *La Transparence du mal*, Paris: Editions Galilée, 1990, p. 112, my translation.

6 'The Theorem of the Accursed Share', in *The Transparency of Evil*, p. 107.

7 After conceptualizing this essay around the figure of this uncanny mirror, I encountered Tom Shone's essay, 'Raider of His Lost Art', *The Modern Review*, vol. 1, no. 10, August–September 1993, in which Shone proposes that the sticker at the bottom of this mirror, reading '"Objects may be closer than they appear" (sic) . . . could be his [Spielberg's] motto', that Spielberg has 'devoted most of his career to perfecting a state-of-the-art way of yelling "He's behind you!"' – his 'monster-in-the-rear-view-mirror joke' (p. 3). I would suggest that what appears in that mirror and its death sentence is what Slavoj Zizek, after Lacan's treatment of Holbein's *The Ambassadors* in terms of the emergence of and in the anamorphic image of the death's head as the making visible of the subject as annihilated, takes up as the phallic anamorphotic uncanny eruption of the real. Or what, after Samuel Weber, I would describe as the parallactic coming-to-pass and passing-to-come of film. See Slavoj Zizek, *Looking Awry*, Cambridge, MA: MIT Press, 1991, pp. 88–91; and Samuel Weber, 'The Parallax View', *assemblage*, no. 20, April 1993, where Weber argues that it is television that installs the parallax view. Parenthetically, it is surprising that Zizek takes up this eruption – of the

'signifier without signified' – in terms of the films of Alfred Hitchcock without citing the film that for me (but not myself alone) more than any other makes of this figure the greatest conundrum in the history of cinema: *Citizen Kane*, and its irresolvable Rosebud. Here, Bernstein's Woman In White weds to Baudelaire's *passante* as a figure of such an eruption. On Martin Heidegger, Walter Benjamin and Baudelaire's *passante* in relation to the mass media, see Weber, 'Mass Mediauras, or: Art, Aura and Media in the Work of Walter Benjamin', in *Mass Mediauras: Form, Technics, Media*, ed. Alan Cholodenko, Sydney/Stanford: Power Publications/Stanford University Press, 1996.

8 See *The Illusion of Life: Essays on Animation*, ed. Alan Cholodenko, Sydney: Power Publications, 1991. 'Speculations on the Animatic Automaton', subsequently presented in long form to the graduate students of Sydney College of the Arts, the Sydney Society for Literature and Aesthetics, the Power Institute Public Education Program and the Critical Studies Program at UCLA, is as yet unpublished.

9 On Baudrillard's notion of the retrospective whitewashing of history, see, for example, 'Operational Whitewash' and 'Necrospective', in *The Transparency of Evil* and 'La décongélation de l'Est', in *L'Illusion de la fin*, Paris: Editions Galilée, 1992.

10 Canetti defines the Dead Point as follows: 'A tormenting thought: as of a certain point, history was no longer *real*. Without noticing it, all mankind suddenly left reality; everything happening since then was supposedly not true; but we supposedly didn't notice. Our task would now be to find that point, and as long as we didn't have it, we would be forced to abide in our present destruction'. *The Human Province*, translated by Joachim Neugroschel, London: André Deutsch, 1985, p. 69.

11 On the Tasaday, see Baudrillard, 'The Precession of Simulacra', translated by Paul Foss and Paul Patton, in Baudrillard, *Simulations*, New York: Semiotext(e), 1983, pp. 13–23.

12 Quoted in Don Shay and Jody Duncan, *The Making of Jurassic Park*, London: Boxtree, 1993, p. 139.

13 On Baudrillard's principle of hypertelia – the pushing of things to their limits – see *Fatal Strategies*, ed. Jim Fleming and translated by Philip Beitchman and W.G.J. Niesluchowski, New York: Semiotext(e), 1990.

14 In terms of this notion of 'pushing the envelope', see Crichton, *Jurassic Park*, p. 51.

15 In terms of delirium, see Baudrillard's English language epigraph to *La Transparence du mal*: 'Since the world drives to a delirious state of things, we must drive to a delirious point of view'. James Benedict, translator of *The Transparency of Evil*, for me inexplicably alters this epigraph to 'Since the world is on a delusional course, we must adopt a delusional standpoint towards the world'.

16 Quoted in *The Making of Jurassic Park*, p. 139.

17 On the process of the increasing indetermination of film and world, see Baudrillard, *The Evil Demon of Images*.

18 On the *deinos*, see Philippe Lacoue-Labarthe, 'Typography', in *Typography*, ed. Christopher Fynsk, Cambridge, MA: Harvard University Press, 1989, p. 93, note 79, where he remarks that Socrates is fond of speaking of the artifice of the

'living statue', the animated statue, and that, as for Plato, 'what unsettles him, in the plastic realm or in "fiction" (whatever form it might take), is, as P.M. Schuhl has suggested, *simultaneously* that the inanimate being should give itself as something alive and that this (falsely or illusorily) living thing should never be sufficiently alive, that is, should always let death show through too much (in other words, "brute" death, the bad death that the sensible world holds – and not that death that marks the "separation of the soul and the body" as the beginning of the true "life of the spirit"). The *deinon*, the *Unheimliche* (as the expatriation or exile of the soul, as well) is this unassignable, this "neither dead nor alive", that disturbs, or always risks disturbing, the fundamental ontological opposition (between the present and the non-present). This is mimesis, the "disquieting strangeness" of fiction: undecidability "itself"'. On this uncanny figure of the living statue – the automaton – as it relates to animation and film, see my 'Speculations on the Animatic Automaton'.

19 In this regard Tom Gunning's essay 'An Aesthetic of Astonishment: Early Film and the (In)credulous Spectator', *Art & Text*, no. 34, Spring 1989, links the advent of the cinema to the aesthetic of attraction, which, though narrative will come to overlay it, never ceases to run its course through the history of cinema. Of course, for me a film like *Jurassic Park* ecstacizes the attraction and, as well, all the more suggests that Gunning's strong piece would benefit from the qualifications that an acknowledgement of his own use of the terms 'canny' and 'uncanny' would call for. That is, for me the advent of the cinema is an uncanny advent, one which necessitates a complex analysis that would avoid simply inverting and replacing the classic passive slave, 'dupe' model of the early film spectator with an active master, 'all-knowing', urban sophisticate model (a reduction Gunning does not always avoid, though it appears he would wish to), one that would acknowledge that all that Gunning says of the character of this advent is already in Freud's 'logics' of the uncanny; that the attraction, film and *a fortiori* animation are of the order of the uncanny (what I characterize as the *animatic*); that when Gunning says that the shock – the simultaneous attraction and repulsion, fascination and dread – at seeing what was still 'come to life' founds the cinema and persists as an undercurrent in narrative cinema, he is saying that the uncanny, the animatic, 'founds' cinema – the inanimate become animate, and vice versa; and that any thinking of cinema cannot delimit itself to the thinking of the subject and its desires and the cinema as only a mode of production and appearance but must at the same time consider what American film theorists have typically ignored, that is, the object and its games, games superior to the subject – the non-organic, artificial life of objects of the cinematic, or rather animatic, apparatus and its modes of seduction, play, dissemination and disappearance. The non-organic life of objects – for me what we mean by 'magic' – is a 'life' coimplicated with the notion of the death drive, for which all uncanny returns are stand-ins, that is, it is death which returns, and more, as it is a life coimplicated with not only a system of explosion but simultaneously one of implosion. And, of course, such a complex analysis would acknowledge the implications of such a model for the very analysis under way, acknowledge the limitations set up thereby to the theorist's ability to account for what he/she seeks to render an account of, so that the theorist would not, like Gunning, on the one hand attempt to forge a sophisticated 'both/and, neither/nor' model for

describing the cinema and its spectator while on the other hand buying into an either/or binary, assuming the position of master demystifying showman-theorist who could simply stand outside the logics of the system being described (in this case the cinematization of the world), who, like his spectator, could find, upon leaving the movie theatre, the world outside the cinema untainted by the world within. For me the radical coimplication of film and world offered by Baudrillard's *The Evil Demon of Images* would call any assumption of such a simple 'leaving', including Barthes', into question (as Barthes' own appeal in his essay, 'Upon Leaving the Movie Theater', to a 'cinematic condition' of 'crepuscular reverie' outside the cinema arguably disturbs his maintenance otherwise in that piece of an opposition of inside versus outside the movie theatre), as it would call for a more complex thinking of the 'suspension of disbelief', one that acknowledges that the cinematization of the world would of necessity incorporate the spectatator and theorist, even the theorist as master demystifier, within it and that the cinematic apparatus is, despite all the '70s discourse and project of the revelation of its mode of production, never givable, producible, as such. Indeed, that the cinema issues a challenge to the either/orism of the master/slave, active/passive model, as it does to all productivist efforts to unveil its/the mode of production. Such banal efforts of demystification are no match for the fatal strategies of the cinema and their seduction of film theory, turning it into a special effect.

20 See 'L'immortalité', in *L'Illusion de la fin*. On Freud's protozoa as the destiny of the 'human', see 'The Hell of the Same', in *The Transparency of Evil* and 'L'Immortalité', in *L'Illusion de la fin*.

21 'The Year 2000 Will Not Take Place', in *FUTUR◊FALL: Excursions into Post-Modernity*, ed. E.A. Grosz *et al.*, Sydney: Power Institute Publications, 1986.

22 On vactors, see Peter Britton, '"Vactors" Grab Starring Roles in Dawn of Film-Making's Digital Age', *The Australian*, Tuesday 19 October 1993, pp. 42–43.

23 On such a cryptic incorporation, one might also consult Jacques Derrida, 'Fors', in Nicolas Abraham and Maria Torok, *The Wolf Man's Magic Word: A Cryptonymy*, translated by Nicholas Rand, Minneapolis: University of Minnesota Press, 1986.

24 See 'The Hell of the Same', in *The Transparency of Evil* and 'L'Immortalité', in *L'Illusion de la fin*.

25 Bazin, 'The Myth of Total Cinema', in *What is Cinema?*, translated by Hugh Gray, Berkeley: University of California Press, 1967. And see Baudrillard, *The Evil Demon of Images*, p. 31, and 'After the Orgy', in *The Transparency of Evil*, p. 4.

26 Quoted in Rufus Sears, 'It's Big!', *Empire*, August 1993, p. 78.

27 'Hystérésie du Millenium', in *L'Illusion de la fin*, p.166, my translation.

28 To Baudrillard's three orders of simulacra (see 'The Orders of Simulacra', translated by Philip Beitchman, in *Simulations*) *The Transparency of Evil* adds this fourth.

29 See *Fatal Strategies* and *The Transparency of Evil*.

30 *Citizen Kane*, a watershed moment for the history, or rather destiny, of cinema, in terms of the hypertelic processes it dramatizes and partakes of, is another film about a potentate who has set up a zoo in his exotic and fenced-in preserve, in this regard (and others) articulating, like *Jurassic Park*, with *King Kong*. See note 7. It is worthy of note that *Citizen Kane* also represents a

watershed moment in cinema for Gilles Deleuze, who characterizes it as 'the first great film of a cinema of time'. *Cinema 2: The Time-Image*, translated by Hugh Tomlinson and Robert Galeta, Minneapolis: University of Minnesota Press, 1989, p. 99.

31 Peter Wollen, 'Theme Park and Variations', *Sight and Sound*, vol. 3, no. 7, July 1993, pp. 7–9. Ostensibly self-declaredly operating as 'cine-palaeontologist tracing the evolutionary history of film', Wollen sees *Jurassic Park* not only as 'a rather obvious hybrid of *Jaws* and writer Michael Crichton's earlier theme-park fantasy *Westworld*' (and through *Jaws* to 'the successful line of monster movies that runs from *The Lost World*, on through *King Kong*, and down to *Jaws*') but also as having as its closest ancestor Alfred Hitchcock's *The Birds*, which film represents for Wollen a merger of the fantastic monster film with the slasher genre.

32 Spielberg is quoted as saying '*Jurassic Park* had a lot of forefathers, and I'm sure *Dr Strangelove* was among them', in Eric Lefcovitz, 'How *Dr Strangelove* inspired Spielberg', *Sydney Morning Herald*, Saturday 5 February 1994, Spectrum, p. 12A. For Baudrillard's discussion of Stanley Kubrick and his *Barry Lyndon* in terms of the filmmaker as purely operational chess player, see *The Evil Demon of Images*, pp. 30–32.

33 Like the 'appropriateness' of the casting of Jeff Goldblum from David Cronenberg's *The Fly* as Ian Malcolm, the 'appropriateness' of Sir Richard Attenborough as Hammond is 'secured' by his earlier role as Blossom in *Dr Dolittle*.

34 On *Apocalypse Now* and *The China Syndrome*, see Baudrillard, *The Evil Demon of Images*.

35 On the artificial paradise of Biosphere 2, see Baudrillard, 'L'écologie maléfique', in *L'Illusion de la fin*. In this regard, the malefic curvature of events – the arrival immanent in the departure at the same time as the departure is immanent in the arrival, indetermining which is which – might be thought to be 'in play' in Peter Wollen's piece on the theme park, 'Theme Park and Variations', wherein he claims, after Michael Sorkin, as 'Ur-form' of the theme park – of which Jurassic Park would be an example, like Disneyland and Disney World before it – the Great Exhibition of the World's Fair of 1851 held at the Crystal Palace in London, 'bringing together the wealth of nations into an enclosed palace for tourists, which [Wollen here quotes Sorkin from his book *Variations on a Theme Park*] "depicted paradise. Not only was it laid out like a great cathedral, with nave and transept, but it was also the largest greenhouse ever built, its interior filled with greenery as well as goods, a climate-controlled reconciliation of Arcadia and industry, a garden for machines"' (pp. 8–9). Wollen notes that Richard Owen, the great palaeontologist who coined the term 'dinosaur', designed an exhibition of dinosaurs – the first such exhibition – on an artificial island in the Exhibition Park when the Crystal Palace moved to Sydenham. Here I would make several points. First, the Crystal Palace is fascinating as a proto-architectural form of the movie theatre in general and the motion picture palace in particular insofar as, like the arcade, it is a form of double invagination, at once the introversion of the exterior and extroversion of the interior, and it is an artificial paradise in which denatured nature is complemented by naturalized machines. And in terms of both it and Owen's prototype of Jurassic Park, I

would claim, against the 'Ur-form' of Wollen and Sorkin, that a prior ancestry for the theme park can be argued: those gardens and grottos of machines – hydraulically driven automata theatres – adjacent to the palaces of the nobility of the sixteenth and seventeenth centuries, which take up a place in a history of automata spectacles whose lineage is well over 2000 years old. See my 'Speculations on the Animatic Automaton'.

36 See 'After the Orgy', in *The Transparency of Evil*. Of Stephen Jay Gould's essay on *Jurassic Park*, 'Dinomania', *New York Review of Books*, 12 August 1993, it could be said that Gould still (and nostalgically) takes as a given what the work of Baudrillard, films like *Jurassic Park* and this essay would suggest are lost referentials: palaeontology, origin, presence, essence, purity, authenticity, the zone of the real and the museum as the sacred site for the real dinosaurs – in the form of fossils. Gould writes: 'theme parks are, in many ways, the antithesis of museums. If each institution respects the other's essence and place, the opposition poses no problem. But theme parks belong to the realm of commerce, museums to the world of education' (pp. 55–56). But I would argue that the theme park has no essence and no place; its 'essence' would be no essence, its 'place' no place. Which suggests that Gould's either/or modelling is naive, displaying insufficient understanding of the logics of the good and bad copy and an unsupportable belief in the candour of the simulacrum and the possibility of it – here in the form of the virtual reality of the theme park – being put outside and kept outside the original, nor does he link the 'reality' of *Jurassic Park* with the virtual reality he attributes to the theme park. The virality of Jurassic Park and *Jurassic Park* wars against Gould's modelling, even as it wars against Hammond's design.

37 See Baudrillard's articulation of the simultaneous processes of acceleration and inertia in the posthistorical in 'The Year 2000 Will Not Take Place'.

38 *Fatal Strategies*, pp. 51, 173. One is reminded of the joke that did the rounds, that the dinosaurs in *Jurassic Park* are better actors than the humans.

39 Baudrillard, 'La danse des fossiles', in *L'Illusion de la fin*, p. 109.

40 On Baudrillard on Disney and/or Disneyland, see, for example, 'The Precession of Simulacra'; *America*, translated by Chris Turner, London: Verso, 1988; and 'L'écologie maléfique' and 'Hystérésie du Millenium' in *L'Illusion de la fin*. See also my Introduction to *The Illusion of Life*.

41 On Telematic Man (what Benedict translates as Telecomputer Man), otherwise called by Baudrillard Virtual Man, see Baudrillard, 'Xerox and Infinity', in *The Transparency of Evil*. The words *virtual* and *virus* contain the Latin *vir*, meaning man, as well as harkening toward the word *virtue*. The computer bug Nedry represents the fall of both man and virtue, though the articulation called for would be a complex one.

42 On the uncanny, see Freud's 'The "Uncanny"', in *Standard Edition*, vol. 17, London: The Hogarth Press and the Institute of Psycho-Analysis, 1955. The uncanny coupling by Nathanael of the lawyer Coppelius and the optician Coppola in the E.T.A. Hoffmann story, 'The Sand Man', is a copulation already marked in their names, a copulation that cannot but perpetuate itself – uncannily – in their coupling with the name already there of the film director Coppola (Francis Ford), whose *Apocalypse Now* Baudrillard characterizes as an example of 'cinema become a vast machine of special effects', the perpetuation of

the Vietnam war by other means, a film become war, as Vietnam is a war become film. *The Evil Demon of Images*, p. 17. In terms of my understanding of film as uncanny, see my Introduction to *The Illusion of Life* and 'Speculations on the Animatic Automaton'. As well, see Thierry Kuntzel's point in 'A Note upon the Filmic Apparatus', *Quarterly Review of Film Studies*, vol. 1, no. 3, August 1976, that in nominating The Mystic Writing Pad as metaphor of the psyche, Freud missed a better model: the cinema. Here Derrida's essays 'Freud and the Scene of Writing', in *Writing and Difference*, translated by Alan Bass, London: Routledge & Kegan Paul, 1978, and 'To Speculate – on "Freud"', in *The Post Card: From Socrates to Freud and Beyond*, translated by Alan Bass, Chicago: The University of Chicago Press, 1987, prove most instructive. On the archaeopterics of the uncanny, see Derrida, 'Fors', in Abraham and Torok, *The Wolf Man's Magic Word*, p. xxvii.

43 *The Evil Demon of Images*, p. 31.

44 Ibid., pp. 33–34.

45 See Baudrillard, 'The Orders of Simulacra', in *Simulations*, p. 109.

46 On Eisenstein's notion of plasmaticness, see Sergei Eisenstein, *Eisenstein on Disney*, ed. Jay Leyda and translated by Alan Upchurch, London: Methuen, 1988. As well, consult Keith Clancy, 'ΠΡΗΣΤΗΡ: The T(r)opology of Pyromania', and Keith Broadfoot and Rex Butler, 'The Illusion of Illusion', in *The Illusion of Life*. My 'Speculations on the Animatic Automaton' also takes up this notion.

47 Such viral indeterminacy takes as one of its pre-eminent forms the facticity of fact generated by the mass media, otherwise known as simulation. See Baudrillard's *America*, p. 85, and *La Guerre du golfe n'a pas eu lieu*, Paris: Editions Galilée, 1991.

48 'Transaesthetics', in *The Transparency of Evil*, p. 15.

49 In terms of Chaos Theory, the Lorenz attractor is here recalled.

50 See 'Superconductive Events', in *The Transparency of Evil*, p. 43.

51 On the multiplicitous meanings – all relevant – of *chez*, see Weber, 'Reading and Writing – *chez* Derrida', in *Institution and Interpretation*, Minneapolis: University of Minnesota Press, 1987. The uncanny nature of the cinema, marked in the event of its advent as described by Gunning, turns the sense of being at home that the spectator felt before the image started to turn from still photograph to mobile cinematograph – the experience of being in a legitimate theatre or at an all too familiar spectacle – into a sense of being homeless – *unheimlich* – with its movement, its turning, its 'coming to life', its coming-to-pass – its animation. (Here, the expression 'coming to life' needs qualification, a curious locution insofar as I would suggest that life can never be come to (nor death); in any case, it is the illusion of life to which for me this expression alludes.) So, too, the relation between film and world becomes homeless, uncanny, as each – film and world – invades, 'inhabits' and indetermines the other. To be in the house (*casa*) of cinema is not to be in the *domus* – the home. Its refuge could never be pure refuge, any more than it could be pure non-refuge. The movie theatre is of the order of the between. To be in it is to be in the haunted house of cinema, *chez* cinema. See notes 19 and 42.

52 On the tele-, see Baudrillard, 'Xerox and Infinity', in *The Transparency of Evil*. See also Weber, 'Television: Set and Screen' and 'Deus ex Media', in *Mass Mediauras: Form, Technics, Media*.

53 Such a process in/and such a medium is, of course, uncanny. Freud's term *unheimlich* can slide all the way into its opposite – *heimlich*, meaning familiar, cosy, friendly – and vice versa.

54 'Superconductive Events', in *The Transparency of Evil*, pp. 36–37.

55 Intriguingly, a tour through the meanings of the French *tour* discloses that it has not one but two forms: the masculine noun, whose meanings include turn, round, twining, winding, revolution, circuit, tour, trip, twist, and notably, trick, dodge, wile; and the feminine noun, meaning tower, rook, castle (chess), taking us to the Devil's Tower of *Close Encounters*. Moreover, *tour* turns up in *tourisme*; *tournée* (the name of the compilation of best animated films that does the rounds, the journey, through movie theatres each year); *tourner*, as in *tourner un film* (to shoot a film), recalling the winding, spooling, of the reel of film in the process not only of shooting but of projection; and as well in *tourbillon*, meaning whirlwind, whirlpool, eddy, vortex. On Heraclitus' fiery whirlwind, see Keith Clancy's essay in *The Illusion of Life*.

56 As Baudrillard points out in 'The Year 2000 Will Not Take Place', pp. 21–23, it is, contrary to Canetti's aspiration, a crossing itself impossible to locate, only ever assumable.

57 Here lies a point of coincidence between Baudrillard's and Derrida's work, implicit in one of Baudrillard's hypotheses in 'The Year 2000 Will Not Take Place': 'But we can just as well suppose that history itself is, or was, nothing but an enormous simulation model' (p. 23).

58 See Bazin's 'The Ontology of the Photographic Image', in *What is Cinema?*. Yet such an uncanny return to cinema's advent is consistent with Bazin's idea that the myth of total cinema, the goal of integral realism, existed fully formed at cinema's conceptual inception, hence the passage to the fulfilment by cinema of its myth must be a movement forwards backwards, or is it backwards forwards? – who could tell? This is to suggest that there are intriguing parallels between Bazin and Baudrillard to be teased out, for example Bazin's model of a cinema bound (albeit ontogenetically) not to man but to the universe and his definition of the job of the film director as not creating a new reality but 'framing the fleeting crystallization of a reality of whose environing presence one is ceaselessly aware'. 'Theater and Cinema – Part One', in *What is Cinema?*, p. 91, quoted in Dudley Andrew, *André Bazin*, New York: Oxford University Press, 1978, p. 123. And for Bazin such a reality is inescapably ambiguous and never given as such. Here, again, it is Welles and *Citizen Kane* that come to the fore. As Andrew writes: 'It is Welles's name and the film *Citizen Kane* that continually resurface in Bazin's ruminations about the environing presence of our spatial universe and the filmmaker's task of crystallizing its fleeting meanings. Probably more than any other film, *Citizen Kane* forced Bazin to locate a metaphysics within a style of photography and narrative' (ibid.). Such would be Bazin's metaphysics of ambiguity.

Jurassic Park redoubles/recapitulates/returns (to) cinema's advent/arrival to complete and annihilate it. The shock attendant upon the arrival of the train of cinema and its doubling of the world is here redoubled by the shock attendant upon the departure of cinema in the pure and empty form of attraction: its fulfillment, death and artificial resurrection in the void. Paralleling acceleration and inertia, exponential instability and stability, the attraction becomes at once more and less attraction than attraction, more and less distraction than distraction, more and less shock than shock, more and less dread than dread, more and less fascination than fascination.

59 'Superconductive Events', in *The Transparency of Evil*, p. 43.

60 Crichton, *Jurassic Park*, p. 133. Note that the word 'turn' hyperproliferates in and hypersaturates the novel.

61 'Superconductive Events', in *The Transparency of Evil*, p. 40.

62 After Lacan one might say of film: film is what it is not and is not what it is.

63 This would indeed be true of any account, including this one, this account of the account.

64 Media virulent in their capability of and complicity in not only challenging, outbidding and seducing reality and the subject but each other.

65 Keeping the tele- in mind.

66 'Le Théorème de la part maudite', in *La Transparence du Mal*, p. 113, my translation. In 'The Theorem of the Accursed Share', *The Transparency of Evil*, p. 108, James Benedict translates *Le film* as 'development', which for me is an infelicitous development. And he translates *jouent* with 'toy', which, while not wrong, for me does not sufficiently capture the play of play (*jouent*).

67 It should be noted that a substantial amount of material in the Kuttna Lecture was drawn from a number of pieces in Baudrillard's *Simulacres et simulation*, Paris: Editions Galilée, 1981.

68 'I Like the Cinema', interview with C. Charbonnier, reproduced in *Baudrillard Live*, ed. Mike Gane, London: Routledge, 1993, p. 31. Indeed, the Hollywood cinema of the last twenty to thirty years seems the pre-eminent filmic exemplar of the logics of certain French 'poststructuralist' and 'postmodernist' thinkers.

69 *Jurassic Park* would suggest that Baudrillard, too, is a great animator who raises the dead to put them into eternal orbit, not merely the whitewashed Hammond but the chaotician Malcolm, and more, for both of them are implicated in the actions of others that demonstrate the limits of the principles Hammond and Malcolm embrace and the actions they undertake: the T-Rex and the Velociraptors. Are the latter not animators, too? Here one is reminded of Chuck Jones' comment in 'What's Up, Down Under?', in *The Illusion of Life*, p. 39, that 'We never made films for adults, and we never made films for children . . . We made pictures for ourselves', suggesting that the Warner Bros. animators could be thought of as both children and adults, neither children nor adults, at the same time and/or, more radically, as not human! It is this latter sense – of something nonhuman at work – that I would suggest is likewise in operation in the animation of Baudrillard.

70 For the Strange Attractor, see *The Transparency of Evil*, especially 'The Object as Strange Attractor', as well as *L'Illusion de la fin*, especially 'Instabilité et stabilité exponentielles'. In terms of the Crystal, see Baudrillard, 'Revenge of the Crystal', in *Fatal Strategies*, itself subtitled: *Crystal Revenge*. The figure of the crystal – be it Bazin's 'fleeting crystallization of a reality', Baudrillard's Crystal, Deleuze's crystal-image or the Crystal Palace – appears to 'reside' at the 'heart' of cinema, in cinema's coming-to-pass, like Baudelaire's *passante*. In the case of Deleuze, the crystal-image of cinema is formed of two sides – actual and virtual – existing in a state of reversibility, that is, where actual and virtual exchange,

thereby producing indiscernibility. The crystal-image for Deleuze finds exemplification in the mirror-image; and when mirror-images proliferate, they absorb the actuality of the character reflected in the mirror, making the virtual images more and more actual in relation to the increasing virtualization of the actual character. Here again Welles surfaces. Deleuze says that 'this situation was prefigured in Welles's *Citizen Kane*, when Kane passes between two facing mirrors, but it comes to the fore in its pure state in the famous palace of mirrors in *The Lady From Shanghai*, where the principle of indiscernibility reaches its peak: a perfect crystal-image'. *Cinema 2: The Time-Image*, p. 70. And a few pages later Deleuze returns to *Citizen Kane* to address the virtual image as seed 'which will crystallize an environment which is at present [*actuellement*] amorphous; but on the other hand the latter must have a structure which is virtually crystallizable, in relation to which the seed now plays the role of actual image' (p. 74), citing the moment Kane utters the word 'Rosebud' and lets slip the snow globe that shatters, that constellation of word and image posing the question of whether the virtual seed 'Rosebud' will be actualized in an environment, and vice versa. Obviously, I would suggest (and have in particular ways suggested) that such issues are intensely and complexly in play in *Jurassic Park*, as exemplified in its constellation of mirror-image and words 'OBJECTS IN MIRROR ARE CLOSER THAN THEY APPEAR', and that the seed implanted by Welles and *Citizen Kane* (and *The Lady From Shanghai*) in Spielberg and *Jurassic Park*, and by the latter in turn, would be a bad seed, having a demonic viral character.

71 Seduction is what is at stake in all of this as fundamental principle for Baudrillard. He writes: 'Seduction does not only turn around the fundamental rule – it IS the fundamental rule'. *L'Autre par lui-même*, Paris: Editions Galilée, 1987, p. 59, my translation. Seduction is the turn. And necessarily, Baudrillard's own work, even in its very movement, would have to be obedient to this principle: for example, one could postulate that it is (and ironically so) with his book *De la Séduction* (1979) that his work uncannily turns from a trajectory that he took to be moving away from the subject of the object – its apparent destination – to one moving toward the subject of the Object! – its destiny. Such an ironical, spiralling movement is what Baudrillard characterizes as not the subjective irony of Adorno but Objective Irony, a movement in and of the destiny of the world. On his strategy of Objective Irony, see the interview between Baudrillard and Edward Colless, David Kelly and Alan Cholodenko in *The Evil Demon of Images*, pp. 39–42, reproduced in *Baudrillard Live*, pp. 137–39.

72 'Game with Vestiges', interview with Salvatore Mele and Mark Titmarsh, *On the Beach*, no. 5, Winter 1984, p. 19, reproduced in *Baudrillard Live*, p. 82.

73 Ibid., p. 19; *Baudrillard Live*, pp. 81–82.

74 'Instabilité et stabilité exponentielles', in *L'Illusion de la fin*, p. 159. Note the shift from 'The Object as Strange Attractor' in *The Transparency of Evil* to 'Instabilité et stabilité exponentielles', where Evil exceeds Chaos Theory.

75 See 'This Beer Isn't a Beer', in *Baudrillard Live*, p. 184. In the same way that Baudrillard describes the work of Andy Warhol in 'Le Snobisme machinal', so would his own work be in accord with the artifice not of art and aesthetics but of Illusion. Hence, in my opinion it is wrong to entitle this conference 'The Art of Theory', insofar as if art is everywhere except in art, it is not art any more, nor is theory simply sustainable outside quotation marks, marking a fatality to theory.

76 See *The Evil Demon of Images*, pp. 31–32; and 'I Don't Belong to the Club, to the Seraglio', interview with Mike Gane and Monique Arnaud in *Baudrillard Live*, pp. 23–24. Such technical virtuosity would link contemporary 'cinema' for Baudrillard with the virtuosity of Virtual Man and his computer as celibate machines, whose 'virtue resides in their transparency, their functionality, their absence of passion and artifice'. 'Xerox and Infinity', in *The Transparency of Evil*, p. 52.

77 'Hystérésie du Millenium', in *L'Illusion de la fin*, p. 166.

78 Baudrillard, *Symbolic Exchange and Death*, translated by Iain Hamilton Grant, London: Sage, p. 74.

79 Baudrillard defines 'hyperreal' in 'The Precession of Simulacra' as 'a real without origin or reality'. *Simulations*, p. 2.

80 As I characterize it in the Introduction to *The Illusion of Life*.

81 'The Year 2000 Will Not Take Place', p. 19.

82 'This Beer Isn't a Beer', *Baudrillard Live*, p. 188.

8

BETWEEN MARX AND DERRIDA: Baudrillard, Art and Technology

GRAHAM COULTER-SMITH

During the 1980s, both Marxism and poststructuralism addressed the complexities of appropriation and the relationship of art to photo-mechanical reproduction: Marxism from the perspective of what might be termed 'ideological deconstruction', and poststructuralism from what might be termed 'counter-rational deconstruction'. Straddling both frameworks, Baudrillard stands out almost by default as one of the few theorists to address the new postmodern technologies. However, his interpretation of these technologies appears unremittingly bleak and of limited value to contemporary visual artists who are beginning to explore the new technology of digital image processing.

For example, Baudrillard's recent deliberations on 'Objects, Images and the Possibilities of Aesthetic Illusion', characteristically refer to the 'cancer of cinema' and the 'pornography' of special effects: concepts which seem somewhat at odds with Alan Cholodenko's more generous suggestion that Baudrillard might virtually be viewed as the genius guiding the allegedly delirious computer-generated imagery of movies such as *Jurassic Park*; a reading typical of that we might term the 'postmodernization' or 'poststructuralization' of Jean Baudrillard. In contrast, Baudrillard himself diagnoses cinema as a 'hyper-efficient' 'hyper-technology' leading to what he derides as the 'useless perfection' and the 'cancerous proliferation of the image'.[1]

In Baudrillard's terms, the more technical dimensions cinema adds to its obscene hyperrealism, the more it seems to depart from the reality of the object. Rather than celebrating the remarkable visual experience offered by the computer-generated imagery in *Jurassic Park*, Baudrillard hints that he now prefers a Zen-like pleasure afforded by the simple meaningless existence of objects freed from representation and to some extent regurgitating 'the mirrors they have swallowed'.[2]

Even if such discourse is ironic, its general tendency is to dismiss technological art, and in the process, I would argue, to underestimate what is potentially one of the key sites of contemporary deconstructive avant-gardism. At this point, two questions may be posited. Firstly, what is it that informs Baudrillard's negativity towards technology and in particular the technology of image production? Secondly, what – if any – alternatives might be offered to Baudrillard's negative analyses of future image processing technologies?

In response to my first question, it would seem that Baudrillard's pessimistic attitude towards technological art stems above all from the way in which his writing has developed out of an unholy marriage between the conflictual frameworks of humanist Marxist and post-structuralist theory. As I will suggest, this attitude derives from the humanist Marxist vestiges which linger on in his theory, and turn his potentially optimistic poststructuralist conclusions sour.

Arguably then, the best alternative to what one might think of as Baudrillard's 'sour' poststructuralism is a 'sweet' poststructuralism untainted by the criticality of humanist Marxism; for example, Derridean poststructuralism, with its emphasis upon the delirious free play of the signifier. Baudrillard's thoughts on aesthetic illusion clearly seem disapproving of such play in so far as it incites a 'pornographic orgy of carcinogenic image proliferation', and merely precipitates 'frozen excrement' and 'garbage'.[3] Nevertheless, as I shall subsequently suggest, it is to Jacques Derrida that we must turn, if we are to seek traces of a more 'sweet' – or optimistic – poststructuralist account of new technological art and information processing systems.

The fundamental premises informing Baudrillard's pessimistic analysis of technology frequently seem to derive from what I would term the predominantly humanist Marxian notions of alienation and reification, or at least hyperrealized versions of those ideas. Discussing the conceptual basis of Baudrillard's *The Society of Consumption* (1970) Charles Levin notes, for example, how the argument of this book both draws upon Marx and qualifies Marx's categories by substituting the notion of consumption for the central premise of labour or production.[4] The Surrealist-Marxist impulse of Guy Debord's *Society of the Spectacle* (1967) was very likely a significant influence upon Baudrillard at that time. In *Society of the Spectacle* Debord posits that the 'incessant expansion of economic power in the form of the commodity . . . transformed human labour into commodity-labour'.[5] Subsequently, Baudrillard's *Critique of the Political Economy of the Sign* (1972) further transformed Marx's economistic analysis by reference to structural linguistics, moving from a productivist to a consumptionist model. In Levin's terms, Baudrillard seems to have understood the primary mode of consumption as the interplay of signs and systems of signification, in so far as he concludes that, 'What is consumed is not the object itself, but the *system* of objects'.[6]

This subsumption or consumption of the human subject into, or by, a commodified and reified signifying system becomes crucial to Baudrillard's theory in so far as it sets up its central dialectical play between humanist notions of alienation and reification and the more anti-humanist register of structuralism. However, in Baudrillard's theory the anti-humanism of structuralism becomes less an alternative to humanism than a means of intensifying the humanistic critique of technological society. Structuralism, with its emphasis upon system and code, allowed Baudrillard to bring humanist Marxist notions of alienation and reification into the late twentieth-century realm of systems, communications networks and information processing. The system, the code and the sign became in effect the most spectacular exemplars of the alienation and reification which pervades capitalist culture. This is particularly evident in 'The Ecstasy of Communication', where Baudrillard elaborates the Marxian notion of alienation into his central concept of 'obscenity'. Arguing that 'as long as there is alienation, there is spectacle, action, scene', Baudrillard continues:

> It is not obscenity – the spectacle is never obscene. Obscenity begins precisely when there is no more spectacle, no more scene, when all becomes transparence and immediate visibility, when everything is exposed to the harsh and inexorable light of information and communication.[7]

As these lines suggest, in Baudrillard's writing, the system, the code and the sign go beyond simply exemplifying alienation and reification. They *exceed* alienation and reification, producing what might be referred to as 'hyper-alienation' and 'hyper-reification'.

Exploring the age of information still further, Baudrillard's theories subsequently deploy the poststructuralist conception of cultural codes and signs in terms of a *mise en abîme* – an infinite regress of self-reference that eventually stretches, conceptually, into the realms of fractal geometry and the Mandelbrot set. Far from sharing the excitement these notions have generated for other intellectuals, Baudrillard laments:

> Where is the freedom in all this? Nowhere! There is no choice here, no final decision. All decisions concerning networks, screens, information or communication are serial in character, partial, fragmentary, fractal.[8]

While most analyses of Baudrillard suggest that he moved in a linear manner from Marxist concepts of alienating and reifying structures to poststructuralist notions of ambiguity and uncertainty, it can be argued that even Baudrillard's most poststructuralist hypotheses resonate with the Marxian notions of alienation and reification, and that it is precisely this inflexion in his thought that accounts for its pessimistic response to present technologies, and hence to technological art. If it is the case that Baudrillard's early writings employ structuralist concepts of systems, signification and codes as quintessential symptoms of alienation and reification, it seems equally evident that his later writings appropriate poststructuralist concepts to a somewhat similar end – albeit in a more complex and ambiguous manner.

The poststructuralist register in Baudrillard's writings is perhaps most striking in his transformation of structuralist notions of the systemic code into his concepts of simulacra, simulation and hyperreality – notions which eventually allowed Baudrillard to project a mutated Marxist theory into the science fiction domain of communications superhighways, virtual reality and cyberspace. Thus in his influential early essay 'The Orders of Simulacra' (1983), Baudrillard's argument characteristically descends from the gravity of the Marxist notion of capital into the vertiginous depths of his own sense of simulacra. In Baudrillard's terms:

> We know that now it [material production] is on the level of reproduction (fashion, media, publicity, information and communication networks), on the level of what Marx negligently called the non-essential sectors of capital . . . that is to say in the sphere of simulacra and of the code.[9]

Throughout 'The Orders of Simulacra' it becomes apparent that Baudrillard's argument has undergone a three-step evolution from the Marxian emphasis upon production, on to a Situationist emphasis upon consumption, and finally to a Benjaminian and McLuhanesque analysis of *reproduction*. So far as Baudrillard is concerned:

> Benjamin and McLuhan saw this matter more clearly than Marx; they saw the true message: *the true ultimatum was in reproduction itself.* And that production no longer has any sense; its social finality is lost in the series. The simulacra win out over history.[10]

Baudrillard's emphasis upon the way in which the concept of 'finality' becomes 'lost in the series' echoes the key poststructuralist notion of the *mise en abîme*.[11] Elaborating his notion of being 'lost in the series' in terms of a world of existential indifference enveloping both the animate and the inanimate, Baudrillard explains:

> The relation is no longer that of an original to its counterfeit – neither analogy nor reflection – but equivalence, indifference.

In a series, objects become undefined simulacra one of the other. And so, along with the objects, do the men that produce them.[12]

Characteristically, Baudrillard uses the poststructuralist notion of a serialist *mise en abîme* to obtain a bleak, apocalyptic effect that might be compared with the rhetorical register of Marxist humanist writers such as Theodor Adorno and Max Horkheimer, or what Jürgen Habermas derides as 'the cynical consciousness of the "black" writers'.[13]

However, as becomes particularly apparent when its most sophisticated formulation is explored, in the theory of Jacques Derrida, the notion of *mise en abîme* is not inherently nihilistic. For Derrida, the simulacral process of representation points to an infinite regress-like structure, or process, of self-reference constituting the ground of all discourse. Writing in *Of Grammatology*, Derrida observes:

> There are things like reflecting pools, and images, an infinite reference from one to the other, but no longer a source, a spring. There is no longer a simple origin. For what is reflected is split *in itself* and not only as an addition to itself of its image. The reflection, the image, the double, splits what it doubles. The origin of the speculation becomes a difference. What can look at itself is not one; and the law of the addition of the origin to its representation, of the thing to its image, is that one plus one makes at least three.[14]

Derrida's notion of a regress of self-reference differs considerably from the nihilism usually implicit in Baudrillard's use of the concept. Indeed, Derrida's theory has important parallels with what might be termed the 'postclassical' paradigm in contemporary science characterized by principles such as non-linearity, indeterminism, holism, recursion or self-referentiality.

To date, the most thorough exploration of the connections between Derrida's theory and postclassical principles in science is offered by Arkady Plotnitsky's *Complementarity: Anti-Epistemology after Bohr and Derrida* (1994). Here Plotnitsky both explores the way in which theorists such as the quantum physicist Niels Bohr and the mathematician Kurt Gödel formulate a logic or 'economy' which seems to contradict classical science, and examines the parallels between these developments and the philosophical alternatives to classical metaphysics elaborated by the theories of Derrida and Bataille. Discussing Derrida's central concept of 'deconstruction' Plotnitsky notes:

> The *anti-epistemology* of my title refers, broadly, to the general possibility of a dislocation, or as we say now, deconstruction of classical or metaphysical theories – epistemologies, ontologies, phenomenologies.[15]

Plotnitsky argues that a fundamental example of such a dislocation of classical epistemology is evident in Bohr's theory of complementarity which addresses the coexistence of opposites such as the wave/particle nature of light. Plotnitsky explains:

> Complementarity entails a radical critique or deconstruction of classical concepts, models, and frameworks, or the entire processes and technologies of measurement and observation.[16]

In order to indicate ways in which Derrida's theory relates to Bohr's concept of complementarity, Plotnitsky first examines the relationship between Derrida's theory and Gödel's Incompleteness Theorem. He shows that there is concrete evidence that Derrida was aware of Gödel's Incompleteness Theorem from the time of writing his first book, *Edmund Husserl's Origin of Geometry: An Introduction* (1962). Succinctly analysing the way in which Gödel's theorem 'springs from a constellation of paradoxes that surround the subject of self-reference', Paul Davies observes:

> Consider as a simple introduction to this tangled topic the disconcerting sentence: 'This statement is a lie'. If the statement is true, then it is false; and if it is false, then it is true. The great mathematician and philosopher Bertrand Russell demonstrated that the existence of such paradoxes strikes at the very heart of logic, and undermines any straightforward attempt to construct mathematics rigorously on a logical foundation.[17]

Clearly, the concept of self-reference which underlies Gödel's theorem has significant parallels with Derrida's notion of recursive self-referentiality in representation. However, in his analysis of Derrida's writings, Plotnitsky stresses the way in which Derrida's use of the concept of 'undecidability' relates to the sense of 'incompleteness' arising from Gödel's notion of self-reference. As Plotnitsky reveals, it is in his *Introduction* to Husserl's 'The Origin of Geometry' that Derrida points out that Gödel's Incompleteness Theorem contradicts Husserl's implication that the epistemological solidity of classical philosophy might be assured by recognizing its critical influence upon the development of the classical mathematical logic of Euclidean geometry. Arguing that 'Undecidability is a key element of Derrida's matrix', Plotnitsky quotes Derrida's observation that 'confidence' in 'the epistemological solidity of classical philosophy':

> did not have long to wait before being contradicted: indeed its vulnerability has been well shown, particularly when Gödel discovered the rich possibility of *'undecidable'* propositions in 1931.[18]

Plotnitsky goes on to show that Derrida's notion of undecidability, like Gödel's theorem, should be understood not so much in metaphorical or metaphysical terms, as in what could be termed a postclassical logic, and quotes from an interview in which Derrida consciously dissociates his theories of the 'pragmatics' of 'undecidability' from the romantic strategy of chance:

> I do not believe I have ever spoken of 'indeterminacy', whether in regard to 'meaning' or anything else. Undecidability is something else again. While referring to what I have said above and elsewhere, I want to recall that undecidability is always a *determinate* oscillation between possibilities (for example, of meaning, but also of acts). These possibilities are themselves highly *determined* in strictly *defined* situations (for example, discursive – syntactical or rhetorical – but also political, ethical, etc.). They are *pragmatically* determined. The analyses that I have devoted to undecidability concern just these determinations and these definitions, not at all some vague 'indeterminacy'.[19]

So far as Plotnitsky is concerned, Derrida's argument in these lines 'clearly strengthens the main point suggested here':

> on the one hand, the proximity between Derridean and Gödelian matrices and, on the other, the juxtaposition between Derridean undecidability and Bohr's quantum mechanical – indeterminate and complementary – anti-epistemology.[20]

As Plotnitsky's examination of the parallels between Derrida's and Gödel and Bohr's priorities indicates, Derridean deconstruction is not so much reducible to nihilism as symptomatic of the forefront of present explorations of a new postclassical logic. Such conceptual correspondences between postclassical science and poststructuralist theory suggest the need for a more positive account of the role of new technologies – both in the development of the visual arts and in the development of late twentieth-century culture as a whole – than the rather negative account of 'fractal' culture that Baudrillard at present provides.

While French poststructural theorists such as Lyotard and Deleuze have already noted such correspondences,[21] Marxian theory frequently seems more comfortable within the paradigms of classical science. With such paradigms in mind, Habermas accuses Derrida of being *insufficiently* 'scientific':

> Despite his transformed gestures, in the end [Derrida] too, promotes only a mystification of palpable social pathologies; he, too, disconnects essential (namely, deconstructive) thinking from scientific analysis; and he, too, lands at an empty, formula-like avowal of some indeterminate authority.[22]

Condemning Derridean deconstruction on the basis of its alleged 'irrationality', Habermas seems unaware that science itself has moved beyond the dominance of classical rationalism.

Baudrillard is one of the few radical theorists with a background in Marxism who does in fact refer to such postclassical developments in science as Heisenberg's Uncertainty Principle. However, such references are usually couched in the same melancholic and apocalyptic register as the following lines from *The Transparency of Evil*, in which Baudrillard characteristically argues that 'Science itself seems to have fallen under the sway of its strange attractors'. For Baudrillard:

> the disappearance of the respective positions of subject and object at the experimental interface . . . has given rise to a definitive state of uncertainty about the reality of the object and the (objective) reality of knowledge.

Accordingly, the 'aim of science and technology' would seem to be that of 'presenting us with a definitively unreal world, beyond all criteria of truth and reality'.[23]

The pessimism and latent humanism underlying such analysis becomes apparent when it is set in the context of Baudrillard's reference to Arthur C. Clarke's fable of the project to decode the 99 billion names of God – a project accelerated by IBM scientists who discover that as their research advances, more and more stars disappear from the sky. From Baudrillard's perspective, it would seem that science and technology will eventually obliterate nature, leaving only a cold empty Cartesian virtuality.[24] In such deliberations, Baudrillard's romantic concern for the loss of the real, the natural and the human seems far closer to the humanist impulse in Marxist theories of alienation than to what I would term the postclassical emphasis of poststructuralist speculation.

A similar concern for a loss of human contact with reality in the face of a burgeoning information processing technology surfaces once again in the following lines from *The Transparency of Evil* in which Baudrillard rather chillingly reflects:

> If men create intelligent machines, or fantasize about them, it is . . . because they secretly despair of their own intelligence . . . By entrusting this burdensome intelligence to machines we are released from any responsibility to knowledge, much as entrusting power to politicians allows us to disdain any aspiration of our own to power.[25]

Whereas Baudrillard predicts the eventual supersession of the human subject by information processing systems such as artificial intelligence, Derrida rather more affirmatively defends the 'necessity' of the self-organizing and nonlinear play of simulacra reaching beyond the controlling grasp of the *cogito*, and of 'present-being'. According to Derrida:

> It was necessary to begin thinking that there was no centre, that the centre could not be thought in the form of a present-being, that the centre had no natural site, that it was not a fixed locus but a function, a sort of non-locus in which an infinite number of sign-substitutions came into play. This was the moment when language invaded the universal problematic, the moment when, in the absence of a centre of origin, everything became discourse . . . that is to say, a system in which the central signified, the original or transcendental signified, is never absolutely present outside a system of differences.[26]

Subsequently celebrating the way in which 'The absence of the transcendental signified extends the domain and the play of signification infinitely',[27] Derrida seems to suggest that this process offers an alternative to the rigidity of classical logic by replacing it with a Gödelian-like logic of 'incompleteness' or 'undecidability'. While Derrida's argument does not refer directly to information processing, it invokes 'language' as a paradigmatic self-referential, self-reflective, self-organizing system of signification, in which the concept of 'writing' might stand in for any system of signifying inscription: tape-recording, photography – or binary data.

Viewed in terms of Derrida's theory, systems of information and image processing might advantageously encourage a broadening of the logic which informs the *cogito* via an application of the paradoxical logic of 'undecidability' and 'complementarity'. This is in stark contrast to Baudrillard's use of the paradoxical logic of the Moebius Strip as a metaphor for the dissolution of the human into the mechanical. Addressing the computer screen – and by extension, contemporary computer technology and computer art in general – Baudrillard associates screen culture with 'an epidermal contiguity of eye and image', and with 'the collapse of the aesthetic distance involved in looking'.

> We draw ever closer to the surface of the screen; our gaze, is as it were, strewn across the image . . . Yet the image is always light years away. It is invariably a tele-image – an image located at a very special kind of distance which can only be described as *unbridgeable by the body* . . . This is why it partakes only of the abstract – definitively abstract – form known as communication.

In Baudrillard's terms, it therefore seems to follow that:

> There is no better model of the way in which the computer screen and the mental screen of our brain are interwoven than

Moebius's topology, with its peculiar contiguity of near and far, inside and outside, object and subject within the same spiral.[28]

Whereas Derrida would doubtless acclaim this interweaving of 'inside and outside, object and subject within the same spiral' as an exemplary dislocation of the classical *cogito*'s 'fixed locus', Baudrillard seems to suggest that such corporeally 'unbridgeable' processes culminate in the definitively 'abstract' and hyperalienating condition beyond what he terms 'the organic sense of touch'. Against this bleakness the only hope that Baudrillard offers is the equally desolate solution of AIDS, crack and computer viruses which he appears to believe are preventing the system from totally taking over. Apparently:

> AIDS, crack and computer viruses are merely outcroppings of the catastrophe, nine-tenths of it remain buried in the virtual. The full-blown, the absolute catastrophe would be a true omnipresence of all networks, a total transparency of all data – something from which, for now, computer viruses preserve us. Thanks to them, we shall not be going straight to the culminating point of the development of information and communications, which is to say: death.[29]

By contrast, the frameworks of Derridean poststructuralism and postclassical science suggest that far from facing the unavoidable 'absolute catastrophe' and the 'death' that Baudrillard associates with information processing technology, we may instead consider such technologies as the site of the alternative, but not necessarily apocalyptic, non-linear logic that we might associate with the beauty of computerized chaos geometry and of the kind of holistic and self-organizing neural networks and cellular automata that Francisco Varela identifies with 'models of cognitive behaviour' for which there is at present 'no unified formal theory.[30]

While such observations indicate that we are now at the beginning of an age of postclassical science and technology, Baudrillard's emphasis upon ever-increasing symptoms of what he takes to be dehumanized virtual hyperreality suggests that his account of the contemporary conditions has yet to come to terms with this more positive postclassical account of technoculture.

Provocatively exaggerating the alienating potential of information technologies, Baudrillard's relentlessly pessimistic – and doubtless partially ironic – speculations are nevertheless notable for the way in which they serve to counterbalance and throw into question the more naive enthusiasms of the zealots of postmodern cyberculture. All the same, it seems reasonable to hope that subsequent assessments of future technologies may look beyond Baudrillard's nightmarish vision of technological hyperalienation, towards the more affirmative prospects concurrently outlined both in the ongoing explorations of postclassical science by Plotnitsky, Davies and Varela, and the evocative resonances that such theory finds within the poststructuralist speculations of philosophers such as Derrida.

NOTES

1 All the quotations in this paragraph are from Baudrillard's keynote address 'Objects, Images and the Possibilities of Aesthetic Illusion' at The Art of Theory: Baudrillard in the Nineties symposium, Institute of Modern Art, Brisbane, 22–24 April 1994. See Chapter 1 in this volume.

2 Ibid.

3 Ibid.

4 Jean Baudrillard, *For a Critique of the Political Economy of the Sign*, translated with an introduction by Charles Levin, St Louis: Telos Press, 1981, p. 5.

5 Debord, Guy, *Society of the Spectacle* (1967), Detroit: Black & Red, 1983, §40.

6 Baudrillard, *For a Critique*, p. 5.

7 Baudrillard, 'The Ecstasy of Communication', in *The Anti-Aesthetic: Essays on Postmodern Culture*, ed. Hal Foster, Port Townsend, WA: Bay Press, 1983, p. 130.

8 Jean Baudrillard, *The Transparency of Evil*, translated by James Benedict, London: Verso, 1993, p. 57.

9 Jean Baudrillard, *Simulations*, translated by Paul Foss, Paul Patton and Philip Beitchman, New York: Semiotext(e), 1983, p. 99.

10 Ibid., p. 100.

11 It appears to have been Craig Owens who introduced the term *mise en abîme* (after Lucien Dallenbach) with reference to Derrida's notion of self-reference. See Craig Owens, 'Photography *en abîme*', *October*, no. 5, Summer 1978, pp. 76–77.

12 Baudrillard, 'The Ecstasy of Communication', p. 97.

13 Jürgen Habermas, *The Philosophical Discourse of Modernity*, Cambridge, MA: MIT Press, 1987, p. 118.

14 Jacques Derrida, *Of Grammatology*, translated by Gayatri Chakravorty Spivak, Baltimore, MD and London: Johns Hopkins University Press, 1974, p. 36.

15 Arkady Plotnitsky, *Complementarity: Anti-Epistemology after Bohr and Derrida*, Durham, NC and London: Duke University Press, 1994, p. 10.

16 Ibid., p. 118.

17 Paul Davies, *The Mind of God: Science and the Search for Ultimate Meaning*, Harmondsworth: Penguin Books, 1992, p. 101.

18 Plotnitsky, *Complementarity*, p. 198.

19 Ibid., p. 209.

20 Ibid., p. 210.

21 Lyotard refers to chaos theory in *The Postmodern Condition*, Manchester: Manchester University Press, 1984, p. 58. Deleuze also refers to chaos theory in *The Fold: Leibniz and the Baroque*, Minneapolis and London: University of Minnesota Press, 1993, p. 16.

22 Habermas, *The Philosophical Discourse of Modernity*, p. 181.

23 Baudrillard, *The Transparency of Evil*, pp. 42–43.

24 This reference is taken from a lecture entitled 'Aesthetic Illusion and Virtual Reality' delivered by Baudrillard at Griffith University, Brisbane, on the occasion of The Art of Theory: Baudrillard in the Nineties symposium, 1994. See Chapter 2 in this volume.

25 Baudrillard, *The Transparency of Evil*, p. 51.

26 Jacques Derrida, *Writing and Difference*, London: Routledge and Kegan Paul, 1981, p. 280.

27 Ibid.

28 Baudrillard, *The Transparency of Evil*, pp. 55–56.

29 Ibid., p. 68.

30 J. Varela, Evan Thomson and Eleanor Rosch, *The Embodied Mind: Cognitive Science and Human Experience*, Cambridge, MA: MIT Press, 1992, p. 88. Varela *et al.* discuss neural networks and cellular automata as holistic, non-linear, and self-organizing models. They explain: 'Take a total number of simple neuron-like elements and connect them reciprocally. Next present this system with a succession of patterns by treating some of its nodes as sensory ends (a retina if you wish). After each presentation let the system reorganize itself by rearranging its connections following a Hebbian principle, that is, by increasing the links between those neurons that happen to be active together for the item presented. The presentation of an entire list of patterns constitutes the system's learning phase. After the learning phase, when the system is presented again with one of these patterns, it recognizes it, in the sense that it falls into a unique global state or internal configuration that is said to represent the learned item. This recognition is possible provided the number of patterns presented is not larger than a fraction of the total number of participating neurons (about 0.15 N). Furthermore, the system performs a correct recognition even if the pattern is presented with added noise or the system is partially mutilated.

'This example is but one of a whole class of neural network or connectionist models, which we shall discuss further. But first we need to broaden the discussion to understand what is at stake in studying these networks. The strategy, as we said, is to build a cognitive system not by starting with symbols and rules but by starting with simple components that would dynamically connect to each other in dense ways. In this approach, each component operates only in its local environment, so that there is no external agent that, as it were, turns the system's axle. But because of the system's network constitution, there is a global cooperation that spontaneously emerges when the states of all participating "neurons" reach a mutually satisfactory state. In such a system, then, there is no need for a central processing unit to guide the entire operation. This passage from local rules to global coherence is the heart of what used to be called self-organization during the cybernetic years. Today people prefer to speak of emergent or global properties, network dynamics, nonlinear networks, complex systems, or even synergetics.

'There is no unified formal theory of emergent properties. It is clear however, that emergent properties have been found across all domains – vortices and lasers, chemical oscillations, genetic network developmental patterns, population genetics, immune network ecology, and geophysics. What all these diverse phenomena have in common is that in each case a network gives rise to new properties' (pp. 87–88). The authors go on to discuss such issues with regard to the operation of 'attractors' (a concept crucial to chaos theory) in cellular automata (pp. 89–91).

9

WHO IS THE 'FRENCH McLUHAN'?

GARY GENOSKO

Two of the major anglophone interpreters of the work of Jean Baudrillard, Mike Gane and Douglas Kellner, have nominated him for the position of the 'French McLuhan'.[1] Any reader of Baudrillard would recognize the important influence McLuhan has had on his work and could not fail to notice the various ways in which this influence has manifested itself over the course of Baudrillard's career to date. This nomination elevates rhetorically McLuhan's influence on Baudrillard above the rest, and it is McLuhan's place that Baudrillard comes to occupy for a new generation of readers, for better or for worse.

Gane's first book on Baudrillard, *Baudrillard: From Critical to Fatal Theory*, quotes George Steiner's remarks on the problem McLuhan himself posed to his readers – that is, how to read him, given both his style and the designscape of his publications. Gane thinks it is 'instructive' to refigure this problem on behalf of Baudrillard for his readers. He approaches the issue with the claim:

> It would be possible to argue that Baudrillard is the French McLuhan, or simply the McLuhan of today . . . But who reads McLuhan now? Perhaps Baudrillard will force people to reread a number of writers – McLuhan, Nietzsche – who are often thought to be unreadable.[2]

Gane's nomination is full of hedges. It places his readers in the paradoxical position of wondering whether there will be anyone in the near or distant future who will provoke one to reread Baudrillard. Like McLuhan, however, Baudrillard poses for Gane the problem of writing as a symbolic practice:

As Baudrillard adopts the full force of McLuhan's notion that the medium is the message, it is to be expected that the medium of the writing style is considered tactically and strategically.[3]

What does it mean for Baudrillard to adopt the 'full force' of McLuhan's most famous slogan 'the medium is the message'? In *La Société de consommation*, Baudrillard translated this slogan into the differential logic of structural value, arguing that it is not content that is consumed, but rather, the coded semiological relations of successive and equivalent signs divorced from the real.[4] Subsequently, the slogan would acquire other meanings in Baudrillard's writings.

Gane's initial nomination, then, acclimatizes readers of Baudrillard to the issue of how his texts establish the critique of the order of simulation from the viewpoint of the symbolic. This critique is said to require specific writing practices beyond the adoption of key terms from the anthropological literature such as 'potlatch'. Symbolic challenges to the semiological order of simulation are developed textually through a variety of concepts (agonistic relations, anagrammatic dispersion, wit, resocialization of death as a counter-gift), all of which serve to annul systems of value (Marxian, semiological, psychoanalytic).

Discussing Baudrillard's style, Gane suggests that what is peculiar to his writing of the symbolic is the ambivalence of his texts. It is not merely that one might respond ambivalently to them, but that they are themselves full of ambivalence. In fact, ambivalence is a key concept in the work of the symbolic because it cannot be positivized and positioned as a stable entity in a logic of value, unlike ambiguity, for instance. Indeed, Baudrillard's relation to McLuhan is itself full of ambivalence.

Little attention was paid to Baudrillard's style of writing before Gane's publications, and this usually pointed in one direction – towards science fiction. Baudrillard has been adopted by the theorists and practitioners of cyberpunk in the same spirit that has recently elevated McLuhan to the status of a patron saint of *Mondo* and *Wired* magazines (among other journals offering glossy attention to hypertextual experiments and virtual reality systems).

For example, for István Csicsery-Ronay, Baudrillard is both stylistically and substantively a philosopher of cyberpunk and a practitioner of cybercriticism.[5] Baudrillard has at times encouraged these comparisons, and in an interview in *Le Monde*, he suggested that his essay on Beaubourg was a vision from science fiction.[6] Baudrillard's interest in the novels of J.G. Ballard, Arthur C. Clarke and Philip K. Dick is not surprising given the claims advanced in his essay 'Simulacres et science fiction' regarding the (con)fusion of science fiction and theory, and the idea that the real has become science fictional, especially in America with its Hollywood presidents such as Ronald Reagan and Spielberg-esque military programmes.[7] Increasingly, both McLuhan and Baudrillard are looked upon as figureheads in the emergence of virtual reality technologies and information highways; the former as the formulator of the basic figures of electronic globalism; the latter as the inventor of a sophisticated language describing the most advanced *simulative* capabilities of new information systems.

The curious simulacral forms populating Dick's novel *The Simulacra* – the simulacral president and the simulacrum of an 'extinct' Martian creature called a papoola (used to instil by thought projection the desire for commodities, in this case used vehicles, in unsuspecting customers)[8] – fit comfortably into the universe Baudrillard describes. In *L'Échange symbolique et la mort*, Baudrillard makes explicit use of Clarke's *Les 99 milliards de noms de Dieu* as an instance of anagrammatic resolution – symbolic writing in the poetic mode.[9] The poetic resolution of the world in this novel, and the intense pleasure which results from an enunciation without remainder, turns on the complete recitation of the 99 billion names of God. Here, salvation is electronic since the task is facilitated by a computer, even though in the end Baudrillard claims that the computer spoils the epiphany because it enables one to reclaim these names.

Gane takes up Baudrillard's concept of anagrammatic resolution without remainder in a short chapter in *Baudrillard's Bestiary* (in which his explication of Ferdinand de Saussure's anagrams closely follows Jean Starobinski's presentation of the unpublished manuscripts),[10] and offers an anagrammatic reading of Baudrillard's little book of poetry, *L'Ange de stuc*, locating the sounds of the theme-words of 'Saussure' and 'Mauss' in certain stanzas.[11] Observing how these fragments are diffracted throughout the poem, Gane notes that there is nothing reclaimable about the theme since its identity cannot be resurrected. The intense symbolic circulation of the fragments exterminates the theme; it can be rearticulated but not reconstituted.

Baudrillard's distinction between these two concepts is critical to his account of the anagram and his strategy of reading Saussure against himself in order to ensure that this so-called revolutionary poetics will be remainderless. The anagrammatic dispersion of the theme in a poem has, then, nothing left over; there is nothing to accumulate and subsequently subject to a structural linguistic law of value. This dispersion itself guarantees theoretically at least that 'the medium is the message' since there is neither a missing or latent reference nor any sort of key remaining to supplement the message.

Baudrillard's reading of Saussure's anagrams, like his use of Sigmund Freud's concept of the *Witz*, emphasizes that the medium cannot be separated from the message. If this was possible, the medium could be subordinated to the demands of depth models of meaning in which disclosure and analysis may be interminable. Media – by which Baudrillard here means the techniques of joking and poetry – are completely resolvable: the technique or medium is the message.

Baudrillard's use of McLuhan's phrase is in the service of these expressions of the symbolic, their destruction of meaning and annihilation of the hermeneutic relevance of linguistic and psychoanalytic systems of value. This is not so much an argument against content as an attack on what Baudrillard calls 'depth models' of interpretation. The symbolic exchange anti-value of the phrase 'the medium is the message' supports a revolutionary poetics the possibility of which neither Saussure nor Freud fully recognized in their concepts of the anagram and the *Witz*.

Baudrillard once again picks up this argument in *A l'Ombre des majorités silencieuses*. The question for Baudrillard is whether or not the masses can function in the mode of the symbolic by preferring the fascination of the medium over the domain of meaning. The terms of this 'probe' are McLuhanesque, but the stakes are quite different: is it possible to communicate, Baudrillard asks, 'outside of the medium of meaning?'[12] The very idea is today untenable, and while Baudrillard cites the neutralization of meaning as an example of the operation of wit, he does not seem to do so simply to support the obvious observation that McLuhan prophesized the rise of a cool phase of mass culture. Rather, for Baudrillard, McLuhan could not have foreseen the symbolic possibilities afforded by his slogan 'the medium is the message'. In Baudrillard's terms, McLuhan, like Freud and Saussure, was blind to the most radical effects of his slogans.

Baudrillard's efforts at expressing the symbolic in print form did not require the construction of an *essai concret* (to use this term from Donald Theall's *The Medium is the RearView Mirror*).[13] Indeed, his long-standing interest in design, taken together with his participation in the groups centred around the journals *Utopie* and *Traverses*, readily lent a number of visual and experimental elements to some of his early essays. While Baudrillard (unlike McLuhan) did not collaborate with a designer such as Harley Parker, design was certainly considered strategically in the S.G.P.P. edition of *La Société de consommation*, although these illustrations were dropped from subsequent pocket-size editions, effectively destroying Baudrillard's most McLuhanesque book-object. The use of print advertisements and photographs illustrates the abundance of chains of object-signs in the society of consumption and fills the text with a busy amalgam of images in a manner similar to the ambiance of what Baudrillard called the 'drugstore'.

By the same token, this concept is not a gloss upon the images: the text engages the phenomena upon which it reflects. The 'drugstore' is a model of a polyvalent commercial complex offering consumers the freedom to design their own everyday environments through the accumulation and combination of homogeneous elements. This de-luxe banality is semiurgical:[14] the participatory sign-work of consumption (shopping, using customer services, seeking entertainment in the climate-controlled interiors of malls) equates maximal comfort and satisfaction with the maximal exclusion of the real, the social, and history.[15]

The 'show and tell' format of La Société de consommation drew the attention of Jean-Claude Giradin, for whom the book seemed to guarantee itself a place in the universe of objects it described, despite its author's warnings about the 'ambiance of repression' in a consumer society in which objects take revenge, slowly, upon those who pursue democracy through them and attempt to alleviate subtle forms of alienation by means of consumption:

> A 16 × 20.5 format, a cover with brocaded borders, the title in gilded letters, this volume adorns itself with a reddish brown jacket on which a car exhibits itself . . . (objective fish-eye photography); a sky-scraper is reflected on the hood and windshield (a wink at the secondary degree of mirroring) giving a foretaste of remarkable iconography; and, it is lined with alluring captions by the author which punctuate the text. In short, for about $7.50 people will want to have this book not for what it is, they will thumb through it without reading it, but rather to leave it sitting casually between the hi-fi set and the bottle of Chivas as an element of worship in the strategy of the surrounding . . . where a sign-mate will not delay in setting a trap.[16]

For Giradin the 'reader' would have wanted the book for what it was not, for its semiological interdependencies and the combinatory possibilities presented by the 'ambiance' of a room pulled together by a certain brand of Scotch and a book by Baudrillard.

In English translation, Baudrillard's books constitute a fetish system of their own: the pretty Verso edition of America beckoned a coffee table on which to display itself and exalt its owner, like an obedient pet;[17] the Agitac edition of Baudrillard's Xerox and Infinity appeared as a chapbook, a photocopied text waiting to be reproduced in turn;[18] Seduction is itself fatal in the sense of being irresistible.[19] With its shocking pink cover featuring Man Ray's photograph Femme au longs cheveux framed with vertical green bands which contribute to the overall vibration of this restless jacket, Marilouise Kroker's design is a lesson in seduction, the key terms of which were culled from Baudrillard's text and expressed in formal terms in the book's design, effectively fetishizing Baudrillard for francophiles. Not even Baudrillard recognized himself in this book-object.

The aestheticized recommodification of Baudrillard for anglophone audiences has all but ignored consideration of those texts in which Baudrillard's writings have been accompanied by images. Gane's focus on the writing of the symbolic contributes indirectly to this critical inattention. Good examples of journal articles were available for more than ten years in *Traverses*, the *Revue trimestrielle du Centre de Création Industrielle* published by the Centre Georges Pompidou, in whose pages essays by Baudrillard were illustrated along thematic lines.

Earlier and more interesting examples may also be found in his contributions to the journal *Utopie, Revue de sociologie de l'urbain*. The large format of the first two issues (1967 and 1969) accommodated typographic heterogeneity and simple uses of collage (clustering and stacking of images of objects and, on occasion, Pop Art inspired graphics expressing the violent explosion of the alienated and hitherto dominated masses),[20] although *Utopie*'s design did not follow straightforwardly from McLuhan's praise of collage, whether it was in terms of the global village understood as an 'animated collage', or as the participatory spirit created by a happening read as a kind of theatre of the electronic age.[21]

In other words, Baudrillard did not uncritically adopt McLuhan's praise for collage and 'participation'. Significantly the German playwright Peter Weiss, four of whose plays Baudrillard translated into French in the 1960s, used collage as a means of breaking through the artificial universe of the media, 'cutting and pasting' existing documentary material in order to re-edit mainstream mediatic representations of current events, and to reveal to the public the latent conflicts, falsifications and political-corporate interests shaping the presentation of information. Such documentary theatre resists the implosive electronic-oral-aural consciousness heralded by McLuhan.

Engaging in subdivision and segmentation (which were for McLuhan outmoded ways of thinking), Weiss's resistance stands alongside the Situationist attacks on happenings as 'naturalistic' spectacles diametrically opposed to the creation of a situation by means of the subversive appropriation and recontextualization of existing materials. Such *détournements* could be reproduced as news or as performance art, losing their critical and transformative edges as diversionary tactics. The spectacularization and repetition of situations was not lost on the Situationists: their work was also subjected to the manufacture of alienation and the self-affirming and self-justifying economy of the spectacle.

For Douglas Kellner, Baudrillard shares the not entirely positive distinction of being a 'new McLuhan' who has repackaged McLuhan into new postmodern cultural capital.[22] Kellner's nomination allows him to identify a trio of 'subordinations' shared by Baudrillard and McLuhan: content and use are subordinate to form; dialectical analysis is subordinate to essentialism and technological determinism; context-specific cultural analyses and alternative political formations are subordinate to a romantic and nostalgic sense of theory. For Kellner, these 'subordinations' occlude the sort of issues he deems apposite but which are absent from McLuhan's and Baudrillard's work: an analysis of the political economy of media production; an entry into a dialectical reading of form with content and media with society.

What makes Kellner's nomination of Baudrillard meta-rhetorical is that the 'subordinations' are themselves subordinate to the arguments advanced in the early 1970s by John Fekete against McLuhan,[23] which Kellner rehearses, but this time directing them against Baudrillard. Simply put, Baudrillard is branded as a new 'McLuhanatic' (a lunatic and counterrevolutionary) collaborating with 'the system', making a fetish of technology, especially television, and furthering the passivity, alienation and domination of consumers by the conservative media-business elites of advanced capitalism.

Fekete's use of the derogatory term 'McLuhanacy' linked eccentricity with culpability – McLuhan was not so 'unsound' as to be considered incapable before the new Left – and furthered a rhetorical practice of discrediting McLuhan already in circulation by the mid-1960s.[24] This term referred both to the enthusiasms of McLuhan's followers (a phenomenon to which they attribute cult status, thereby diminishing these persons' mental capacities by branding them as irrational), and to McLuhan's own penchant for wit, paradox and glib talk. The 'Cult of McLuhanacy' was a precursor of the 'Baudrillard Scene' on the level of a pop-philosophical phenomenon; and the latter has certainly not lacked intimations of mind control and feeble-mindedness.

One of the effects of Kellner's nomination is to render moot comparative and contrastive textual insights into the Baudrillard–McLuhan ligature. For instance, Kellner notes that in his 'later writings' Baudrillard adopts literary practices similar to those of McLuhan (probes and mosaic constellations of images and concepts) which prevent the articulation of a 'well-defined theoretical position'.[25] Unlike Gane, Kellner does not connect these 'McLuhanite' strategies with Baudrillard's project of establishing the symbolic as a revolutionary concept with which to challenge the one-dimensional society of simulations; neither does the mention of such strategies suggest the variety of uses Baudrillard finds for McLuhan's concepts.

In order to secure the nomination on behalf of Baudrillard, Kellner downplays the theoretical significance of the anti-semiological and anti-simulational concept of the symbolic in its so-called 'early' and 'later' manifestations. There is no equivalent concept in McLuhan's work. McLuhan's notions find a place in Baudrillard's work in relation to his own most important but least critically recognized concept of the symbolic and its manifestations.

It would be pointless to deny, however, that there is a superficial resemblance in the relation expressed by McLuhan's idea of participation and Baudrillard's concept of symbolic exchange. The concept of participation is subject to general critical remarks in Baudrillard's *Le Miroir de la production*.[26] As McLuhan explained in *Understanding Media*, media are extensions of psychic and sensory capacities.[27] A hot medium (photography and radio) extends a single sense in 'high definition', that is, one filled with data. A cool or 'low definition' medium (telephone and television) provides a meagre amount of information and extends several senses at once. Hot media are low, while cool media are high in participation, which is defined in terms of what a receiver has to bring to the medium to complete its message: more involvement means the medium is 'inclusive'; a less involving medium is 'exclusive'.

The concept of symbolic exchange takes many forms in Baudrillard's writings, and it is in general incommensurable with any system of value. It is in addition anti-productivist and involves the sumptuary destruction of signs. It is also potlatch-like, a 'tribal' custom, governed by obligation and agonistic reciprocity, of gift exchange, returning what is given or destroyed in kind or with interest. The fatal malady of capitalism is, Baudrillard argues, its inability to reproduce itself symbolically. Yet capital, understood as a code, can and does simulate symbolic processes by admitting as differential value every form of liberation, no matter how strange such social movements and initially non-marked forces make it seem to itself.

Like McLuhan, Baudrillard valorizes, by means of an explicit archaism, so-called primitive and tribal cultures. While McLuhan gleefully announces the retribalization of the post-Gutenbergian world, Baudrillard uses 'primitive' practices to attack the highest order of simulation. Both eschew ethnographic detail for the sake of their dominant conceptual figures. In some instances, their views momentarily converge. For McLuhan practical jokes and aphorisms are physically and mentally involving. Baudrillard, too, treats jokes and aphorisms as cool phenomena. But these convergences quickly break down, since for Baudrillard participation reproduces the system of the capitalist code: participation 'has a connotation that is much too contractual and rationalist to express what is symbolic'.[28]

Put another way, Baudrillard attempts to explain that the code of capital integrates a symbolic variable under the rubric of participation, as sign-value. In spite of this, Baudrillard still holds out the symbolic's radical, irreducible alterity in the forms of the incessant circulation of speech which takes responsibility for itself and the personal relations it cements, the festive destruction of riches elevating *consumation* over *consommation*, and the release of anti-productive potential against the structural inability of systems defined by their internal logic to realize human potential other than in terms of productive forces.

It makes little difference for Baudrillard that McLuhan is thought of as a dupe of capital since the alternative offered by Marxism, including Marxist critiques of McLuhan, is itself mired in the simulation of the capitalist mandate of production and the projection of its categories on to 'primitive' societies. Baudrillard, albeit unwillingly, commits a similar projection in the name of the symbolic akin to McLuhan's own myth of the anxiety-free state of 'backward and nonindustrial countries' whose very backwardness and coolness prepare them for the electric revolution.[29] While McLuhan recognized that the arrival of electric technologies created a series of minor irritations (anxiety and boredom), there is nothing quite as volatile as the 'break and entry' of the Baudrillardian symbolic into the semiurgy, at least in theory.[30]

Inspired by McLuhan's focus on the medium, the experimental artist Fred Forest received permission from Le Monde in 1972 to provide a 150 cm^2 blank space in one issue of the newspaper in which readers could 'speak in response' to largely unidirectional messages.[31] Some 800 responses were returned to the artist. Forest repeated this exercise in several other media, including radio and television. By opening a space for the responses of readers, Forest did not break what Baudrillard calls the 'fundamental rule of non-response of all media'. Forest's experiment is an example of 'fragile manipulatory practices' that do not challenge the medium but, rather, stage responses in terms the medium can accommodate.[32] In this case, the newspaper served as a medium in the sense of an intermediary channel for the delivery of letters to the artist, and maintained the abstract separateness of its readers and their mode of participation.

Baudrillard's general critical remarks on participation do not, however, address McLuhan's specific claims about the media user's involvement with cool and hot media. In an article co-written with Derrick de Kerckhove on television and radio for the Encyclopaedia universalis (France), McLuhan and his co-author maintain that television totally engages the viewer.[33] One is involved in a 'process of configuration that is always in progress' with regard to the relatively small number of the luminous points on the screen out of which the image is, according to this 'perceptualist' position, constructed. Theorizing against the etymological grain of television as the domain of the eye, the active participation of the viewer is primarily tactile, a concept defined constitutively in terms of the interplay of all the senses.

Taken in this way, the television viewer takes an interior trip that appears by external critieria to be one that is passive. Even so, the idea that one is glued to the screen brings home McLuhan's fascination with the tactility of the television experience. This interior voyage of the central nervous system into the magnetic field gives television its communal flavour and puts it on a continuum with the psychedelic drug trip. There are no bad trips in the cool world of McLuhan's vision. The case of television is the most extreme and the most important example of participatory experience in McLuhan's writings.

Baudrillard understands participation ideologically in the context of his critique of models of communication that merely simulate communication, usually by means of consumption. His approach does not illumine the specific problems of McLuhan's definition, but succeeds in drawing attention to the ideological nature of participation in general, which in its turn may be used to reconsider certain ambiguities and problems in McLuhan's account.

Francis Balle took precisely this tack in his book *MacLuhan*. Participation became a buzzword of sorts and circulated widely in the late 1960s and early 1970s according to various theories of 'unfinished' or 'open' works, especially the new cinema and novel of Alain Resnais and Alain Robbe-Grillet. The destruction of linear narrative placed new demands on the audience. But the polysemic fluctuations of the term have emptied it, Balle claims, of all signification, since it is not clear whether it concerns the messages conveyed, their stylistic differences and the conditions of reception, or the use made of a given medium. Balle continues:

> We never know on which of these three levels MacLuhan situates his observations; moreover, the examples which serve as illustrations show, rather, that he passes from one to the other without paying attention to them.[34]

Further, Balle thinks the distinction between cool and hot media expresses McLuhan's hostility towards print culture and has little to do with verifiable insights:

> the distinction has been put to work only to justify the disrepute into which the techniques and the arts contemporary to the age of print at one and the same time have fallen.[35]

The cool/hot typology is ideological, Balle asserts, because it substitutes values for facts and desire and fear for sociological observations of the media. McLuhan's sociology of the media is in the service of his prophetism or, in other words, *media* serve the interests and preferences of the *médium*.

As I have suggested, McLuhan's most famous slogan supported Baudrillard's understanding of anagrammatic dispersion and the *Witz* in *L'Échange symbolique*. *L'Échange symbolique* is often considered the last book of Baudrillard's 'early writings', after which, it would appear, he adopted more fully McLuhan's ideas, if we are to believe his critics. But this conventional reading tells us little about the details of Baudrillard's appropriations of McLuhan's work. What it does not tell us is that *L'Échange symbolique* was not translated into English in its entirety until 1993, precisely seventeen years after it was written. There are still no studies of this important, indeed pivotal, text available for English readers. One can only imagine what the 'Baudrillard Scene' would have looked like if this important book had appeared before the terms postmodernist and Baudrillard became synonymous.

It is in *L'Échange symbolique* that Baudrillard grafts McLuhan's distinction between hot and cool media on to the logic of the sign's reference. In a hot and referential semiological regime, the medium is not the message. When the medium becomes the message, one enters the cool era of operational simulation and, in Baudrillard's terms, an era characterized semiologically by the referentless Saussurean signs of the structural revolution of value.[36] Monetary signs are cool for Baudrillard: affectless, commutable, tied to the rules of the structural system, unconnected with parasystemic real referents, and hence 'messageless'. Money has not, however, become only a medium whose circulation and disconnectedness is its message:

> It is no longer a medium, a means for the circulation of goods,
> it is the *circulation itself*, that is to say, the realized form of the
> system in its abstract rotation.[37]

Baudrillard's use of 'coolness' in this passage adheres to an often neglected aspect of the concept which McLuhan specified in terms of 'rending' and 'wracking'.[38] Cool money is circulation itself, liberated from both use value and exchange value, and thus relieved of exchangist messages. It is its own message.[39] This kind of money has, then, the power to 'rend and wrack' any national economy, Baudrillard adds, because it is no longer tied to a market, to a local equilibrium, to a mode of production, to a common measure, etc.[40] Cool money relates only to itself, 'participates' in its own inflationary spiral and periodic crashes, and as McLuhan himself noted and Baudrillard emphasizes, in its abstractness and speed it surpasses hot hardware – and even credit – with anarchic consequences.

Baudrillard's attention to McLuhan is for the most part limited to textual skirmishes with certain slogans and concepts. He often stretches the limits of concepts such as cool and hot. This tactic involves, for instance, the infusion of a recurring issue in his writing such as the flotation of money and of signs without referential anchors with McLuhan's concepts. This infusion neither elucidates the concepts nor does it add substantively to the issue at hand. Rather, they are introduced with a calculated abandon, quickly saturating an issue so as to heighten the sense that it is perfecting itself and in so doing spiralling out of control.

Baudrillard's working hypothesis with respect to the slogan 'the medium is the message' is, on the one hand, that McLuhan's 'prophecy' has been realized. This acknowledgement does not mean that Baudrillard supports this state of affairs. On the contrary, this hypothesis is a first step toward pushing the terms of the slogan to the very limits of sense in order to describe the development of media in a society of simulations. On the other hand, the hypothesis that McLuhan was right and remains more correct than he perhaps should have been is an exaggeration which Baudrillard hopes will, in a second step, destabilize the very development the slogan captures.

Baudrillard has attempted to theorize this 'final straw' (the straw that broke 'the system's' back) by various means throughout his career. He continued to use the revolutionary rhetoric of beating 'the system' into the mid-1970s, even though by this time 'the system' in question was defined structurally and included diverse phenomena such as models of communication and the power of biocrats to control the distinction between life and death from the Thanatos centres of the hospital and the laboratory. Paradoxically, McLuhan's slogan defines the field against which symbolic violence must be applied, and may be used to read Freud and Saussure against themselves, thereby articulating certain modes of symbolic exchange. This is the central contradiction in Baudrillard's use of McLuhan's ideas.

A further, clearly parodic way of acknowledging McLuhan appears in Baudrillard's notion of 'the generalization of McLuhan's theory of the "extensions of man"'.[41] The emphasis on electronic extensions of the brain has reached, Baudrillard thinks, a critical point of reversal in which the brain becomes an 'extension' or internal prosthetic device of the body. The prosthetic brain is internal to the body but no longer centred by it. It seems to be pursuing an orbit independent of its individual body!

It is at this point that Baudrillard denies he is writing science fiction. It is purely parodic to suggest that McLuhan's well-known optimism about technological extensions of bodies has resulted in the concentric orbit of these extensions around the bodies from which they were launched. Baudrillard's reason for this travesty is clear enough: he claims that it is the work of theory to play a game of oneupmanship, of going to extremes with the goal of destabilizing 'the system'.

Baudrillard's guiding principle is, as McLuhan believed, breakdown as breakthrough, though he does not subscribe to the hypothesis that a hitherto unacknowledged depth may be disclosed through an interruption drawing attention to the medium. Rather, for Baudrillard 'the system' is challenged by a symbolic violence which consists in returning to it the principle of its own power (the power to give unilaterally and irreversibly without return) and thereby driving it to a point of breakdown because it can neither respond nor retort except by its own collapse.[42] In addition, the symbolic enters the semiurgical universe with the violence of a break and entry, an *effraction*. In Baudrillard's theorizing breakdown takes the form of a break-in.

Whereas Baudrillard was clearly critical of McLuhan's work in the late 1960s, focusing on the illogicality of the hot–cool distinction, the implicit finality of American culture, and the problem of technological idealism, and then reading the formula 'the medium is the message' into the logic of sign value, breaking the spell of McLuhan's optimism; it would seem that optimism returned to Baudrillard's thought in the mid-1970s as he came to consider McLuhan's slogan in terms complementary to the vehicles of symbolic exchange. Scattered throughout Baudrillard's writings one finds both instances of parodic extensions of McLuhan's concepts and places at which their language overlaps.

For McLuhan, 'implosion' – or the 'pulling out of the spaces [and time] between components' – is brought about by revolutions in tele-communications, primarily by the speed of new media, and reconfigures 'all operations, all information, all associations'.[43] As Barry Smart remarks, in Baudrillard's hands McLuhan's 'dictum' works itself out in an emphasis on form, the meaning of which is 'far from exhausted'.[44] Put another way, Baudrillard's concern with form – in particular, in his analyses of the object and mass society – culminates for Smart in the implosion of the media and the masses, yielding the Baudrillardian dictum 'mass(age) is the message'.

As becomes evident, Baudrillard uses his version of the dictum both to show that the 'medium is the message' is of the third order of simulation and to deliver his message that the mass form refuses socialization. Accordingly, implosion indicates the catastrophe of the collapse of new media toward the mass form. For Baudrillard, implosion does not produce the intimacy of the 'global village'; rather, the new patterns of inclusive structuration postulated by McLuhan yield their inverse: inertia, silence, indifference. Saturated by communication, human relations are reduced to points of 'contact'.

Here, Baudrillard turns McLuhan's sense of implosion inside out, but not towards explosion, by burying it in the indifference of the mass form. Such indifference as a kind of resistance has little to do with the paradise of involvement in the social process. This is also, on another level of analysis, precisely how McLuhan worked, since he claimed that a kind of proto-Baudrillardian 'fatal reversibility' reigns over events:

One of the observations of the I Ching, the *Book of Changes*, some 3,000 years old, is 'when a thing reaches its limit, it turns around' – it reverses its characteristics.[45]

Reversibility or a flip is a key to Baudrillard's critical practice of reading thinkers against themselves. On a generous reading of the relationship between Baudrillard and McLuhan, one might conclude that the apparent contradictions of Baudrillard's use of McLuhan's concepts are really only examples of a series of flips or inversions as a given concept exhausts itself and reverses its characteristics.

The nomination of Baudrillard for the position of the 'French McLuhan' has not resulted in a move to close nominations. The floor was already open. Indeed, considered in terms of the pataphysical effects of reversibility: isn't McLuhan a Canadian Baudrillard? As absurd as this seems, McLuhan's contemporary return to relevance in the diverse area of new information technologies has a distinctive Baudrillardian glow about it, especially now that he is being updated for a new generation in the largely borrowed, but inflated and exaggerated, conceptual language that Baudrillard put into circulation throughout the 1980s – the time of his most widespread influence in the English-speaking world, to be sure. At times more McLuhan than McLuhan himself, and at others anti-McLuhanite to the core, Baudrillard's ambivalence toward McLuhan reveals the limits of the nomination, no matter how it is phrased.

NOTES

1 The research for this chapter was funded by a Social Sciences and Humanities Research Council of Canada Postdoctoral Fellowship (1992–94). The bulk of the work was completed while I was a McLuhan Research Fellow (1992–93) at the McLuhan Program in Culture and Technology at the University of Toronto. I presented an earlier version of this chapter in the Department of Sociology, Goldsmiths' College, University of London, while I was a Visiting Research Fellow (1993–94). It is taken from a manuscript in preparation entitled 'The Masters of Implosion: McLuhan and Baudrillard'.

2 Mike Gane, *Baudrillard: Critical and Fatal Theory*, London: Routledge, 1991, p. 3.

3 Ibid., p. 13.

4 Baudrillard, *La Société de consommation*, Paris: S.G.P.P., 1970, p. 189.

5 See István Csicsery-Ronay, 'Cyberpunk and Neuromanticism', *Mississippi Review*, no. 47–48, 1988: 266–78; and 'The SF of Theory: Baudrillard and Haraway', *Science Fiction Studies*, no. 55, 1991, pp. 387–404.

6 See Christian Deschamps' interview with Baudrillard in *Entretiens avec Le Monde 3. Idées contemporaines*, Paris: Editions la Découverte, 1984.

7 See Baudrillard, 'Simulacres et science fiction', *Simulacres et simulations*, Paris: Galilée, 1981.

8 Philip K. Dick, *The Simulacra*, London: Methuen, 1964.

9 Baudrillard, *L'échange symbolique et la mort*, Paris: Gallimard, 1976, pp. 305–6.

10 Jean Starobinski, *Words Upon Words: The Anagrams of Ferdinand de Saussure*, translated by Olivia Emmet, New Haven: Yale University Press, 1979.

11 Baudrillard, *L'Ange de stuc*, Paris: Galilée, 1978; Gane, *Baudrillard's Bestiary*, London: Routledge, 1991, pp. 121–25.

12 Baudrillard, *A l'Ombre des majorités silencieuses*, Paris: Utopie, 1978, p. 41.

13 Donald Theall, *The Medium is the RearView Mirror: Understanding McLuhan*, Montreal: McGill-Queen's University Press, 1971, pp. 240–41.

14 Space does not permit me to elaborate upon the importance of the concept of semiurgy in considering the relationship between McLuhan and Baudrillard. Suffice to say it is commonplace for postmodernists to draw a direct line of influence from McLuhan's concept of massage to Baudrillard's sense of semiurgy, thereby not only overlooking the contributions of René Berger and Roland Barthes to semiologically inspired neologisms, but obscuring some important differences. *Sémiurgie* is a French neologism which came into use in substantive and adjectival forms in the early 1970s. It designates the logic of mass-mediated environments and is modelled on 'demiurgy', in some usages adding evil to artifice. Literally part 'sign' and part 'work', the concept appeared at once in Baudrillard's description of the philosophy of design of the Bauhaus school and Berger's distinction between sciences which take the suffix '-logies' (imposition of a model in a cognitive attitude) and '-urgies' (implementation of a creative attitude; see Berger's *La Mutation des signes*, Paris: Denoël, 1972.

Baudrillard argued that the Bauhaus' vision of a universal system of functional objects entailed a designed environment in which participation is completely controlled. Hence, semiurgy simulates participation by reducing it to moves in a functional calculus. Human experience is alienated from the signification of objects whose meaning is determined by their interdependent and oppositional relations with other objects in a closed system. The combinatorial possibilities of the system are dictated by the Bauhaus' ultimate signified of functionality. Conversely, Berger cleansed semiurgy of its negative attributes by connecting it with creative involvement through appeals to the ideas of McLuhan. Accordingly, semiologists must become sign readers and makers, seizing the opportunities of the communications revolution, for signs are said to shift in the direction of those who act upon them and influence their work of signification.

Semiurgy is a key term in the description of the endless self-reflexive play of signs in postmodern theory. In this literature the origin of semiurgy is located in McLuhan's idea of massage, or how media intensify certain faculties, diminish others, and establish new proportions between them. The stresses and pains of massage are overcome in favour of stimulating social communication. Semiurgy and massage both name powerful forces shaping social experience. Contrary to McLuhan and his followers, Baudrillardian semiurgy impoverishes social experience and prevents genuine – that is, symbolic – communication between persons.

15 Baudrillard, *La Société de consommation*, p. 34.

16 Jean-Claude Giradin, 'Toward a Politics of Signs', translated by David Pugh, *Telos*, no. 20, 1974, p. 131, n. 6.

17 Baudrillard, *America*, translated by Chris Turner, London: Verso, 1988.

18 Baudrillard, *Xerox and Infinity*, translated by Agitac, London: Touchepas, 1988.

19 Baudrillard, *Seduction*, translated by Brian Singer, Montreal: New World Perspectives, 1990.

20 I am thinking of the graphic representation of the explosiveness of proletarian revolt in Baudrillard's 'Le Ludique et le policier', *Utopie*, vol. 2, no. 3, 1969, pp. 8–9.

21 McLuhan and Wilfred Watson, *From Cliché to Archetype*, New York: Viking, 1970, pp. 198–99.

22 Douglas Kellner, *Jean Baudrillard: From Marxism to Postmodernism and Beyond*, Stanford: Stanford University Press, 1989, p. 73.

23 John Fekete, 'McLuhanacy: Counterrevolution in Cultural Theory', *Telos*, no. 15, 1973, pp. 72–123.

24 See Jack Behar and Ben Lieberman, 'Paradise Regained or McLuhanacy?' in *The McLuhan Explosion: A Casebook on Marshall McLuhan and Understanding Media*, eds Harry H. Crosby and George R. Bond, New York: American Book Co., 1968.

25 Kellner, *Baudrillard*, p. 70.

26 Baudrillard, *Le Miroir de la production*, Tournai: Casterman, 1973.

27 McLuhan, *Understanding Media: The Extensions of Man*, New York: McGraw-Hill, 1964, pp. 22–24.

28 Baudrillard, *Le Miroir*, p. 123.

29 McLuhan, *Understanding Media*, p. 40.

30 For a detailed discussion of Baudrillard's idea of *effraction*, see my *Baudrillard and Signs*, London: Routledge, 1994, Chapter 1.

31 In Hervé Fischer, Fred Forest and Jean-Paul Thenot, *Collectif art sociologique: Théorie-pratique-critique*, Paris: Musée Galliera, 1975, pp. 213–14.

32 Baudrillard, *Pour une Critique de l'économie politique du signe*, Paris: Gallimard, 1972, p. 228.

33 McLuhan and Derrick de Kerckhove, 'Télévision et radiodiffusion, 4: Mythologie et utopie', in *Encyclopedia universalis*, vol. 15, Paris: Encyclopedia universalis France, 1968, pp. 898–99.

34 Francis Balle, *MacLuhan*, Paris: Hatier, 1972, p. 56.

35 Ibid., p. 58.

36 Baudrillard, *L'Échange symbolique*, p. 41.

37 Ibid.

38 See McLuhan, 'Inflation as New Rim-Spin', *The McLuhan Dew-Line Newsletter*, vol. 2, no. 2 September–October 1969, unpaginated.

39 Baudrillard, *L'Échange symbolique*, p. 41.

40 Ibid., p. 42.

41 Baudrillard, 'Transpolitics, Transsexuality, Transaesthetics', in *Jean Baudrillard: The Disappearance of Art and Politics*, eds W. Stearns and W. Chaloupka, New York: St Martin's Press, 1992, p. 17.

42 Baudrillard, *L'Échange symbolique*, pp. 64–65.

43 McLuhan, 'The Mini-State and the Future of Organizations', *The McLuhan Dew-Line Newsletter*, vol. 1, no. 8, February 1969, p. 12.

44 Barry Smart, *Modern Conditions, Postmodern Controversies*, London: Routledge, 1992, pp. 126–28.

45 McLuhan, 'Media and the Structured Society' *The McLuhan Dew-Line Newsletter*, vol. 2, no. 1, July 1969, p. 8.

10
THIS IS NOT A WAR

PAUL PATTON

In many respects, the 1991 Gulf war represented a qualitative shift in the impact of communications technology upon world events. It was not the first time that images of war had appeared on TV screens, but it was the first time that they were relayed 'live' from the battlefront. It was not the first occasion on which the military censored what could be reported, but it did involve a new level of military control of reportage and images. Military planners had clearly learnt a great deal since Vietnam: procedures for controlling the media were developed and tested in the Falklands, Grenada and Panama.

As a result, what we saw was for the most part a 'clean' war, with lots of pictures of weaponry, including the amazing footage from the nose-cameras of 'smart bombs', and relatively few images of human casualties, none from the Allied forces. In the words of one commentator, for the first time 'the power to create a crisis merges with the power to direct the movie about it . . . Desert Storm was the first major global media crisis orchestration that made instant history'.[1]

The Gulf war movie was instant history in the sense that the selected images which were broadcast worldwide provoked immediate responses and then became frozen into the accepted story of the war: high-tech weapons, ecological disaster, the liberation of Kuwait. In case anyone missed the first release, CNN produced its own edited documentary, *CNN: War in the Gulf* which was shown on TV around the world. Within weeks of the end of hostilities, Time Warner produced a CD ROM disk on Desert Storm which enabled published text, unedited correspondents' reports, photos and eyewitness accounts that would fill 500 floppy disks to be distributed in the form of a single hypertext document to school libraries and retail outlets across the US. In their publicity, they described this interactive multimedia disk as a 'first draft of history'.

But the Gulf war movie was also an influential part of history even as it unfolded. Reports before and during the conflict phase directly influenced public opinion in support of the war. Film coverage of the bombing of retreating Iraqi forces was fundamental to the decision to end the war, since it was feared that such images would adversely affect public sentiment. The images of destruction and death along the road to Basra did not fit the script of the world's first high-tech clean war. The impact of this new feedback loop upon strategic planning is evident in the comment by one military analyst that 'curiously, this is counter to traditional military thinking, as the best time to strike an enemy is when he is disorganised and retreating'.[2]

Despite such interference, the images and the reality of events in the Gulf bled into one another, producing a new kind of composite event composed at once of digital images and bodies and machines. The war witnessed the birth of a new kind of military apparatus which incorporates the power to control the production and circulation of images as well as the power to direct the actions of bodies and machines. A new kind of event and a new kind of power which is at once both real and simulacral. In view of these developments, even at the time, the Gulf war seemed to many of us a pure product of Baudrillardian hyperreality in which the distinction between reality and its representation had become increasingly difficult to sustain. Fascination and horror at the reality which seemed to unfold before our very eyes mingled with a pervasive sense of unreality as we recognized the elements of Hollywood script which had preceded the real, and as the signifiers of other events faded into those of the present (for example, the oil-soaked bird from the *Exxon Valdez* recycled to warn us of impending eco-disaster in the Gulf). Occasionally, the absurdity of the media's self-representation as purveyor of reality and immediacy broke through, in moments such as those when the CNN cameras crossed live to a group of reporters assembled somewhere in the Gulf, only to have them confess that they were also sitting around watching CNN in order to find out what was happening. With 'Gulf war the movie', television news coverage finally appeared to have caught up with the logic of simulation.

Jean Baudrillard's article, 'The Gulf War Will Not Take Place', was published in *Libération* on 4 January 1991, a little over one month after the UN Security Council had voted to authorize the use of force if Iraq had not begun to remove its troops from Kuwait by 15 January, and a little under two weeks before the American and British air attack on Baghdad and Iraqi positions in Kuwait. Far from being deterred by the reality of the unfolding situation, he wrote two more pieces along similar lines: 'The Gulf War: Is It Really Taking Place?', which referred to the events during February 1991, and 'The Gulf War Did Not Take

Place', which was written after the end of hostilities on 28 February. Part of the second article appeared in *Libération* on 6 February while a fragment of the third article appeared in *Libération* on 29 March 1991. All three pieces first appeared in extended form in the book published in May 1991.[3]

The central assertion of 'The Gulf War Will Not Take Place' appears to be directly contradicted by the facts. What took place over the ensuing weeks was a massive aerial bombardment of Iraq's military and civil infrastructure. According to some accounts, the amount of high explosive unleashed in the first month of the conflict exceeded that of the entire Allied air offensive during the Second World War.[4] This was followed by a systematic air and artillery assault on the Iraqi forces left in Kuwait, which culminated in the infamous 'turkey shoot' carried out on the troops and others fleeing along the road to Basra. Official estimates of lives lost as direct casualties of these attacks are in the order of 100,000, not to mention the subsequent loss of life to hunger and disease. On the face of it, Baudrillard could not have been more wrong. So why did he write this piece, and then pursue the line of argument which appears to deny the reality of the Gulf war? Pure provocation, perhaps? A symbolic challenge to this new modality of power? Not irony so much as that black humour which seeks to subvert what is being said by pursuing its implicit logic to extremes: so you want us to believe that this was a clean, minimalist war, with little collateral damage and few Allied casualties. Why stop there: war? what war?

Whatever the effects of this polemical strategy upon those who wield this simulacral power, and they may be negligible, some critics of the war were strongly provoked. Christopher Norris set out to write a polemical response to 'The Gulf War Will Not Take Place' and ended up producing a book against the whole 'postmodern tendency' in contemporary theory, for which he takes Baudrillard to be the prime spokesman and 'purveyor of some of the silliest ideas yet to gain a hearing among disciples of French intellectual fashion'.[5] Norris charges Baudrillard with peddling a brand of 'theory' which is not only 'ill-equipped to mount any kind of effective critical resistance',[6] but also conducive to a '"postmodern" mood of widespread cynical acquies-cence' in events such as the Gulf war.[7] As such, he argues, this postmodern theory betrays the deep 'ideological complicity' which obtains between its anti-realist or irrationalist doctrines and the 'crisis of moral and political nerve' which Norris discerns among the Western intelligentsia.[8]

One may wonder what it means when one intellectual who published polemical pieces about the Gulf war and its media representation is accused of failure of moral and political nerve by another who seized the occasion to write a polemic about postmodern theory. I will return to Norris' arguments against what he takes to be Baudrillardian doctrines below. In order to fully appreciate the force of these arguments, we need to understand more fully the position they are directed against. These are occasional essays, written in the heat of the moment, but they are grounded in an implicit theory of the nature of those disturbing events.

In fact, Baudrillard offers another reason besides provocation for undertaking what he calls the 'stupid gamble' of attempting to demonstrate the impossibility of war in the Gulf just at the moment when all the signs were pointing in the direction of its occurrence, namely the stupidity of not doing so (G, 28). 'Stupidity' in this context assumes a variety of forms. In addition to the particular stupidity of war itself, Baudrillard mentions:

> [the] professional and functional stupidity of those who pontificate in perpetual commentary on the event: all the Bouvards and Pécuchets for hire, the would-be raiders of the lost image, the CNN types and all the master singers of strategy and information who make us experience the emptiness of television as never before. (G, 51)

But the particular form of stupidity against which he wrote these articles was that of those critics who uncritically participate in the supposed realism of the information industry. With this goes the stupidity of taking a position for or against the war without first interrogating the nature and type of 'reality' proper to events such as those which unfolded in the Gulf and on our TV screens. Critics of the war typically sought to denounce it as an outrage against humanitarian and democratic values. Baudrillard's refusal of stupidity is grounded in a different ethic:

> Resist the probability of any image or information whatever. Be more virtual than events themselves, do not seek to to re-establish the truth, we do not have the means, but do not be duped, and to that end re-immerse the war and all information in the virtuality from whence they come. Turn deterrence back against itself. Be meteorologically sensitive to stupidity. (G, 66–67)

Battlefield Simulation

The terms of this injunction bring us to the heart of Baudrillard's analysis of the war which did not take place. What is the 'deterrence' which must be turned back on itself and in what sense are events 'virtual'? In current usage, 'virtual' reality is generally opposed to 'actual' reality and applied to several features of electronic technology: the virtual desktop on my screen is not a real desk, even though I can interact with it to store and retrieve real files, and send messages to real destinations. In this sense, much of what took place in the Gulf was virtual but nonetheless bound up with the reality of high-tech warfare. Just as it marked a new level of military control over the public representation of combat operations, so the Gulf war displayed a new level of military deployment of simulation technology. In this sense, simulacra neither displace nor deter the violent reality of war: they have become an integral part of its operational procedures. The development of flight simulators provided an early example of the computer technology which allows trainee pilots to be immersed in a virtual environment. With the increasing strategic reliance upon data from radar and computer screens, Manuel De Landa points out, the boundaries between simulation and reality become blurred: the images and information which furnish the material for exercises and war games are indistinguishable from that which would be encountered in a real conflict.[9]

The same technology now applies to ground vehicles such as tanks, in which access to external environments is similarly electronically mediated. This allows not only the creation of simulated environments in which to train individual crews, but also the possibility of connected simulators in which virtual tank battles can be fought out. An article in the first issue of *Wired*, a magazine devoted to virtual reality technology, recounts developments in the use of networked simulation machines as training devices. Current research aims to achieve what is called 'seamless manipulation' in which 'the seams between reality and virtuality will be deliberately blurred' and 'real tanks can engage simulator crews on real terrain which is simultaneously virtual'.[10] Within months of the end of the war, army historians and simulation modellers had produced their own multimedia, fully interactive, network capable digital simulation of one of the tank battles from the closing stages of the conflict: 'armchair strategists can now fly over the virtual battlefield in the "stealth vehicle", the so-called "SIMNET flying carpet", viewing the 3-D virtual landscape from any angle during any moment of the battle. They can even change the parameters – give the Iraqis infrared targeting scopes, for instance, which they lacked at the time . . . this is virtual reality as a new way of knowledge: a new and terrible kind of transcendent military power'.[11]

As the Gulf war showed, the military application of simulation technology is no longer confined to training and war games. Virtual environments are now incorporated into operational warplanes:

> When you are flying low in an F-16 Falcon at supersonic speeds over a mountainous terrain, the less you see of the real

world the more control you can have over your aircraft. A virtual cockpit filters the real scene and represents a more readable world.[12]

Here, there is no opposition between simulacra and the real but a new and more powerful assemblage of the two: simulation augments the effectiveness of military technology. In 'The Precession of Simulacra', Baudrillard took as an allegory of simulation the Borges story in which the cartographers of an empire draw up a map so detailed that it exactly covered the territory.[13] Thanks to the geographical data collected by the US Defense Mapping Agency, remote corners of the American empire such as Kuwait already exist on hard disk. But this technological notion of the virtual readily accommodates belief in a reality outside the virtual image which represents it more or less truthfully. Our access to reality is often mediated by electronic signals, and for all we know the images on the TV screen may be the results of studio production techniques rather than the representation of 'real' events. In this sense, Baudrillard reminds us, the direct transmission by CNN of information in real time does not prove that war is taking place (G, 61–62). However, his claim that the Gulf war did not take place does not depend upon the possibility of such technological fraud. Rather, it relies upon two distinct notions of virtual war and two distinct forms of the simulation of war: the virtual 'informational' war and the virtual war which results from the transformation of war into deterrence.

Media War

The first sense in which Baudrillard speaks of events as virtual is related to the idea that at a certain speed, that of information under the present technological conditions of its generation and dissemination, events lose their identity and fade into hyperreality. 'Real' events lose their identity when they attain the velocity of real time information, or to use another metaphor, when they become encrusted with the information which represents them. In this sense, while televisual information claims to provide immediate access to real events, in fact what it does is to produce informational events which stand in for the real, and which 'inform' public opinion which in turn affects the course of subsequent events, both real and informational. As consumers of mass media, we never experience the bare material event but only the informational coating which renders it 'sticky and unintelligible' like the oil-soaked sea bird (G, 32). Where was this image captured and what oil spill caused it? Who caused the oil spill to begin with? To the extent that events are mediated and portrayed by such selected images, they become contaminated by what Baudrillard calls 'the structural unreality of the image'. At the same time, the images themselves have real effects and become enmeshed in the ensuing material and social reality. 'The closer we approach the real time of the event, the more we fall into the illusion of the virtual. God save us from the illusion of war' (G, 49).

In this sense, we live in a hyperreality which results from the fusion of the virtual and the real into a third order of reality. Virtual media events are a new kind of entity, qualitatively different to 'real' or 'imaginary' events as these were understood prior to the advent of modern communications technology. They are informational entities and one of their defining characteristics is to be always open to interpretation. Information events are thus the objects of endless speculation: because a range of interpretations is always possible, the identity of such events becomes vague or undecidable. Thus, the Iraqi invasion of Kuwait may be represented as the outcome of the megalomaniac ambitions of a local dictator, or as the result of a deliberate ploy on the part of the Americans in order to legitimize their projection of force into the region. Baudrillard's Gulf war essays provide many examples of such aporia: for example, the Americans are unable to perceive the Other in any terms but their own, and as a result they misrecognize the strategic aims of Saddam Hussein, or alternatively Hussein is entirely a mercenary beholden to outside forces and it is the West which is in conflict with itself in Iraq.

Norris represents the argument somewhat differently, preferring to treat it as a confused epistemological thesis which begins by denying that we have any means of access to 'what happens' other than what is provided by the media, and ends by concluding on this basis that there is no 'operative difference between truth and falsehood, veridical knowledge and its semblance as created by the feed-back mechanisms of media reporting, opinion-polls etc'.[14] This makes it easy to present Baudrillard as the most extreme case of the supposed poststructuralist thesis that reality is textual or discursive all the way down, and then to show that he is guilty of the most elementary philosophical confusions, such as confusing the ontological issue of what is the case with the epistemological issue of what we can know about what is the case.

As Norris puts it, 'the main confusion in Baudrillard's thought is his habit of equating what is currently, contingently "good in the way of belief" with the limit of what can possibly be known from a critical or truth-seeking standpoint'.[15] Understood in this manner, the thesis that the Gulf war did not take place is readily disproved, and the confusions which lie behind such claims rapidly exposed. Readers may wonder why Norris has to call in the heavy artillery of technical argumentation drawn from 'the province of epistemology, philosophy of language and truth-conditional semantics',[16] when all that is required is a couple of distinctions known to every student of Philosophy I.

More to the point, if it were to be understood in this manner, the thesis that the Gulf war did not take place would indeed be ludicrous, and would hardly justify the effort of a lengthy essay in reply. Norris betrays an awareness of this ground for embarrassment by the manner in which he defensively repeats his justification for embarking on this polemic – these notions are taken seriously, even in the pages of *Marxism Today* and the *New Left Review* – and by the disclaimers he makes with regard to the descriptive value of Baudrillard's account of the present sociocultural condition: for example, he allows that 'this is indeed in some sense a "postmodern" war, an exercise in mass-manipulative rhetoric and "hyperreal" suasive techniques, which does undoubtedly confirm some of Baudrillard's more canny diagnostic observations'.[17] Why then does Norris choose to attack the straw man version rather than take up what he concedes to be accurate diagnosis? Perhaps because he can find no purchase in this account of the postmodern condition for the kind of principled denunciation of the facts which is crucial to his self-image as a critical intellectual, or because he is unwilling to consider the possibility that changes to our sociocultural condition might have a bearing on what constitutes effective critical resistance.

I recommend a different interpretative strategy in relation to Baudrillard's text: instead of treating the hyperreality thesis as a universal claim about the collapse of the real into its forms of representation, which leads only to the futile hypothesis of a generalized solipsism, treat it as a specific ontological claim about social reality. Informational events such as the Gulf crisis are a feature of postmodern public life. Since they are by definition always open to interpretation, they may serve a variety of political ends. They are an important vector of power. What matters is to control the production and meaning of information in a given context.

Much has been written since the Gulf crisis about the role of the media in promoting the military option, and about the practice of misinformation, lies and propaganda on both sides. There is no doubt that such things occurred. One of the more effective propaganda stories about Iraqi atrocities in Kuwait was the eyewitness account before a Congressional human rights caucus of soldiers removing babies from incubators and leaving them to die. It later emerged that the witness was the daughter of the Kuwaiti ambassador to the US, and that she had been coached by a public relations firm hired by the Kuwaiti government.[18]

However, the danger in confining one's critical response to the denunciation of such abuses of the democratic right to information is that this also serves to sustain what Baudrillard calls a 'hypocritical vision of television and information' (G, 46). It judges the media by reference to a moral ideal, namely that of a good or truthful use of images and signs. In fact, there is nothing inherently good about images or signs, and they can just as readily be employed to deceive as to tell the truth. As Deleuze argues with respect to Plato,[19] the attempt to distinguish between good and bad copies of reality may be seen to found a system of moral defence against the principle of simulation which governs all forms of representation. In this sense, Baudrillard argues, it is cynics such as Saddam Hussein and the US military commanders who are less naive and hypocritical in their willingness to control information and images in whatever ways best serve their strategic ends: 'We believe that they immorally pervert images' when 'They alone are conscious of the profound immorality of images' (G, 47).

In effect, at least two strategies are in play with regard to the control of information in contemporary public life. During the 'live' phase of a significant event such as the Gulf conflict or an election campaign, the strictest control of information is necessary in order to influence future developments. Wherever public opinion can feed back into a political process which includes the event in question, image and interpretation or 'spin' upon current developments is vital. Once that phase is passed, however, another strategy takes over. The proliferation of archival information including taped audiovisual records allows the event to become utterly dispersed into conflicting interpretations and hypotheses about what really happened. Did Saddam Hussein undertake the invasion of Kuwait against all indications or was he lured into a trap by US policy makers? Who was really responsible for the assassination of JFK? And who killed Laura Palmer? Not only does the real vanish into the virtual through an excess of information, it leaves an archival deposit such that 'generations of video-zombies . . . will never cease reconstituting the event' (G, 47).

It is this latter effect of the proliferation of information which sets limits to the effectiveness of the kind of critical media analysis which seeks to discover the truth of events. The author of *The Persian Gulf TV War*, Douglas Kellner, recounts his accumulation of hundreds of hours of videotape of the Gulf crisis even before the bombing began. Thereafter, he videotaped and analysed at least sixteen hours of television a day, and systematically studied mainstream US print media as well as foreign newspapers and journals, along with computer databases and peace networks on the Internet. Despite this herculean effort, his book opens with an admission of failure: he cannot decide conclusively for or against the conspiracy theory according to which the US enticed Iraq to invade Kuwait, since 'other accounts are also plausible'.[20]

It is the desire to avoid this kind of informational aporia which lies behind Baudrillard's injunction : do not seek to re-establish the truth, we do not have the means. And even if we did, what difference would this make? For every book exposing the lies and inhumanity of US policy in the Gulf there are two more which champion it as the defence of democracy and the new world order.

Pure War

Baudrillard's alternative is to be more virtual than events themselves. Only one thing could be more virtual than an informational war approved by the UN and broadcast live on prime-time TV, namely a non-war, an empty war or a war that never took place. In part, the point being made in the article published in January 1991 is that the events which were unfolding did not and would not correspond to the 'archaic imaginary of media hysteria' (G, 56). This imaginary object of media speculation was total war in the 1940s sense, including the use of chemical and perhaps even nuclear weapons. Baudrillard's argument was that war in that sense would not take place. On the one hand, this response is a kind of *fuite en avant*, a sardonic challenge to the media hype surrounding the Gulf crisis. On the other, it points to an irony in events themselves which derives from the fact that war itself has become virtual.

The underlying argument of that article is that the logic of deterrence has transformed the nature of war. Deterrence is a matter of the virtual exercise of power, action upon the action of the other by immaterial means. It is a means of waging war, but one in which the aim is precisely non-engagement or the avoidance of direct encounter between the parties involved. The cold war was indeed a war, one that has been fought and won, but increasingly by economic, informational and electronic means. It was a war fought on the principle of deterrence, on the basis of an economic, R&D and informational effort to deter any use of material force by the other side. It was won when the Soviet economic and political system could no longer maintain the effort. In the process, war evolved in a manner parallel to the evolution of capital:

> Just as wealth is no longer measured by the ostentation of wealth but by the secret circulation of speculative capital, so war is not measured by being waged but by its speculative unfolding in an abstract, electronic and informational space, the same space in which capital moves. (G, 56)

This does not mean that it is unreal in the sense of not having real effects, any more than a capital crisis is unreal because it takes place in the electronic and informational space of digitalized and networked financial markets. Rather, it means that military power is now virtual in the sense that it is deployed in an abstract, electronic and informational space, and in the sense that its primary mechanism is no longer the use of force. Virtual war is therefore not simply the image or imaginary representation of real war, but a qualitatively different kind of war, the effects of which include the suppression of war in the old sense.

The hypothesis of 'The Gulf War Will Not Take Place' is that the deterrence of war in the traditional sense has been internalized and turned back upon the Western powers, producing a form of self-deterrence which renders them incapable of realizing their own power in the form of relations of force. Under present conditions, Baudrillard argues, the virtual has overtaken the actual, it functions to deter the real event and leaves only the simulacrum of war which will never advance to the use of force: 'We are no longer in a logic of the passage from virtual to actual but in a hyperrealist logic of the deterrence of the real by the virtual' (G, 27). Shortly after the publication of 'The Gulf War Will Not Take Place' the bombing began in earnest. Does this constitute a refutation of the hypothesis that there was no Gulf war? Only if we accept that what did take place out there in the desert beyond the reach of the TV cameras was in fact a war. Baudrillard's argument in 'The Gulf War: Is It Really Taking Place?' and 'The Gulf War Did Not Take Place' is not that nothing took place, but that what took place was not a war.

In the past, war has always involved an antagonistic and destructive confrontation between adversaries, a dual relation between warring parties. In several respects, this was not the case in the Gulf conflict. On the level of military technology, the disparity between US and Iraqi forces was so great that direct engagement rarely took place, and when it did the outcome was entirely predictable. The complete absence of any engagement by Iraqi planes, and the fate of their technologically inferior tanks, testify to the one-sided nature of the conflict:

> It is as though the Iraqis were electrocuted, lobotomised, running towards the television journalists in order to surrender or immobilised beside their tanks . . . can this be called a war? (G, 67–68)

On the level of military and political strategy, the disparity between the aims and methods of the two sides was also such that no real encounter took place. With respect to military strategy, one commentator has argued that Iraq was still fighting in the manner of its previous war with Iran, while the US and its allies were fighting an altogether different war. While they were 'preparing to deploy high-technology, precision guided "smart" weapons and the latest developments in air power in order to win the war as quickly and "cleanly" as possible, Iraq was digging in for a long war of attrition, preparing to tolerate massive casualties and employing weapons from the old Cold War era'.[21] Similarly, with respect to political strategy, there was an equivalent failure of communication between the two sides (G, 64–66). Saddam Hussein's war was a gigantic bluff, a political and diplomatic opening gambit from which he showed every sign of being willing to retreat in return for concessions. George Bush's war was a calculated operation which refused negotiation at every point as it progressed relentlessly towards its pre-programmed goal of teaching the 'lying son of a bitch' a lesson.

As a result, what took place was a failure to engage in adversarial fashion, a non-event or non-war. The imbalance of military means was such that this was not a conflict in which the survival of both sides was in play, but an entirely asymmetrical operation, an exercise in domination rather than an act of war. The point is analogous to Foucault's argument that a body enslaved is subject not to relations of power but to relations of force.[22] Foucault defines the exercise of power in terms of action upon the action of others, and domination as the situation in which one party can act upon the other without the possibility of any reciprocal effect: see without being seen, act upon the other without the other being able to act upon oneself. This situation is the goal of every tactician of power, embodied in technologies of power like Bentham's Panopticon. Overwhelming superior force is another way of establishing a relation of domination, one which has its own particular advantages and costs.

To make this distinction is not to suggest that being subject to force relations is somehow less offensive than being subject to power, or that domination is an acceptable situation. On the contrary, it provides a basis upon which to begin to explain the peculiar horror that is involved in being treated not as an agent but as a body, or in finding oneself trapped in a situation from which there is no possibility of escape. In the case of the Gulf conflict, as Baudrillard points out, it provides a basis on which to appreciate the peculiar insult that is involved in the refusal to recognize the other as interlocutor, in the refusal to negotiate and the recourse to ultimata. It also explains the particular horror of the air assault on Iraqi troops in the final stages of the conflict, and the hasty end to hostilities to prevent the images of the atrocity causing political damage at home.

In his defence of the rationalist outlook which rejects the postmodern reduction of truth to consensus belief, Norris upholds the figure of Chomsky against Baudrillard, Foucault and others, as a model of the liberal and critical intellectual. Here is someone who is both a defender of Enlightenment ideals in morality and the philosophy of language, and a staunch critic of US foreign policy. How surprising it is then to find that Chomsky has also questioned whether what took place in the Gulf in 1990–91 was a war:

> As I understand the concept 'war', it involves two sides in combat, say, shooting at each other. That did not happen in the Gulf.[23]

He goes on to describe the successive phases of the conflict as involving varieties of state terrorism practised on both sides, and a form of slaughter practised by US and UK air and ground forces upon Iraqi soldiers and civilians. Does this mean that the argument is largely semantic, a matter of pointing out that the events in the Gulf did not amount to a war in the sense that this term had previously been understood, and is largely ineffective as a result? Not necessarily, since to draw attention to the more unsavoury and less heroic aspects of these events by renaming them is a form of resistance to the prevailing information. *Contra* Norris, it is not clear that the issue of whether or not what took place in the Gulf was a war is one which could be settled, even in principle, by an appeal to the fact of the matter.

However, to challenge the informational event in this manner is to adopt a modest critical stance which does not overestimate the power that intellectual commentators can exercise over such events. Baudrillard reminds us that the real power of subversion and ironic reversal lies in the events themselves. Reality produces its own viral effects, which can undermine the meaning and 'reality' of events from within.

The claim that war itself has become virtual does not mean that military conflicts do not occur: they do and with increasing frequency and savagery in the new world order. But these are secondary phenomena, like the persistence of sweatshops alongside fully automated production facilities. They are the consequences of a law of uneven development, located for the most part in a political and military third world. Where they do involve first world powers such as the US or UK, it is because they are in conflict with third world forces who do not recognize that the rules of the game have changed, or who, like Saddam Hussein, operate according to different rules. They are police operations rather than wars. The crucial stake in the Gulf affair, Baudrillard argues, was the subordination of Islam to the global order.

> Our wars thus have less to do with the confrontation of warriors than with the domestication of the refractory forces on the planet . . . All that is singular and irreducible must be reduced and absorbed. This is the law of democracy and the New World Order. (*G*, 86)

In these cases, deterrence breaks down for lack of any common ground, and it is this failure of communication which leads to the use of force. However, the use of force remains carefully circumscribed, a lever of last resort employed only to the extent that is necessary to bring the recalcitrant party into line. This is not war, and even if it was, in the case of the Gulf conflict, it is as though it never happened.

The final irony of the whole episode is that, apart from the massive damage and suffering inflicted upon Iraq, and the political and economic benefits at home, very little has changed. The Iraqi regime remains intact. The rights of Kuwait may have been restored, but in exchange for the rights of minorities in Iraq. A perfect semblance of victory for the Americans has been exchanged for the perfect semblance of defeat for Iraq (G, 71). In short, the Gulf war did not take place.

NOTES

1 George Gerbner, 'Persian Gulf War, the Movie' in *Triumph of the Image: The Media's War in the Persian Gulf – A Global Perspective*, ed. by H. Mowlana, G. Gerbner and H.I. Schiller, Boulder, CO and Oxford: Westview Press, 1992, pp. 244, 247.

2 Lieutenant-Colonel Jeffrey D. McCausland, *Adelphi Paper 282*, London: The International Institute for Strategic Studies, 1993, p. 66.

3 Jean Baudrillard, *La Guerre du Golfe n'a pas eu lieu*, Paris: Éditions Galilée; translated by Paul Patton as *The Gulf War Did Not Take Place*, Sydney: Power Publications, 1995. Henceforth abbreviated as G.

4 Gerbner, 'Persian Gulf War', p. 252.

5 Christopher Norris, *Uncritical Theory: Postmodernism, Intellectuals and the Gulf War*, London: Lawrence and Wishart, 1992, p. 11.

6 Ibid., p. 30.

7 Ibid., p. 29.

8 Ibid., p. 27.

9 Manuel De Landa, *War in the Age of Intelligent Machines*, New York: Zone Books (Swerve Editions), 1991, pp. 101, 189.

10 Bruce Sterling, 'War is Virtual Hell', *Wired*, vol. 1, no. 1, 1993, p. 95.

11 Ibid., pp. 95–6.

12 Michael Heim, *The Metaphysics of Virtual Reality*, New York and Oxford: Oxford University Press, 1993, p. 113.

13 Baudrillard, *Selected Writings*, ed. Mark Poster, Cambridge: Polity Press, 1988, p. 166.

14 Norris, *Uncritical Theory*, p. 12.

15 Ibid., p. 16.

16 Ibid., p. 20.

17 Ibid., pp. 25–6.

18 Douglas Kellner, *The Persian Gulf TV War*, Boulder, CO and Oxford: Westview Press, 1992, pp. 67–68.

19 Gilles Deleuze, 'Overturning Platonism', in *The Logic of Sense*, New York: Columbia University Press, 1990, pp. 253–66.

20 Kellner, *The Persian Gulf TV War*, pp. 7, 13.

21 Philip M. Taylor, *War and the Media: Propaganda and Persuasion in the Gulf War*, Manchester and New York: Manchester University Press, 1992, p. 28.

22 Michel Foucault, 'The Subject and Power', afterword to H. Dreyfus and P. Rabinow, *Michel Foucault: Beyond Structuralism and Hermeneutics*, Chicago: University of Chicago Press, 1984.

23 Noam Chomsky, 'The Media and the War: What War?', in H. Mowlana *et al.*, *Triumph of the Image*, p. 51.

11

AFTER THE AFTERIMAGE OF JEAN BAUDRILLARD:
Photography, the Object, Ecology and Design

ANNE-MARIE WILLIS

I was invited to participate at this symposium because of my writings on photography – it was thought I might have something to say about the photographic activity of Jean Baudrillard. My reasons for accepting the invitation are somewhat different, in that my own interests have in recent years extended beyond photography, into a consideration of its spheres of activity, particularly consumption and the sign economy, so Baudrillard's work has been important for me in this regard. However I find what he has to *say* about photography more problematic – as I will explain later.

But I have still to set up the scene. It is with trepidation that I declare that what I most want to explore are the possibilities and limits of using Baudrillard's work to think about something which I imagine is of little concern to him – that is, a relational thinking of the object, consumption, and an ecology of the artificial – in fact to use the word ecology is to evoke what he disparagingly refers to as 'The New Political Ecology' in *The Transparency of Evil*.[1]

The Baudrillard I refer to of course is nothing more than an authorial persona I have constructed out of my own erratic reading of his texts, with varying degrees of involvement over a number of years – a bit of a casual affair you might say. My Baudrillard is probably not your Baudrillard – and it may well have nothing to do with the corporeal presence of the same name. My confessed desire to *use* his *work* – calling on that obsolete category of use value – immediately creates a chasm between my disposition and his, which I would characterize as a weary delight in advocating a position of ironic immobilization. Where I too often feel immobilized, I do have a compulsion to act.

Why bother with him, then? We probably really are incompatible. Well, this remains to be seen.

In writing this essay I also set out to discover why it was that I could have found the earlier work of Jean Baudrillard so rich, suggestive and useful for what I was seeking to understand, but then how I could lose interest in the later work. There are two possible answers to this. Maybe I was seduced by someone else. Or maybe Baudrillard's work became less able to deal with what I came to see as the vital concerns of now. Here I will explore the second of these possibilities.

My approach will be to take two extracts from *The Transparency of Evil*, one on photography, in which the object is present in several senses, the other on ecology, in which the object is absent, and then by referring to aspects of Baudrillard's earlier work, suggest my own project of a relational re-thinking of the object and the 'environment'.

I wish to point to the limitations of his photographic activity, in terms of its genre and location, rather than the imagery itself. And I would like to take issue with his recent characterization of ecology (the 'New Political Ecology') and the futility of doing anything about ecological crisis. Here I will argue that the possibilities for action are not delimited in terms of actualities/potentialities, but in terms of how he sets up the argument. However at this point it needs to be made clear that no consensus on an understanding of the ecological can be assumed.

The object is a constantly mutating thing in Baudrillard's discourse. Sometimes paired with subject as its binary, the object may be animate or inanimate, human, non-human, natural or artificial. In his earliest writings it is part of a *System of Objects* (as one of his books was called),[2] which creates a system of needs based not on necessity or utility, but on sign values transmuted into a code, in which meaning is the function of an endless play of difference. As he becomes preoccupied with the code and the condition of hyperreality, the object metamorphoses into pure sign. Then it returns vengefully in *Fatal Strategies*, exercising its power of proliferation.[3] It is now a phantom object – powerful, mysterious, in control of the subject, wreaking its revenge – but it is completely dematerialized: Baudrillard's objects have in fact become holograms. And now the object migrates from simulation to illusion – a slippery and ill-lit passage indeed.

On the Issue of Criticism

The Transparency of Evil, along with Baudrillard's other more recent writings, *America* and *Cool Memories*,[4] could be regarded as little more than strings of aphorisms, and thus not worthy of critical engagement. They are less dense, layered and complex than what preceded them. Blending travelogue, anecdote and commentary they are congealed truisms that restate and extend earlier themes. Here are the bare bones of Baudrillard. Some claim that these writings mark his shift into 'the art of theory', and as such they should only be engaged on their own terms, and certainly not according to their possible correspondence with an assumed 'reality'.

At the same time, many who make these claims would use Derrida (for example) to assert the validity of multiple readings of texts. Equally there is the problem that all criticism of Baudrillard is cast by his fans as either outdated or ill-informed, so the actual value of Baudrillard's work is devalued because it is put outside of the possibility of a productive critical relation – which is certainly what I am attempting to do. Baudrillard's third constituency, his critical readers, are rendered invisible by the binary of 'supporters' versus 'the outdated/ill-informed' (much in the same way that binaries operate in Baudrillard' s own discourse).

Of course all bodies of writing/theories create their own 'realities'/ objects of engagement, and therefore it is not possible to compare them to a 'state of things' assumed to be objectively present and thus able to be called up unproblematically. Nevertheless bodies of work do have effects. They become objects of exchange, people make investments in them. They become operational by going into circulation, by becoming inscribed into social relations and practices (such as symposia, lectures, as pedagogical material, and as objects of casual conversation that eventually transmute into 'common sense').

Baudrillard's recent work is not in fact read as pure fiction. For many readers his pronouncements are taken as authorative (if troubling) statements on 'the state of things', because of the authority that has accumulated around the name 'Baudrillard'. For these reasons, and despite its 'thinness', it is important to engage his more recent work in terms beyond those it sets up itself. To register Baudrillard as proper name is also to cite 'the Baudrillard effect'. Thus Baudrillard can be returned to Baudrillard as an object of analysis or equally, one can declare that Baudrillard never happened, that he is an illusion or that Baudrillard is over. (The standard joke in Sydney, in both 1984 and 1994, was that those who watched his lectures relayed by television to an adjacent lecture theatre because of lack of room in the theatre where he appeared 'live', were the ones who saw 'the real Baudrillard'.)

The First Move: Photography

In the essay 'Radical Exoticism' in *The Transparency of Evil* Baudrillard's object is an isolated and splendid thing, willing hostage of the camera's cool eye, object of fascination rather than an object of theoretical speculation as an item of exchange in the sign economy. In fact it seems as if there is a game of alternating seduction now on, an exchange being played out between object and photography, with the subject (now designated as photographer) no more than a hapless accomplice. For example, Baudrillard writes:

> You think you are photographing a scene for the pleasure of it, but in fact the scene demands to be photographed, and you are merely part of the decor in the pictorial order it dictates. The subject is no more than a funnel through which things in their irony make their appearance.
> A photographic image must have this quality of a universe from which the subject has withdrawn. The very detail of the object, of line and light, should signify this suspension of the subject, and hence also of the world, which is what creates the photograph's tension. By means of the image the world imposes its discontinuity, its fragmentation, its distention, its artificial instantaneousness. From this point the photograph is the purest of images, for it simulates neither time nor motion and is thus unrealistic in the strictest sense.[5]

While I would agree with this decentring of the subject, the rest of the statement could be characterized as a naive ontology of photography. Baudrillard's insistence on the human subject suspending gaze and aesthetic judgement is an utterance that echoes through American art photography of the last fifty years. Unwittingly he reiterates the familiar stance of the art photographer whose deliberate self-construction as a sensitive presence, camera in hand, makes statements like 'the human subject is a good photographic medium, moreover, only if he enters into the spirit of this game, if he suspends his own gaze, and his own aesthetic judgment, if he takes pleasure in his own absence'.[6] This is the replay of an exhausted aesthetic strategy, firmly within the tradition of the anti-aesthetic (which itself always becomes another aesthetic).

With his privileging of detail, suspension, tension, the fragment, intensity, 'the purest of images', of 'pure objectality', Baudrillard's photographic aesthetic is virtually and accidentally interchangeable with that formulated by John Szarkowski (former curator of photography at the Museum of Modern Art, New York) in his influential book and exhibition of 1966 *The Photographer's Eye*,[7] in which the essential characteristics of the photographic medium were defined as 'The Thing Itself', 'The Frame', 'Time', 'The Detail', 'Time and Vantage Point'. Of course the title of Szarkowski's book indicates its difference from Baudrillard's sensibility in its privileging of subject (the photographer) over object. For Baudrillard the object is the privileged term, because it exercises a mysterious power over subjects.

Baudrillard's irony can also be contrasted with Szarkoswki's earnestness. But it is an irony that erases culture's authoring of subject positions of photographer and viewer. And here it's not a matter of the photographer's eye, but the authoring of the photographer's eye (or anti-eye, in terms of an advocated suspension of gaze) by the technology of photography, which in its turn is authored by an epistemological tradition founded on and founding the subject/object split.

Because neither Szarkowski nor Baudrillard is working with a dialectical understanding of subject/object/culture the effect of their discourse on photography is remarkably similar even though separated by nearly thirty years. Both circulate only within the restricted economy of valorized art practice. Their function is, by intention for Szarkoswki, by default for Baudrillard, the valorization of the photograph as aestheticized object. In his Australian press interviews Baudrillard declared that his own photographs are not art. Nevertheless their audience is almost exclusively an art audience (of what interest would they be to anyone else?). His disclaimer makes sense in the context of his 'Transaesthetics' (also in *The Transparency of Evil*), in which he states that art has disappeared and seeks only to duplicate itself by simulation, 'leaving behind an immense museum of artificial art and abandoning the field completely to advertising'.[8] Art may have disappeared (I am in full agreement with him here) yet its institutions live on to appropriate the corpus of Jean Baudrillard in last-gasp efforts to reanimate the corpse of art.

The critique I have offered so far can itself perhaps be seen as not moving beyond the restrictive aesthetic economy as I have defined it.

Another way I would offer of understanding Baudrillard's turn to photography is as the latest manifestation of his nostalgia. His writing is shot through with nostalgia. Earlier on, it is nostalgia for pre-modern systems of exchange, reciprocity and the gift manifested in his taking up of the work of Marcel Mauss and Georges Bataille.[9] Nostalgia is also pervasive in the rhythms and structures of his incantations – the repeated 'no longer', the constant evocation of 'today' which always implies a yesterday which was otherwise. But now it is nostalgia for an imaging technology based upon a principle of referentiality (even if only at the level of its optical operations), a principle no longer operative in the digital technologies that are swallowing up traditional photography, in which there are no longer first or final instances, and the image simply becomes information, amongst data fields in constant flux.

Baudrillard is led to talking about photography by way of a discussion of exoticism, the death of which he laments. Nostalgia envelops his discourse again. He makes the provocative statement, 'the most beautiful of all photographs are those taken of savages in their natural surroundings',[10] a statement which seems to be straight from the editorial thinking that informed the project of *National Geographic*.

However, his pose is again ironic (or is it?). His racism here is a strategy of deliberate reversal, a recoil I suspect from identity politics, from political correctness. He has always attacked the current 'progressive' orthodoxies, in this case the liberal demand for the expression of difference which, he argues (and I would agree), can be just as coercive as more overtly racist strategies in its policing of the boundaries of acceptable difference, which it usually wants as appearance rather than operationality.

Baudrillard claims that exoticism is dead (while desperately trying to reanimate it) but this is not because there are no more 'innocent primitives' left as he suggests, but because its terms have been deconstructed. We are all familiar now with the notion of primitive as a construction of the West and that posited innocence is no more than the projection of a regretfully self-aware subject who yearns for something other. And in that yearning violence is done – for the knowing Western subject is never, in the last instance, willing to relinquish the power that comes with his privileged knowing. This so many have told us – Frantz Fanon, Pierre Clastres, Edward Said, Gayatri Chakravorty Spivak, Homi Bhabha, James Clifford, Hal Foster.[11]

The price that must be paid for the loss of our innocence about innocence is the burden of responsibility – thus ethics is born. This is not intended as an injunction, or a demand; rather, to use one of Baudrillard's phrases, 'it simply is so'. Radical forgetting is not possible. Once belief is shattered – in God, the sovereignty of the subject, the transformatory power of art, or whatever – it is never possible to be or to act in the same way again, except in bad faith. Radical exoticism is dead, radical forgetting is not possible, thus radical denial becomes the only available strategy – this to avoid the burdensome task of working out where to go from here?

Which leads me to where I go from here (and by coincidence my narrative takes an autobiographical turn, in terms of my own shifting interest from photography to an ecology of the artificial, in which I would seek a location for photography).

The Second Move: Ecology

Here I will address the way in which Baudrillard figures the ecological in 'The Fate of Energy' essay in *The Transparency of Evil*. Underscored by his earlier rejection of an economics of scarcity and his embrace of a Bataillian economy of excess, this essay states:

> The dangers threatening the human species are thus less risks of default (exhaustion of natural resources, dilapidation of the

environment, etc.) than risks of excess: runaway energy flows, chain reactions, or frenzied autonomous developments. This distinction is a vital one, for while risks of default can be addressed by a New Political Ecology ... there is absolutely nothing to counter this other immanent logic, this speeding up of everything, which plays double or nothing with nature.[12]

Further on he refers to 'a sort of Great Game whose rules are unknown to us' and warns that 'we should entertain no illusions about the effectiveness of any kind of rational intervention'. For Baudrillard, intervention 'can have only the slightest validity within the tiny marginal sphere contributed by our rational model'.

Inside these bounds ethical reflection and practical determinations are feasible; beyond them, at the level of the overall process which we have ourselves set in motion, but which from now on marches on independently of us with the ineluctability of a natural catastrophe, there reigns – for better or worse – the inseparability of good and evil, and hence the impossibility of mobilising one without the other.[13]

I see a number of problems with these views. The possibilities for intervention to avert destruction are not delimited in terms of actualities/potentialities, but in terms of how the argument is set up. The diagnosis is limited by the simplicity of the binary – problems of damage and exhaustion that can be controlled vs. runaway reactions that cannot. Even within the limited terms of the reformist environmentalism of which he is critical (the New Political Ecology) measures to reduce the impact of runaway reactions in climate and atmosphere such as the effects of ozone depletion and global warming are either underway, being contemplated and/or are the stake of political contestation. This links to his singular characterization of environmentalist positions (as if there were only one). Contrarily, I would identify three: (1) the idealism of moral appeal linked to an unreconstructed view of 'nature' of the political environmental movement; (2) reformist environmentalism, seeking moderate interventions which will not impede economic growth; and (3) a way of thinking environment beyond the binary of human(ity)/nature, which proposes the interrelation of human and non-human life in what has become a pervasive condition of artificiality, and which requires protection/enhancement for the benefit of all life, through materialized practices. This encompasses (or perhaps glimpses) a paradigm shift to another economy not based on the assumption of productivism, nor the reform of the restrictive (money) economy. Eco-design is one available, but not fully adequate, naming of this position.

His evocation of 'playing double or nothing with nature' is another problem: Baudrillard is talking here as if nature existed. Yet he himself had already banished it in the 'Design and Environment' essay in *For a Critique of the Political Economy of the Sign* written over twenty years ago where he stated, 'everywhere the right to (nature, the environment) countersigns the demise of . . .', and went on to assert the displacement of nature by environment, which is the sphere of design.[14] But more fundamentally than this, nature ceased to exist at its very moment of naming, in the contradictory move that designated a cultural idea (nature) as natural.

There are two ways to think nature now – as an imaginary that fuels fantasies of a non/pre-cultural tradition, or in terms of 'state of being' or condition – and here we could say that the human condition has increasingly become a naturalized artificial, the artificial is our nature: it is that in which we dwell, that which is nearest to hand.

Continuing his diagnosis of 'The Fate of Energy' Baudrillard speaks of the possibility of 'the restoration of equilibrium to our ecological niche . . . the energies in play could still be rebalanced'. This ushers in further problems. First, 'our ecological niche' suggests a separation of human activity from other life forms and the means of their sustainment. Yet this is untenable given the scale of productive activities and pressure of population upon every aspect of the ecosphere; the runaway effects of the burning of fossil fuels on the atmosphere; and the chain reaction effects of air-, water- and soil-borne chemicals on the biology and reproductive systems of many species, the effects of which are only beginning to be confronted and described.

Similarly, 'rebalancing' suggests that at one time an equilibrium did prevail, yet the larger ecology of the human and non-human, the living and non-living, can be better thought of as a cybernetic system of *constant change*. This relational way of thinking the ecological could draw on and extend Georges Bataille's notion of general economy as that which lies beyond the restricted sphere of the money economy. But this could be taken further, beyond Bataille's thinking of systems only of *human* exchange towards economy rethought as the wider exchange relations between the organic and the inorganic. What I have in mind here is what Tony Fry names the 'Aeonic Economy'.[15]

For Baudrillard the risks of runaway excess are beyond human control or rational intervention. They are the subject of destiny, 'a secret destination', 'a destiny for the human species', 'a Great Game whose rules are unknown to us'. It could be asked: Whose secret? Whose rules? Those of God the Father? Of Mother Nature? While not denying the possibility of uncontrollable change, the notion of destiny itself can only be ours.

As well, we could note the variety of claimed destinies in circulation predicted by science and science fiction, which compete for our attention, not all of them environmental catastrophe, but all as dramatic in their own ways – from disembodied existence in cyberspace, to genetic engineering, to the end of consciousness as we know it with the escalation of the breakdown of the human/machine distinction, to the opposite of total annihilation with nanotechnology's 'engines of creation' with their possibilities of endless life in self-repairing systems.

Do destinies become self-fulfilling prophecies? Do they prefigure? Are they desire?

A condition of ever advancing artificiality could be named as human destiny, but the precise nature of that artificiality itself is not predetermined. Crucial to the condition of artificiality is the prefigurative activity of design, something which Baudrillard has dealt with previously (in his above-mentioned essay on 'Design and Environment'), but which is not present in this latest evocation of environment. But to speak about design I'll have to return to the object.

The Third Move: The Object and Design

Baudrillard writes of the pull of the object. In the case of the object that calls out to be photographed, and the pull of the photographic object itself (that is, the photograph, with its compelling frozenness, its surreal stillness), we are in a hermetic space of exchange between camera, object, photographer and viewer – a variety of actors for sure, but a space and activity sealed off from, apparently disconnected to, the larger ecology and its crisis. This is the effect of Baudrillard's discourse, yet another geometry of the object could be described – a relational thinking of the object – which places the object within a sign economy, an informational matrix, a postnatural cybernetic system incorporating the living and non-living.

What is needed is a thinking of the object which no longer rests upon a taken for granted anthropocentrism which assumes that the relation between the object and the human subject is the most significant area of concern.

Baudrillard has repeatedly evoked the seemingly maniacal proliferation of the objects of our making: the object that wreaks revenge by endless duplication. But that willing of objects, which is (none other than) the willing of technology, does not only wreak havoc upon the human subject (that is, the domain of the psychosocial) but on all that is living and non-living in its interconnectedness. As Baudrillard acknowledges, the object as sign is implicated in the process of the liquidation of value(s) as meanings proliferate in an outbidding process of the cannibalization of meaning in order for objects to be differentiated within the political economy of the sign. (The power of photography and other imaging technologies is well known here.)

But the sign economy, rather than being conceived of as a realm of dematerialized production (images, the televisual, information networks etc.) can be thought of as *driving* industrial production (even when it is named postindustrial) and its material effects extend well beyond the human. Raw materials are extracted, the nature of water flows and composition are altered, the characteristics of air and atmosphere are all affected by the literal object's processes of manufacture, its manner of use, whether it is ultimately used up, whether it stays around, or whether it decomposes, and then whether it does this in a manner which enhances or harms life (here the decomposition of matter which feeds life processes can be contrasted with toxic decomposition). This then is a way of thinking of the power of objects that goes beyond what Baudrillard has presented in his recent work, yet which is consistent with some of his earlier analyses but also seeks to add in that which is left out because of his 'ecological blind spot'.

What is being advocated is a thinking of the object within an ecology of the artificial. This can provide an understanding of the object's relation to ecological crisis. Here we need only follow the logic of something Baudrillard has already put in place: that is, if sign values have assumed ascendancy, if *they* are what is consumed, rather than use values, and if these sign values are attached to objects, you have a situation in which objects in fact never get used up. Once sign value is consumed, the material residue remains: the object that is no longer an object of desire; the object whose magic is exhausted; the out of fashion object; the packaging that contained the object. The fallout of the non-consumption of objects litters the landscape – land-fill sites, intractable waste dumps – here are the sites of the excess of the sign economy. This is so even with so-called immaterial production (the cultural economy, the information economy). Ironically the excessive productivity of the information economy is creating one of the greatest waste problems post-2000: how to manage the sheer volume of outdated, discarded and potentially toxic hardware of PCs and TVs.

Such a thinking of the object in terms of an ecology of the artificial also implies a questioning of the categories of consumer society/consumer culture. The last thing consumers do is consume or use up the objects they have purchased. We are a culture of serial users. Like serial killers, or serial monogamists, we have serial relations with objects. In fact this is the way objects are 'in control'.

The manufactured materiality of commodity culture is the delimitation of our lifeworld. That which is de-signed and manufactured, purchased, used, whether hardware or software, is not just an object of fascination or contemplation (to cite aesthetic models of the agency of objects), or of display, status, or a marker of group membership (to cite sociological models of the function of objects); rather, they circumscribe our sphere of knowing and being. We may name them but they also name us: mechanic, keyboard operator, programmer, handyman, networker. Objects make us operational. They regulate what we (can) do. Use value hasn't disappeared, objects create uses and users. Use value no longer prefigures objects; it's the other way round, objects prefigure uses. Use remains, intricately bound up with sign value, but use no longer connected to utility as a fundamental or pre-existing state – this much Baudrillard usefully asserted many years ago. But he hasn't brought this to a thinking of the agency of the object in ecological terms.

To talk of the object sooner or later leads to talking of design. And here again recall Baudrillard in 'Design and Environment':

> everything belongs to design, everything springs from it, whether it says so or not: the body is designed, sexuality is designed, political, social, human relations are designed, just as are needs and aspirations.[16]

This occurs not because of some kind of masterminding, but through processes whereby design is simultaneously everywhere and nowhere, visible and invisible. The activity of the design is itself designed by the history of design practices that precede it; the designed object designs specific needs, desires, uses, particularly in terms of the assigning of sign values. The intentionality of the designed object also carries with it before and after-effects, that extend beyond effects upon the human to all living things, because of their interconnectedness.[17]

This 'system of objects' I have sketched out, which views the object as an actor in a cybernetic process, an artificial ecology which incorporates all living and non-living in a network of exchange relations, is at present nevertheless under the sway of anthropocentrism (this is so whether one posits 'the code' or the restricted money economy as the lubricant of the system).

Once the agency of the designed object is recognized it becomes possible to conceive of a materialized ethical practice of the object (a contingent pragmatic ethics, ethics as something to set out to embody as an ontological feature of the object). The aim of such a practice would be to work against anthropocentrism, to design for the protection of (bio)diverse life. But of course this is not a singular practice, restricted to design as it is understood as a delimited area of professional practice; it rests upon a notion of design understood as all prefigurative activity which has agency.

The already cited 'eco-design' is one available, but perhaps transitional, term that names this materialized ethical practice. In its more advanced (as opposed to reformist) manifestations it is conceived of as an aesthetic practice. Here, I don't just mean at the level of the styling of objects, but as an activity of invention/reinvention, making/remaking, which requires a remaking of thinking, with this being linked to practices of materiality. Recognizing the power of the sign, it involves itself in recoding practices, ranging from the recovery and assigning of new ecological meanings to forgotten objects to the coding of technologically complex objects as ecologically preferable on the basis of what has been designed in or designed out.

This talk of an ethical practice, be it an ethics reconstructed beyond a humanist frame or based upon a valuing of life (as being alive, that is, as more than the biological), must be ringing alarm bells for many. While to explore it fully would require a lot more time than is available now, I will make some qualifications. 'Life' is evoked in the context of a critique of anthropocentrism, in which human life is not being privileged, nor life thought of as a linear and individual journey from birth to death. What a materialized ethics of eco-design would protect is the continuity, thought of in relational, interdependent terms, of the possibility of life itself, in its bio and cultural diversity. This is not to evoke a naturalistic philosophy, for the imbrication of all life in conditions of artificiality is fully acknowledged.

Nor is the banishment of death implied, that constant warding off of death that haunts our culture, and which simply inscribes death's power, about which Baudrillard writes in *Symbolic Exchange and Death*.[18] In ecological terms death can be seen as necessary for the continuity of life: a life comes to an end, but is replaced by another life – thus life continues through individual lives. DNA is the ultimate code that writes us. Individual instances of life can be seen as no more than receivers and transmitters of the code, each having its fleeting efflorescence, its fifteen minutes, or in the case of this particular socioeconomic group of humanity, seventy-plus years of fame. The only possibility for a replacing of death in an order of symbolic exchange (something Baudrillard once desired) lies in death rethought in terms of the error of anthropocentrism which elevated that named as human above all else. In recognition of that error also lies the possibility of the sacred, and of the making/coding of sacred objects by design.

Departing/Parting Company

I have travelled a long way from where I began with Baudrillard's photographic object. And I guess by now our paths have diverged to such an extent that despite a corporeal presence, I can see only a figure in the distance. A ghost maybe? Certainly other ghosts loom, Georges Bataille for example, in my attempt to think exchange, life and economy. But perhaps Jean Baudrillard and I have grown apart, and we really are incompatible now. And all that is left is to say goodbye, thank you . . . and thanks for the memory.

NOTES

1 Jean Baudrillard, *The Transparency of Evil: Essays on Extreme Phenomena*, translated by James Benedict, London: Verso, 1993, p. 104.

2 Jean Baudrillard, *Le Système des objets*, Paris: Denoël-Gonthier, 1968. Extracts translated in *Jean Baudrillard: Selected Writings*, ed. Mark Poster, Stanford: Stanford University Press, 1988 and Jean Baudrillard, *Revenge of the Crystal: Selected Writings on the Modern Object and its Destiny, 1968–1983*, translated by Paul Foss and Julian Pefanis, London: Pluto, 1990.

3 Jean Baudrillard, *Les Stratégies fatales*, Paris: Grasset, 1983. Extracts translated in *Selected Writings* and *Revenge of the Crystal*.

4 Jean Baudrillard, *America* (1986) London: Verso, 1988 and *Cool Memories*, Paris: Editions Galilée, 1987.

5 *The Transparency of Evil*, pp. 153, 154.

6 Ibid.

7 John Szarkowski, *The Photographer's Eye*, New York: Museum of Modern Art, 1966.

8 *The Transparency of Evil*, p. 17.

9 See especially Marcel Mauss *The Gift: Forms and Functions of Exchange in Archaic Societies* (1925), translated by Ian Cunnison, introduction, E.E. Evans-Pritchard, London: Routledge and Kegan Paul, 1974, and Georges Bataille, *The Accursed Share* (1967), New York: Urzone/Zone Books, 1988.

10 *The Transparency of Evil*, p. 151.

11 These names indicate a diverse literature. Key works include: Frantz Fanon, *Black Skin, White Masks* (1952) London: Pluto Press, 1986 and The *Wretched of the Earth*, preface by Jean-Paul Sartre, New York: Grove Press, 1963; Pierre Clastres, 'On Ethnocide' (1974), *Art & Text*, no. 28, 1988; Edward Said, *Orientalism* (1978), Harmondsworth: Penguin 1985; Gayatri Chakravorty Spivak *The Post-Colonial Critic*, New York: Routledge and Kegan Paul, 1990; Homi K. Bhabha (ed.), *Nation and Narration*, London: Routledge, 1990; James Clifford, *The Predicament of Culture: Twentieth Century Ethnography, Literature, and Art*, Cambridge, MA: Harvard University Press, 1988; Hal Foster, 'The Primitive Unconscious', in *Recodings: Art, Spectacle, Cultural Politics*, Port Townsend, WA: Bay Press, 1985.

12 *The Transparency of Evil*, pp. 103–4.

13 Ibid., p. 105.

14 Jean Baudrillard, *For a Critique of the Political Economy of the Sign* (1972), translated by Charles Levin, St Louis: Telos Press, 1981, p. 202.

15 Tony Fry, *Remakings: Ecology, Design, Philosophy*, Sydney: Envirobook, 1994. My essay, particularly the second half, owes a large debt to this work.

16 *For a Critique of the Political Economy of the Sign*, p. 201.

17 Fry, *Remakings, passim*.

18 Jean Baudrillard, *Symbolic Exchange and Death* (1976), translated by Iain Hamilton Grant, introduction by Mike Gane, London: Sage, 1993.

12

BAUDRILLARD, BARTHES, BURROUGHS, AND 'ABSOLUTE' PHOTOGRAPHY

NICHOLAS ZURBRUGG

'Mr D., would you care to make a statement?'

'A statement. Any "statement" I might make would be meaningless to you who cannot think in terms of white hot gas, nebulae, light years and anti-matter. Your technicians can write the formulae I dictate but they cannot think in these terms. My statement, if complete, would be incomprehensible.'

'Please make an attempt, Mr D.'

'Very well but if you are to understand even partially you must suspend all human feelings and value judgements.'

Reading this fragment from the American novelist William Burroughs' early text *Ancient Face Gone Out*,[1] it is extremely tempting to reverse the poles of theory and fiction, by treating these lines as an extract from an interview – some time, some place – with Jean Baudrillard.

Pursuing this comparison, one might add that just as Burroughs' fictional 'Mr D.' is identified as 'the man who gave the orders' in 'Nova terms' on behalf of an intergalactic terrorist organization classified as the 'Nova Mob' (*BF*, 44), 'Monsieur B.' is perhaps most commonly recognized as the man who has given 'the orders' in 'Hyper terms' on behalf of the international 'Hyper Mob'.[2]

By the 'Hyper Mob' I mean those intellectuals, critics, artists and readers who have enthusiastically welcomed Baudrillard's every word – frequently – as Baudrillard himself specifies, *'with such misunderstanding'* (*BL*, 189). To be precise, it now seems increasingly evident – particularly when one considers Baudrillard's reflections on photography – that both negative and positive responses to his work consistently overemphasize the iconoclastic impulse within his attempts to look beyond all 'formulae' and beyond 'all human feelings and value judgements'.

To be sure, Baudrillard's reservations before the 'formulae' of 'human feelings' and 'value judgements' usually provoke his rather tiresome complaint that we now confront 'the loss of the real, the absolute distance of the real' (BL, 103), within a 'profoundly melancholic' condition in which it seems more often than not that 'Death . . . has . . . already taken place' (BL, 104). But an equally persistent – if less frequently acknowledged – affirmative current in Baudrillard's writings suggests that they are perhaps most significant as pointers towards 'enchanted' or 'initiatory' ante-matter, rather than as diagnoses of terminal or entropic anti-matter.

Describing his general most positive aspirations as the wish to identify 'an enchanted space', a 'highly initiatory space', 'another space which would be without limit (contrary to the former one) with a rule of play, a caprice' (BL, 61), Baudrillard, like Burroughs – and as I shall suggest, like Barthes – increasingly emphasizes the possibility of inaugurating *new* forms of thought, *new* forms of being and *new* forms of creativity.

Significantly, Baudrillard speculates that of all discourses, those of art may perhaps be the most rewarding in the present circumstances. Somewhat reluctantly drawing towards this conclusion in a recent interview, he comments:

> Personally, I'm no longer involved in political analysis, nor in philosophy, nor in sociology . . . Whereas the artists, as I see them, are still fascinated by art. They don't leave behind the exercise of art, they're still within a history, a will to create, to communicate.[3]

In much the same way, Félix Guattari's last book of essays, *Chaosmose*, identified the conceptual relevance of what he called 'le maquis de l'art' – 'the artistic underground', and identified the convergence between his own calls for the positive 'miniaturization and personalization of machinery' and Burroughs' attempts to 'create new universes of mutated and mutating meanings'.[4]

For his part, Burroughs never seems to have doubted that artists and creative thinkers are the most likely astronauts of the kind of 'enchanted space' advocated by the more affirmative currents in late postmodern art and writing.[5]

> Artists and creative thinkers will lead the way into space because they are already writing, painting and filming space. They are providing us with the only maps for space travel. We are not setting out to explore static pre-existing data. We are

setting out to create new worlds, new beings, new modes of consciousness.

Elaborating his sense of the conditions of such change, Burroughs speculates that the transcendence of pre-existing data and prior discourse may well involve the abandonment of language as we know it and the exploration of some kind of postverbal or non-verbal thought.

> In the beginning was the word and the word was God. And what does that make us? Ventriloquist dummies. Time to leave the Word-God behind. 'He atrophied and fell off me like horrible old gills' a survivor reported. 'And I feel ever so much better'. (*AM*, 103)

In much the same way, Baudrillard argues that it may be necessary 'to pass through all disciplines' (*BL*, 81) in order to shake off the 'horrible old gills' of atrophied theoretical discourse.

If I have thus far compared Baudrillard's and Burroughs' general priorities this is not to establish any order of originality in their writing. Rather, I wish to suggest the ways in which Baudrillard's writings contain a highly subtle utopian current, often at odds with his more influential apocalyptic pronouncements. Arguably, it is precisely this understated – but increasingly emphatic – counter-current in Baudrillard's thought that most of his admirers and opponents have overlooked or undervalued. Somewhat as the interrogators of Burroughs' 'Mr D.' find his ideas 'interesting and uh enlightening' but 'not altogether convincing' (*BF*, 46), Baudrillard is frequently dismissed as 'brilliant, intelligent, but not serious' (*BL*, 189). For the New York artist Hans Haacke, for example, much of Baudrillard's recent writings 'seem increasingly symptomatic of mental disorder'.[6]

In a sense of course, it could be argued that Baudrillard's provocations, like Haacke's provocations, aim precisely at nothing less than 'mental disorder', if this concept is taken in the Rimbaudian sense of a positive disordering – or reordering – of what Burroughs calls 'static pre-existing data'. What one witnesses in Baudrillard's recent writings, particularly in his writings about the postverbal or non-verbal domain of photography, is the fascinating dilemma of the mind attempting as it were to extricate itself from what Burroughs calls 'the Word-God', in order to identify – one way or another – the 'magic' quality of those alternative perceptions that Baudrillard finds most 'at stake'.

The general terms of this dilemma become particularly clear in an interview of 1983 in which Baudrillard acknowledges that the very function of writing may now be redundant; that he is partially, but not entirely, conditioned by a 'coercive culture'; but that he still considers writing to be 'worthwhile'.

At the limit the effect of something written is nil today. I can choose not to go on writing because I am not caught up in a coercive culture that compels a writer to write, and an intellectual to think. I began to write when I wanted to, and I will stop if it ceases to be worthwhile. I need a challenge myself, there's got to be something at stake. If that is taken away, then I will stop writing. I'm not mad. At a given moment, however, you cause things to exist, not by producing them in the material sense of the term, but by defying them, by confronting them. Then at that moment it's magic. (*BL*, 44)

A little later in the same interview, Baudrillard once again emphasizes his sense that the most effective and valid form of writing is a kind of calculated invocation – an act as it were of defiance, confrontation, and yet also a process animated by 'a rule of play, a caprice' (*BL*, 61) which the writer knows how to manipulate. Extending this sense of playing a 'magic' game to the more general fields of culture and of existence itself, Baudrillard adds:

And it's not only writing that functions like that . . . There is a game . . . in which things demand to be solicited, diverted, seduced. You've got to be able to make them appear as well as disappear; to play the whole game. Writing is nothing but that, and theory as well. It is knowing how to conjure up concepts, effects, and knowing how to resolve them. Culture is not just a simple question of producing ideas or differences. It's also a question of knowing how to cast a spell. (*BL*, 45)

At this point, Baudrillard's argument distinguishes between two related but crucially distinct levels of verbal and conceptual subversion. The first and more elementary of these two strategies is a kind of intellectual war-game which exploits certain rules to generate confrontational 'ideas or differences'. Those playing this war-game contest the discursive context that Burroughs defines as 'static pre-existing data', and function as a kind of virus or foreign agent, sabotaging cultural conventions, but never really replacing any aspect of the status quo with the kind of utterly radical alternative that Burroughs defines as 'new modes of consciousness' (*AM*, 102).

Discussing the dynamics of the related field of avant-garde art (as opposed say, to avant-garde theory), Renato Poggioli helpfully defines this strategy as 'anti-art' (or a predominantly oppositional strategy and iconoclastic strategy), as opposed to 'ante-art' (or a more constructive strategy introducing new alternatives to the targets of anti-art).[7] If Baudrillard's anti-theory generates radical 'differences', Baudrillard's ante-theory and ante-photography suggest the 'magic' quality of radical otherness.

Like Barthes, and to some extent like Burroughs, Baudrillard now seems to posit that radical otherness is more likely to emerge within the domain of photography than within that of writing. If the dominant myth of the late nineteenth century's Symbolist mentality contrasted the elementary differences conveyed by prosaic language's 'meaningful coins' with the radical otherness of the new poetic consciousness that Mallarmé conceived of as realizing language's 'full potential . . . in dream and song',[8] the post-textual temper of the late twentieth century might well prove to be at least partially dominated by the cultural myth that radical otherness most readily finds its 'full potential' in the domains of dream and photograph.

The dichotomy and frequent incompatibility between these two forms of conceptual destabilization – the logical guerrilla warfare of anti-theory foregrounding paradoxical 'differences', and the magical invocation of ante-theory annunciating, adumbrating and inaugurating 'new modes of consciousness' – is nicely pinpointed towards the end of *The Transparency of Evil*. Specifying that the detailed impact of photography permits the observer to look beyond the disappointing vistas of the general postmodern condition and to reattain contact with the 'stunning clarity' of particular exceptions to such general rules, Baudrillard memorably observes:

> Perhaps the desire to take photographs arises from the obser-vations that on the broadest view, from the standpoint of reason, the world is a great disappointment. In its details, however, and caught by surprise, the world has a stunning clarity.[9]

This distinction seems to offer a refreshing alternative to Virilio's more pessimistic assumption that we can seldom escape the blinding impact of increasingly accelerated imagery. According to Virilio, the techno-world seems far too fast for us ever to appreciate the clarity of life's stunning details. Thus, for Virilio,

> We have gone from the esthetics of appearance, stable forms, to the esthetics of disappearance, unstable forms . . . There is . . . the possibility of disappearance in excessive speed: disappear-ance of the world's peculiarities and of the consciousness we have of them to the extent that over-accelerated speed renders us unconscious.[10]

For Baudrillard, photography seems to be most significant in terms of its capacity to offer genuine alternatives to the frustrating circularity of subversive writing. For if language allows us to juggle with ideas and to twist them around like sections of a Rubik cube until they implode or explode, such rhetorical exercises do little more than dutifully – and on occasion, beautifully – self-deconstruct and self-destruct. Once it turns upon itself, language is the ultimate vicious circle.

Baudrillard's predictably disappointing, if stylishly elegant 'Rubik' use of language is nicely evidenced in his recent notes on sex, art and media icons. Successively comparing and contrasting La Cicciolina, Madonna, Michael Jackson and Andy Warhol as various types of transvestite, transexual and artificial mutant, Baudrillard provocatively concludes:

> We are all agnostics, transvestites of art and or of sex. None of us has either aesthetic or sexual convictions any longer – yet we all profess to have them. (*T*, 22)

If we now return to Baudrillard's discussion of issues 'at stake' in his interview of 1983, and his aspiration to master the process of 'knowing how to cast a spell' (*BL*, 45) and thereby inaugurate a 'magic' process which can 'cause things to exist' (*BL*, 44), I think it becomes clear that Baudrillard's finest writings derive from something rather more subtle than the fairly mechanical inversion/implosion formulae which he distinguishes as 'the most trivial form of exoticism' as opposed to 'Radical exoticism' (*T*, 147) exemplifying 'the fundamental law of the intensity of sensations, of the exaltation of the senses, and thus of living itself' (*T*, 148).

Elaborating this concept of radical exoticism, or radical otherness, Baudrillard contrasts it with what he calls 'the pimping of differences' (*T*, 147). Citing structuralist theory as an example of this modish process, Baudrillard observes:

> These days everything is described in terms of difference, but otherness is not the same thing as difference. One might even say that difference is what destroys otherness. When language is broken down into a set of differences . . . the radical otherness of language is abolished . . . The existence of this level accounts for the play in language, for its appeal in its materiality, for its susceptibility to chance; and it is what makes language not just a set of trivial differences, as in the eyes of structural analysis, but symbolically speaking, truly a matter of life and death. (*T*, 127)

Somewhat as Nabokov's postface 'On a Book Entitled *Lolita*' suggests that his novel is perhaps most significant in terms of certain scenes and incidents, destined to be 'skimmed over or not noticed', which constitute the 'nerves', the 'subliminal co-ordinates' and the 'secret points . . . by means of which the book is plotted',[11] Baudrillard's concern in *The Transparency of Evil* seems to be that of identifying traces of *radical otherness* within what he calls 'that strange form from elsewhere, *that secret form* which orders not only chains of events but also existences in their singularity' (*T*, 174; my italics).

For Baudrillard, such secret and singular forces afford crucial exceptions to his general reservations regarding 'the childish notion of self-transcendence' (*T*, 8) and the apparent 'impossibility of a self-transcendence of the social relationship' (*T*, 12). Fundamental symptoms of 'the intoxication, the sheer pleasure, that humans get from functioning', they constitute:

> that ironical surplus or excess functioning which contributes the pleasure, or suffering, thanks to which human beings transcend their determinations – and thus come closer to their *raison d'être*. (*T*, 53)

As becomes evident, Baudrillard variously recommends both the objective rhetorical techniques of ironic reversal and contradiction, and the more subjective surprise of perceiving objects in all their clarity. Dismissing 'the objective idiocy of the probabilities', he initially insists upon the centrality of the intellectual's 'ironic function'.

> When a forecast is made, no matter what it may be, it is always tempting to prove it wrong. Events themselves often help us out in this regard. There are overpredicted events, for instance, that obligingly decline to occur; and then there are the exactly opposite kind – those which occur without forewarning. We must bet on the *Witz* of events themselves. If we lose, we shall have had the satisfaction of defying the objective idiocy of the probabilities. This obligation is a vital function . . . the only genuine function of the intellect: to embrace contradiction, to experience irony, to take the opposite tack, to exploit rifts and reversibility – even to fly in the face of the lawful and the factual. (*T*, 39)

While this conclusion places considerable – if not exclusive – emphasis upon the active intellectual strategies of contradiction, irony, opposition, reversal and flight from laws and facts, Baudrillard's concluding pages to *The Transparency of Evil* suggest that the experience of radical otherness is not so much an intellectual achievement as a happy coincidence which one can at best confront rather than contrive, when one involuntarily rediscovers

> That otherness which erupts into our life, with stunning clarity, in the shape of a gesture, a face, a form, a word, a prophetic dream, a witticism, an object, a woman, or a desert. (*T*, 174)

Surprisingly, perhaps, Baudrillard's list of those extreme phenomena which evoke radical otherness – gestures, faces, forms, words, dreams, witticisms, objects, women, deserts – seems entirely continuous with the

155

utopian modernism of writers such as Mallarmé, Pater and Proust. Pater's 'Conclusion' to his *Studies in the History of the Renaissance* (1873), for example, offers an uncanny precursor to the conclusion to *The Transparency of Evil*. Condemning those 'habits . . . relative to a stereotyped world', Pater adds:

> To burn always with [a] hard gem-like flame, to maintain this ecstasy, is success in life. Failure is to form habits: for habit is relative to a stereotyped world . . . while all melts under our feet, we may well catch at any exquisite passion, or any contribution to knowledge that seems, by a lifted horizon, to set the spirit free.[12]

For his part, Proust, rather similarly dwells upon the impact of inhabitual insight, when, animated by 'some generous impulse', and thus transfigured by the kind of 'lifted horizon' evoked by Pater, the most indifferent human face may become 'illuminated like a grey, overcast horizon, which the clouds unveil, for its transfiguration'.[13]

Predictably enough, Proust also repeatedly emphasizes the way in which art may convey what Baudrillard might term this quality of 'stunning clarity', going so far as to suggest that even when an artist or critic such as Ruskin is dead, their light may still continue to irradiate those who contemplate or read their work. According to Proust,

> Though dead, he continues to shine upon us, like one of those extinguished stars whose light still reaches us, so that as he remarked upon Turner's death, 'It is through these eyes, now closed forever in the grave, that generations yet unborn will look upon nature.'[14]

On occasion, Baudrillard seems to evoke 'radical otherness' in precisely this kind of astral imagery, concluding *The Transparency of Evil* with the comment:

> The other . . . is not the locus of desire, not the locus of alienation, but the locus of vertiginousness, of eclipse, of appearing and disappearing – the locus, one might say (but we must not), of the scintillation of being. (T, 173–76)

Were this the whole story, one might well think of Baudrillard's recent work as a comforting coda to the utopian modernist tradition. Predictably, Baudrillard's agenda is rather more complex.

In the first place, Baudrillard insists that his use of the term 'scintillation of being' is consciously ambiguous:

> I use the term 'scintillation' in terms of the way it is used with reference to . . . very distant stars which have perhaps died, but which still seem to scintillate or shine . . . there seems to be

light, but perhaps there isn't light, and perhaps it's just an apparition . . . It's not so much something positive, as something alternative.[15]

Secondly, in both *The Transparency of Evil*, and its successor, *L'Illusion de la fin*, Baudrillard seems to take particular pains to discredit the possibility of asserting any kind of existential or aesthetic value. For example, discussing 'the Fate of Value' in *The Transparency of Evil*, in terms of four ever-decreasing categories, Baudrillard identifies the present, 'fractal' stage, as an era successively preceded by:

a natural stage (use-value);
a commodity stage (exchange-value);
and a structural stage (sign-value).

At this fourth 'fractal' stage of value,

There is no point of reference at all, and value radiates in all directions, occupying all interstices, without reference to anything whatsoever, by virtue of pure contiguity . . . there is no longer any equivalence, whether natural or general . . . no law of value, merely a sort of *epidemic of value*, a sort of general metastasis of value, a haphazard proliferation and dispersal of value . . . [a] chain reaction [which] makes all valuation impossible. (*T*, 5)

Assuming that 'our culture' as a whole conveniently corresponds to the fractal quality of microphysics, Baudrillard announces the extinction of all ethical and aesthetic value:

It is as impossible to make estimations between beautiful and ugly, true and false, or good and evil, as it is simultaneously to calculate a particle's speed and position. Good is no longer the opposite of evil, nothing can now be plotted on a graph or analysed . . . Just as each particle follows its own trajectory, each value or fragment of value shines for a moment in the heavens of simulation, then disappears into the void along a crooked path that only rarely happens to intersect with other such paths. This is the crooked pattern of the fractal – and hence the current pattern of our culture. (*T*, 6)

Such sweeping analysis seems a far cry from Baudrillard's alternative emphasis upon the more positive 'pattern' or 'secret form' informing both 'events' and 'existences in their singularity' (*T*, 174), motivating the 'genuine' (*T*, 39) functions of the intellect, revealing our *raison d'être*, and prompting us to 'transcend' our 'determinations' (*T*, 53).

Put more plainly, somewhat as Émile Zola naively invoked 'the objective idiocy of possibilities' (*T*, 39) when citing the 'decisive authority' of science in defence of his claim that the 'Experimental Novel' might confidently 'analyse the facts and become master of them',[16] Baudrillard's recent microphysical generalizations reverse this process by citing the 'decisive authority' of science as proof that each 'fragment of value' can shine only 'for a moment' in the apparently virtually void postmodern cosmos.

Not surprisingly, Baudrillard's *L'Illusion de la fin* characterizes the present as the era of the lost soul, or of lost existence, without value, without time, and without any sense or possibility of an ending.

> We experience the impossibility of dreaming either of a past or future state of things. Quite literally, the state of things is definite – neither finite, nor infinite but de-finite, that is to say, deprived of an ending. And the sentiment of the de-finite . . . is melancholia. And whereas a state of mourning contains both a sense of the end of things and the possibility of eventual renewal, this state of melancholia engenders neither the possibility of an ending nor the possibility of renewal, but merely the resentment of our disappearance.[17]

At this point, like the Prince d'Aquitaine in De Nerval's poem 'El Desdichado', Baudrillard evokes existence as disenfranchized melancholia, and might just as well lament,

> Je suis le Ténébreux, – le Veuf, – l'Inconsolé,
> Le Prince d'Aquitaine à la tour abolie:
> Ma seule *Étoile* est morte, et mon luth constellé
> Porte le *Soleil noir* de la *Mélancolie*.

> I am the Shadow, – the Widower, – the Unconsoled,
> The Aquitanian Prince with the ruined tower:
> My only *Star* is dead, and my star-strewn lute
> Bears the *Black Sun* of *Melancholy*.[18]

Like the speaker in De Nerval's poem, Baudrillard situates himself in a world devoid of value, overshadowed by the 'Black Sun of Melancholy' and bereft of his 'only Star'.

But from such a low point, the only way is up, and the final pages of *L'Illusion de la fin* suggest that the fourth phase of value – that of fractal culture – may perhaps be complemented by a fifth possibility – poetic culture, or what Baudrillard calls 'a poetic reversal of events'. If it is the case that reliance upon analogies with microphysics leads to a sense of the apocalyptic reversal and neutralization of events, Baudrillard finally hints that the 'existence' of more positive mutations within the domain of literature may well imply that positive mutations also occur within a wider existential arena.

Reassessing his 'objective' conviction that all is lost, Baudrillard speculates:

> Against this general tendency, there remains the completely improbable, and doubtless unverifiable hypothesis of a *poetic reversal of events*, a possibility at best quasi-evidenced by the existence of its counterpart within language. (*IF*, 168)

According to Baudrillard, this kind of poetic impulse 'exists in the predestination, in the imminence of its own ending', and is thus 'an unconditional event, without significance or consequence, apparent in the vertigo of its own final resolution' (ibid.).

All of the late work of Burroughs, Baudrillard and Barthes shares this utopian concern for the discovery of new modes of consciousness – and to this extent seems entirely continuous with the modernist project of Proust, Pater and Mallarmé. Put another way, Burroughs, Baudrillard and Barthes all seem survivors of a preliminary anti-modern, or post-modern, *rite de passage* during which they analysed the paradoxes and mythologies of the 1960s, 1970s and 1980s within predominantly formulaic and predominantly neutral modes of subversive discourse – the cut-ups of Burroughs, the studied reversals of Baudrillard and the structuralist categories of Barthes – offering what Burroughs calls 'a broad general view of things'.[19]

To equate postmodern culture as a whole with the strategies and assumptions of such early postmodern subversive discourses is to miss the point that the liveliest manifestations of late postmodern culture evince a far less aggressive register informed by what one might think of as an almost Oriental sense of quietude, patience and acceptance: a process, as it were, of accepting perceptual revelation, rather than of attempting to systematize conceptual revolution.

Barthes speaks of this transition in the early pages of his late essays on photography in *Camera Lucida*, where he comments that none of the available 'broad general' accounts of photography offered his 'primitive' sensibility any specific satisfaction.

> Some are technical . . . others are historical or sociological . . . none discussed precisely the photographs which interest me, which give me pleasure or emotion. What did I care about the rules of composition . . . or, at the other end, about the photograph as family rite? Each time I would read about photography, I would think of some photograph I loved, and this made me furious . . . [a] voice urged me to dismiss . . . sociological commentary; looking at certain photographs, I wanted to be a primitive, without culture.[20]

Discussing his rather different approach to photographs, Baudrillard employs remarkably similar argument:

On the one hand there's a kind of material that I know and can manipulate quite well – writing, literary forms, and so on . . . The other is something else. It's a foreign domain, and I want to retain this foreign quality. I want to remain a foreigner there. (*BL*, 168)

Why should this 'primitive' or 'foreign' aspect of photography have appealed so much to Barthes and Baudrillard? Perhaps, after all, despite their initial confidence in their capacity to defy and confront language and 'cause things to exist', they realized that the language of structural analysis and of structured ironic contradiction offers few surprises, and really is an all too familiar, all too colonized domain.

Barthes' *Camera Lucida*, for example, traces his gradual discovery that his favourite analytical concepts – while indomitable within the domain of language – appeared only of partial relevance in the domain of photography. Barthes describes these elementary structural relations between continuous and discontinuous objects and beings as 'studium', or the clearly coded relations explaining 'an average effect' (*CL*, 26), or 'a general and, so to speak polite interest' (*CL*, 27), such as the paradoxical, but otherwise entirely formulable, co-presence of nuns and soldiers in Koen Wessing's photograph, *Nicaragua, 1979*.

A photograph made me pause. Nothing very extraordinary: the (photographic) banality of a rebellion in Nicaragua: a ruined street, two helmeted solders on patrol; behind them, two nuns. Did this photograph please me? Interest me? Intrigue me? Not even. Simply, it existed (for me). I understood at once that its existence . . . derived from the co-presence of two discontinuous elements . . . I foresaw a structural rule. (*CL*, 23)

In so far as this photograph makes Barthes 'pause' in terms of its slightly unusual juxtaposition of soldiers with nuns behind them, it also partakes in a 'quite elementary' (*CL*, 47) way in the more disturbing domain of 'punctum'. A realm of photographic experiences 'which pricks me (but also bruises me, is poignant to me) (*CL*, 27), 'punctum' is not so much a quality that Barthes can voluntarily 'seek . . . out', as an element 'which rises from the scene, shoots out of it like an arrow, and pierces me' (*CL*, 26).

For Baudrillard too, the process of taking photographs is at best the discovery of a kind of punctum which seems both involuntary and unexpected, in so far as 'it is the scene that demands to be photographed, and you are merely part of the décor in the pictorial order it dictates' (*T*, 153). Baudrillard further explains:

In a way an object creates a sense of emptiness, as it were. When one finds something like that, an object imposes itself – suddenly, one sees it, because of certain effects of light, of contrasts and things like that, it isolates itself and it creates a sense of emptiness. Everything around it seems to disappear, and nothing exists but this particular thing, which you capture technologically objectively.

Discussing this process in still more detail, Baudrillard characterizes the 'drama' of photography as one of 'silence' and 'immobility':

> The photographic image is . . . Dramatic by virtue of its silence. Dramatic by virtue of its immobility. What things dream of, what we dream of, is not motion, but this more intense immobility. (*T*, 155)

This 'intense immobility' arising from the silent object is at once the very antithesis of the 'violence of speed' that Virilio envisages as 'the world's destiny',[21] and the very counterpart of the more subjective sense of 'intense immobility' that Barthes associates with the haiku-like 'punctum' emanating from the photographic subject. As becomes evident, the photographic agendas of Barthes and Baudrillard seem to be two sides of the same 'absolute' coin: transcendent subjectivity and transcendent objectivity.

Using analogy with the haiku to evoke precisely the sense of 'predestination', 'imminence' and vertiginous 'final resolution' (*IF*, 168) with which Baudrillard associates the poetic impulse, Barthes suggests that the quality of 'punctum' is 'at once inevitable and delightful', an aspect of the photograph that the photographer 'could not not photograph' (*CL*, 47), and a source of energy 'close to the Haiku', wherein,

> everything is given, without provoking the desire for or even the possibility of a rhetorical expansion. In both cases . . . [we must] speak of an intense immobility: linked to a detail (to a detonator), an explosion makes a little star on the pane of the text or the photograph. (*CL*, 49)

Conceiving of what one might think of as objective 'punctum' which similarly resists 'rhetorical expansion' and interpretation, Baudrillard freely aligns himself with Barthes' general terminology:

> Yes, I'm considerably in favour of 'punctum', in the sense of the singularity of the object at a given moment. Or the singularity of the instant outside of its interpretative context, at the point where things have no meaning – or do not yet have meaning – but appear all the same.

For Barthes, this lack of meaning, of sign and of name culminates in states of 'Absolute subjectivity', as an image, withdrawn from what he calls 'its usual blah-blah', rises 'of its own accord into affective consciousness' (*CL*, 55). Robert Mapplethorpe's portrait of Robert Wilson and Philip Glass thus offers a quintessential site of subjective or affective 'punctum' in the sense that

> Wilson holds me, though I cannot say why, i.e., say where: is it the eyes, the skin, the position of the hands, the track shoes? The effect is certain but unlocatable, it does not find its sign, its name; it is sharp and yet lands in a vague zone of myself; it is acute yet muffled, it cries out in silence. (*CL*, 52–53)

What seems to fascinate Baudrillard, Barthes and Burroughs most of all in photography is its sense of unambiguous reality and immediacy: qualities virtually exterminated by the apocalyptic 'objective idiocy' of much postmodern theory. For Barthes,

> The photograph . . . is the absolute Particular . . . the This . . . in short what Lacan calls the *Tuché*, the Occasion, the Encounter, the Real, in its indefatigable expression. (*CL*, 4)

For Burroughs, photographs such as Robert Walker's images of New York similarly identify 'something quite definite', 'a point where inner and outer reality intersect',[22] although as in Barthesian 'punctum', this 'point' may be extremely mysterious. Contemplating Walker's photograph *New York, 1983*, for example, Burroughs emphasizes photography's capacity to generate highly subjective 'punctum' – effects both 'certain' but 'unlocatable', save in the world of subsequent dreams.

> Here is a young man in a striped black-and-white T-shirt and blue jeans. His right hand is extended, the thumb separated from the four fingers in a curious stylized gesture. In front of him is a slovenly girl in shorts with a shoulder bag that has slid down over her buttocks. His expression is blank. What is he looking at? He doesn't seem to be looking at her at all or even be aware of her presence. No, something else we can't see is engaging his attention. I had a dream about this picture in which I touched his arm and found it cold, dead cold, and started back exclaiming, 'He is an Empty One! A walking corpse, a body without a soul!' (*RW*, 66)

Responding as it were to an image *withdrawn* from what Barthes calls 'its usual blah-blah' (*CL*, 55), or usual contextual detail, Burroughs seems to consider such 'punctum' a catalyst for highly subjective dream discoveries.

But whereas Barthes and Burroughs associate the unlocatable 'This' of photography with conscious or unconscious zones of 'Absolute subjectivity' (*CL*, 55), Baudrillard, by contrast, argues that the specificity of 'Good photography . . . captures . . . the radical exoticism of the object' (*T*, 152); becomes 'the conduit of pure objectality'; and in this way perhaps constitutes 'the purest of images'. Firstly, by presenting 'a universe from which the subject has withdrawn', and secondly, by 'stripping the object of all its features one by one: weight, outline, feel, depth, time, continuity – and, of course, meaning' (*T*, 154).

As Baudrillard concedes, this quest for 'the purest of images' is not necessarily feasible within writing, although it may be more possible to approximate to such 'pure objectality' within the realm of photography.

> With photography it is considerably easier to make the object appear, and to disappear as a subject. Obviously, that's rather a utopian ambition – to disappear as a subject, and to reappear as an object. To be sure, one is always there, but in this case one's mediated by an insignificant object – it's in this way that one appears.

Perhaps something of this kind occurs in a work like *Paris, 1989*: the image of a chair in Baudrillard's apartment in which an object appears (the chair), a subject disappears (Baudrillard), and in which a subject (Baudrillard) reappears as an object (the trace of absent presence suggested by the wrinkles in the chair's cover). What one sees here is at one and the same time less conceptual than hard-core conceptual art and less surreal than hard-core Surrealism; an image less objective and less neutral than Kosuth's deconstructive *One and Three Chairs*, but at the same time, an image less ornate and less paradoxical than Magritte's parallel exploration of folded fabric in *The Gatherer*.

Responding to the suggestion that this photograph is almost a self-portrait in the manner of Magritte, Baudrillard admits that this is partially the case in so far as this photograph evokes 'the absence of the subject – absence modelled within a certain form'. But he also insists that such comparisons are of secondary rather than of primary significance.

> One can find these correspondences retrospectively, but when I'm taking photographs I don't have any kind of references in mind . . . There's no unity of coherence in my photographs, except perhaps at a secondary level. They're all taken according to my caprice or my pleasure.

'Exactly,' one might add. But again, it is perhaps this level of 'caprice or pleasure' which unifies Baudrillard's language and Baudrillard's photographic images at the 'most radical level', rather than the more explicit coherence of conscious 'references in mind'. In this respect, one might argue that radical language, like radical photographic imagery, and like radical computer art, manifests the unexpected process by which, to paraphrase and modify Peter Callas' paraphrase of Erkki Huhtamo, the caprice, pleasure and subconscious (of the maker) speaks to the caprice, pleasure and subconscious (of the audience) on the shared domain of verbal, photographic or computerized culture.[23]

As becomes evident, Baudrillard's photographs occasionally reveal striking unities of radical register and reference with his writings, especially his most explicitly capricious fragments in *Cool Memories*. Here, for example, Baudrillard's writing seems to offer a number of sketches of the photographic effect which *Paris, 1989* so forcefully articulates: 'the absence of the subject – absence modelled within a certain form'; be this the way in which cats 'leave the total imprint of their sleeping bodies on the sand or the bed',[24] or the ways in which the human imprint achieves a still more astonishing conjunction of absence and presence.

For example, contemplating the mystery of the sleeping body, Baudrillard observes:

> Even in a very large bed she sleeps on the outer edge and her light body leaves no trace. I cannot succeed in taming this fragile, distant body. (*CM*, 210)

To invoke Nabokov once again, these are perhaps 'the nerves . . . the secret points, the subliminal co-ordinates' (*L*, 334), by means of which *Cool Memories* is plotted; the subliminal co-ordinates of erotic 'caprice and pleasure' which underlie and underline Baudrillard's most compelling photographic images and most compelling poetic images. Put another way, such details are perhaps manifestations of what he calls 'that secret form which orders . . . existences in their singularity' (*T*, 174); or of what Burroughs, speaking of the subliminal co-ordinates in Robert Walker's photographs, terms 'the pattern of chaos, the underlying unities of disparate elements' (*RW*, 66).

It is perhaps possible to invoke the specific quality of Baudrillard's photographs by fleeting reference to Manet's *Olympia*. For Griselda Pollock, the most interesting aspect of this work is its depiction of social 'studium', in so far as its image of Olympia's maid offers useful documentation of the nineteenth-century 'domestic service industry'.[25] For Barthes, the most interesting detail of the painting might be the 'punctum' generated by the position of Olympia's fingers, half relaxed, half holding the sheet against the artist's or the viewer's gaze.

For Baudrillard, the most interesting detail of this work might be the more impersonal *'punctum'* evoked by the delicate pressure of Olympia's elbow upon her pillow – a presence of pressure which in its lightness is also at once a certain absence of pressure. Of Olympia, as of one of the subjects of *Cool Memories*, Baudrillard might perhaps observe:

Her head is so light that it leaves no mark upon the pillow. The bed from which she rises is not at all unmade, the sheets have hardly moved, they have barely assumed her shape. (CM, 78)

What seems most striking in Baudrillard's recent writings on photography is their insistence upon art's capacity to displace the 'chaos' and 'the violence, the speed or the noise of its surroundings' by distilling an inward sense of the 'unities' of silence, immobility and seemingly transcendent quietude; a paradoxical synthesis of presence, absence and lightness of being. Photography appears unique in its capacity to register the almost mystical quality of 'The silence of photographs', or what he distinguishes as:

The silence not only of the image which surpasses . . . all discourse, all commentary, in order to be perceived and read 'inwardly' as it were – but also the silence into which the image plunges the objects that it seizes, wrenching them from the thunderous context of the real world.[26]

For Baudrillard, 'Irrespective of the violence, the speed or the noise of its surroundings, the photograph restores the object to the immobility and the silence of the image'.[27]

As we have seen, Barthes posits that photography transcends the 'nauseated boredom' of 'universalized' images by revealing traces of 'terrified consciousness' within the highly subjective 'punctum' that he associates with 'photographic ecstasy' (CL, 119). In turn, Baudrillard posits that photography offers the possibility of encountering what he too describes as the 'ecstasy of photography', within 'pure objectality' (T, 154); a tranquil zone affording unexpected alternatives to 'universal banality' (T, 151).

Melancholic diagnoses of postmodern banality are ever with us, and as Baudrillard himself acknowledges, the disappointing generalities of the postmodern condition seem predestined to proliferate analysis of its technologies, patterns, probabilities and determinations in terms of 'aberration and depersonalization'.

That's what we've done, and that's what we're continuing to do in analyses of virtual reality – it's possible to continue forever in this sort of direction . . . But it's also necessary to identify another form of analysis – a more subtle form of analysis than that one.

As becomes evident, Baudrillard's theories operate at several conflicting levels, registers and speeds. Baudrillard's 'broad general' appropriations from the arguments of microphysics clearly persuade him that value judgements are as 'impossible' as the plotting of particle values 'on a graph' (T, 6). But his more detailed attention to the 'punctum' of specific photographs leads him to speculate – still more interestingly, surely – that even if particle values cannot be graphed, they may at times be both photographed and evaluated according to the 'clarity' of their 'objectality'.

Reading between the lines – or perhaps against the lines – of Baudrillard's most explicitly apocalyptic arguments, one finds traces – apparitions, perhaps – of a surprisingly affirmative 'secret' logic. Substantially at odds with Baudrillard's more influential forecasts and fictions, this logic seems substantially at one with both utopian modernism and with more recent utopian currents – or counter-currents – within the writings of such chronologically postmodern writers and theorists as Nabokov, Burroughs and Barthes.

Perhaps I have overemphasized the significance of these traces of utopian thought and creativity within the late postmodern cosmos. Perhaps not. My sense is that Baudrillard's more melancholic generalizations have for too long been taken too literally, and that his recent writings on photography at last suggest 'a more subtle form of analysis' than his habitual, all too predictable, predictions. This transition is both timely and welcome. As Baudrillard advises,

> When a forecast is made, no matter what it may be, it is always tempting to prove it wrong. (T, 39)

NOTES

1 William S. Burroughs, *Ancient Face Gone Out* (first published in *Gnaoua*, no. 1, Spring 1964, Tangier), collected in *The Burroughs File*, San Francisco: City Lights, 1984, pp. 44–47. Henceforth abbreviated as BF.

2 Baudrillard describes himself as a theoretical 'terrorist' in *Baudrillard Live: Selected Interviews*, ed. Mike Gane, London: Routledge, 1993, p. 168. Henceforth abbreviated as BL.

3 Serge Bramly, 'Cover Story: Jean Baudrillard', interview with Baudrillard, translated by Brian Holmes, *Galeries Magazine*, no. 53, February–March 1993, p. 85.

4 Félix Guattari, *Chaosmose*, Paris: Galilée, 1992, p. 126, my translation; 'The Postmodern Dead End', translated by Nancy Blake, *Flash Art*, no. 128, May/June 1986, p. 41; and 'Postmodernism and Ethical Abdication', interview with Nicholas Zurbrugg, *Photofile*, no. 39, July 1993, p. 12.

5 William S. Burroughs, *The Adding Machine: Selected Essays*, New York: Seaver Books, 1986, p. 102. Henceforth abbreviated as AM.

6 Hans Haacke, in Pierre Bourdieu and Hans Haacke, *Libre-Échange*, Paris: Editions du Seuil, 1994, p. 47, my translation.

7 Renato Poggioli, *The Theory of the Avant-Garde*, translated by Gerald Fitzgerald, Cambridge, MA: Harvard University Press, Belknap Press, 1968, pp. 136–37.

8 Stéphane Mallarmé, 'Crisis in Verse' (1886–96), translated by Thomas West, in *Symbolism: An Anthology*, ed. West, London: Methuen, 1980, p. 10.

9 Jean Baudrillard, *The Transparency of Evil*, translated by James Benedict, London: Verso, 1993, p. 155. Henceforth abbreviated as *T*.

10 Paul Virilio and Sylvère Lotringer, *Pure War*, translated by Mark Polizotti, New York: Semiotext(e), 1983, pp. 84–85. Henceforth abbreviated as *PW*.

11 Vladimir Nabokov, 'On a Book Entitled *Lolita*', in *Lolita* (1955), London: Corgi, 1967, p.334. Henceforth abbreviated as *L*.

12 Walter Pater, 'Conclusion', *Studies in the History of the Renaissance* (1873), in *The Portable Victorian Reader*, ed. Gordon S. Haight, Harmondsworth: Penguin, 1976, p. 631.

13 Marcel Proust, *A la recherche du temps perdu* (1913), ed. Pierre Clarac and André Ferré, Paris: Gallimard, Bibliothèque de la Pléiade, 1968, vol. 1, p. 314, my translation.

14 Marcel Proust, 'John Ruskin' (1900), in *Proust, Contre Sainte-Beuve*, ed. Pierre Clarac and Yves Sandre, Paris: Gallimard, Bibliothèque de la Pléiade, 1971, p. 129, my translation.

15 Jean Baudrillard, Interview with Nicholas Zurbrugg, 4 June 1993, see Chapter 4 in this volume. All subsequent unreferenced quotations by Baudrillard refer to this interview.

16 Émile Zola, 'The Experimental Novel' (1880), in *Documents of Modern Literary Realism*, ed. G.J. Becker, Princeton, NJ: Princeton University Press, 1967, pp. 162, 169.

17 Jean Baudrillard, *L'Illusion de la fin*. Paris: Galilée, 1992, pp. 167–68, my translation. Henceforth abbreviated as *IF*.

18 Gérard de Nerval, 'El Desdichado', text and translation by Anthony Hartley, in *The Penguin Book of French Verse: The Nineteenth Century*, ed. Hartley, Harmondsworth: Penguin, 1963, p. 96.

19 William S. Burroughs, *Exterminator!*, London: Calder and Boyars, 1974, p. 115.

20 Roland Barthes, *Camera Lucida: Reflections on Photography*, translated by Richard Howard, New York: Hill and Wang, 1983, pp. 6–7. Henceforth abbreviated as *CL*.

21 Paul Virilio, *Speed and Politics*, translated by Mark Polizzotti, New York: Semiotext(e), 1986, p. 151.

22 William S. Burroughs, 'Robert Walker's Spliced New York', *Aperture*, no. 101, Winter 1985, p. 66. Henceforth abbreviated as *RW*.

23 Peter Callas, Interview with Nicholas Zurbrugg, *Continuum*, vol. 8, no. 1, 1994, p. 118. (Huhtamo suggests: 'the subconscious (of the maker)' is 'speaking to the subconscious (of the audience) on the shared domain of media(ted) culture'.)

24 Jean Baudrillard, *Cool Memories*, translated by Chris Turner, London: Verso, 1990, p. 48. Henceforth abbreviated as *CM*.

25 Griselda Pollock, *Avant-Garde Gambits 1888–1893: Gender and the Colour of Art History*, London: Thames and Hudson, 1992, p. 21.

26 Jean Baudrillard, 'The Art of Disappearance', my translation, see Chapter 3 in this volume.

27 Ibid.

FOLLOWING
BAUDRILLARD:
A Bibliography of Writings
on Jean Baudrillard

RICHARD G. SMITH

Adair, G., 'Did the Gulf War Really Take Place?', in *The Postmodernist Always Rings Twice*, London: Fourth Estate, 1992, pp. 154–56.

Albert, C., 'The Year 2000 Will Not Occur – Lecture by Baudrillard within a Framework on the Interdisciplinary Course of Lectures on the Theory of the Fantasy at the Freire-Universitat-Erkin, 24 January 1984', *Argument*, vol. 26, July 1984, pp. 610–11.

Anon, 'A French Thinker in the Land of the Unreal: Jean Baudrillard's *America*', *The Economist*, 309/7578, 26 November 1988, pp. 143–44.

Anon, 'Review of *America*', *London Review of Books*, 26 March 1989, p. 13.

Anon, 'Review of *America*', *New York Review of Books*, 16 December 1989, p. 1391.

Anon, '*Cool Memories* by Jean Baudrillard', *Virginia Quarterly Review*, vol. 67, no. 2, 1991, p. 50.

Anon, '*Baudrillard Live* – Selected Interviews by M. Gane', *Times Literary Supplement*, no. 4708, 32, 1993.

Arditi, J., *Revenge of the Crystal – Selected Writings on the Modern Object and its Destiny, 1968–1983* by Jean Baudrillard and *Critical Fatal Theory* by M. Gane', *Contemporary Sociology – An International Journal of Reviews*, vol. 22, no. 1, 1993, pp. 19–23.

Armitage, J., 'The Transparency of Evil: Essays on Extreme Phenomena by Jean Baudrillard', *Media, Culture & Society*, vol. 16, 1994, pp. 699–702.

Aubert, J., 'Jean Baudrillard, *Le Système des objets*', *L'Homme et la Société*, no. 11, pp. 229–30.

Baier, L., 'The Fraud of Simulation – An Attempt to Stay on the Trail of the Latest – Baudrillard', *Merkur Deutsche Zeitschrift für Europaisches Denken*, vol. 40, no. 9–10, 1986, pp. 807–24.

Ballion, R., 'Sur la Société de consommation', Revue Française de Sociologie, vol. 12, no. 4, 1971, pp. 557–68.

Bauman, Z., 'America and Selected Writings by Jean Baudrillard', Times Literary Supplement, no. 4472, 1988, p. 1391.

Bauman, Z., 'Disappearing into the Desert', Times Literary Supplement, December, 1988, pp. 16–22.

Bauman, Z., 'Douglas Kellner, Jean Baudrillard: From Marxism to Postmodernism and Beyond', Sociology, vol. 24, no. 4, November 1990, pp. 697–99.

Bauman, Z., 'The World According to Jean Baudrillard', in Intimations of Postmodernity, London: Routledge, 1992, pp. 149–55.

Bauman, Z., 'La Gauche divine and Les Strategies fatales by Jean Baudrillard', Theory, Culture and Society, vol. 5, no. 4, November, 1988, pp. 738–43.

Beard, S. and McClellan, J. 'Watch Out Baudrillard's About', Face Magazine, January 1989, pp. 61–62.

Beniger, J.R., 'Baudrillard: From Marxism to Postmodernism and Beyond by D. Kellner', Communication Research, vol. 18, no. 1, 1991, p. 118.

Benison, J., 'Jean Baudrillard on the Current State of SF', Foundation, no. 32, 1984, pp. 25–42.

Bennington, G.P., 'Seduced and Abandoned – The Baudrillard Scene by Frankovits', French Studies, vol. 42, no. 3, 1988, pp. 369–70.

Best, S., 'The Commodification of Reality and the Reality of Commodification: Jean Baudrillard and Postmodernism', Critical Perspectives in Social Theory, vol. 19, 1989, pp. 23–51.

Bidaud, A.M., 'America by Baudrillard', Revue Française d'Études Américanes, no. 33, 1987, pp. 447–49.

Billig, M., 'Sod Baudrillard! Or Ideology Critique in Disney World', in After Postmodernism: Reconstructing Ideology Critique, ed. H.W. Simons and M. Billig, Sage: London, 1994.

Bogard, W., 'Sociology in the Absence of the Social: The Significance of Baudrillard for Contemporary Thought', Philosophy and Social Criticism, vol. 13, no. 3, 1987, pp. 227–42.

Bogard, W., 'Cool Memories by Baudrillard', Philosophy and Literature, vol. 15, no. 1, 1991, pp. 155–57.

Bohlke, E., 'The Transparency of Evil by Jean Baudrillard', Deutsche Zeitschrift für Philosophie, vol. 40, no. 4, 1992, pp. 447–49.

Bollon, P., 'Les Séductions de Baudrillard', Magazine Littéraire, 193, March 1983, pp. 80–85.

Bonnaud, R., 'The Illusion of the End by Jean Baudrillard', Quinzaine Littéraire, no. 632, 1993, pp. 27–28.

Boyne, F., 'Baudrillard: Critical and Fatal Theory by M. Gane', History of the Human Sciences, vol. 5, no. 4, 1992, pp. 70–73.

Breuer, S., 'Structural Law of Value and Revolt of Death – Skeptical Remarks on Baudrillard', Merkur Deutsche Zeitschrift für Europäisches Denke, vol. 38, no. 4, 1984, pp. 477–82.

Buhle, P., 'America: Postmodernity?', New Left Review, no. 180, March–April 1990, pp. 163–75.

Callinicos, A., 'The Mirror of Commodity Fetishism: Baudrillard and Late

Capitalist Culture', in *Against Postmodernism: A Marxist Critique*, Oxford: Polity, 1989, pp. 144–53.

Cardin, A., 'Seduction without Seduction (Baudrillard's Views on Society)', *Cuadernos del Norte*, vol. 5, no. 26, 1984, pp. 26–28.

Carmagnola, F., 'A Dream of Commodities – Jean Baudrillard', *Domus*, no. 701, 1989.

Carrier, D., 'Baudrillard as Philosopher or, The End of Abstract Painting', *Arts Magazine*, vol. 63, no. 1, 1988, pp. 52–60.

Caygill, H., 'The Plight of a *paysan* de Paris', *The Times Higher Education Supplement*, 14 May 1993, p. 29.

Chang, B., 'Mass Media, Mass Mediation: Baudrillard's Implosive Critique of Modern Mass-mediated Culture', *Current Perspectives in Social Theory*, no. 17, 1986, pp. 157–81.

Chen, K.H. 'The Masses and the Media: Baudrillard's Implosive Postmodernism', *Theory, Culture and Society*, vol. 4, 1987, pp. 71–88.

Cioran, P., 'The Ethnographer as Geologist – Tocqueville, Lévi-Strauss, Baudrillard and the American Dilemma', *Social Science Information*, vol. 31, no. 2, 1992, pp. 267–92.

Clarke, D.B. and Doel, M.A., 'The Perfection of Geography as an Aesthetic of Disappearance: Baudrillard's *America*', *Eucumene*, vol. 1, no. 4, 1994, pp. 317–23.

Cohen, E., 'The "Hyperreal" v. The "Really Real": If European Intellectuals Stop Making Sense of American Culture Can We Still Dance?', *Cultural Studies*, 1989, pp. 25–37.

Cook, D., 'Ruses de Guerre – Baudrillard and Fiske on Media Reception', *Journal for the Theory of Social Behaviour*, vol. 22, no. 2, 1992, pp. 227–38.

Coward, R., 'Marvellous to be a woman? *Cool Memories* and *Seduction* by Jean Baudrillard', *New Statesman and Society*, vol. 3, no. 109, 1990, pp. 35–36.

Cronel, H., 'Seeing through Evil – Esssay on Extreme Phenomena', *Nouvelle Revue Française*, no. 453, 1990, pp. 120–22.

Csicsery-Ronay, I.R., 'The SF of Theory: Baudrillard and Haraway', *Science Fiction Studies*, vol. 18, 1991, pp. 387–404.

Csicsery-Ronay, I.R., '*Baudrillard: Critical and Fatal Theory* by M. Gane', *Science Fiction Studies*, vol. 18, November 1991, pp. 420–30.

D'Amico, R., '*Oublier Foucault*', *Telos*, no. 36, Summer 1978, pp. 169–83.

D'Amico, R., 'Objects and Utility', in *Marx and Philosophy of Culture*, Gainesville: University of Florida Press, 1981, pp. 44–57.

Danto, A.C., 'The Hyper-Intellectual: *America* by Jean Baudrillard, *Baudrillard from Marxism to Postmodernism and Beyond* by D. Kellner and *Selected Writings* by Baudrillard', *New Republic*, vol. 203, no. 11–1, 1990, pp. 44–48.

de, P.B., 'Notes Bibliographies: *le Système des objets*', *Revue Française de Sociologie*, vol. x, no. 1, 1969, p. 97.

Denzin, N.K., 'Paris, Texas and Baudrillard on America', *Theory, Culture and Society*, vol. 8, no. 2, May 1991, pp. 121–33.

Denzin, N.K., 'Takes on the Postmodern: Baudrillard, Lyotard, and Jameson', in *Images of Postmodern Society: Social Theory and Contemporary Cinema*, London: Sage, 1991, pp. 29–52.

Deschamps, C., 'Jean Baudrillard', in *Entretiens avec le Monde*, vol. 3. Idées Contemporaines, Paris: Editions la Découverte, 1984.

Diani, M., 'The Desert of Democracy, from Tocqueville to Baudrillard', *L'Esprit Créateur*, vol. 30, no. 3, 1990, pp. 67–80.

Dobson, S. and Gundersen, R., *Baudrillard's Journey to America*, London: Minerva Press, 1996.

Donahue, N.H., 'From Worringer to Baudrillard and Back: Ancient Americans and (Post)modern Culture in Weimar Germany', *Deutsche Vierteljahr und Geistesgeschichte*, vol. 66, no. 4, 1992, pp. 765–82.

Duncan, J.S., '*America* by Jean Baudrillard', *Geographical Review*, vol. 80, no. 1, 1990, pp. 85–87.

Englert, K., 'The System of Things – Our Relationship to Everyday Objects – Jean Baudrillard', *Deutsche Zeitschrift für Philosophie*, vol. 40, no. 8, 1992, pp. 977–80.

Ewald, F., 'Baudrillard: le sujet et son double', *Magazine Littéraire*, no. 264, April 1989, pp. 18–23.

Faye, J.P., 'La Gauche infernale', *Change International*, no. 3, 1985, pp. 5–6.

Fernandez, J.B., 'The Great Seduction (Baudrillard)', *Cuadernos del Norte*, vol. 5, no. 26, 1984, pp. 17–19.

Frankovits, A. (ed.) *Seduced and Abandoned: The Baudrillard Scene*, New York: Semiotext(e)/Autonomedia and Glebe: Stonemoss, 1984.

Frith, S., 'What is a Washing Machine', *New Statesman*, vol. 115, June 3, 1988, pp. 23–24.

Gablik, S., 'Dancing with Baudrillard', *Art in America*, June 1988, pp. 27–29.

Gaillard, F., 'Pour un renversement du point de vue', *Quinzaine Littéraire*, no. 398, 1983, pp. 18–19.

Gallop, J., 'French Theory and the Seduction of Feminism', in *Men in Feminism*, eds A. Jardine and P. Smith, London: Methuen, 1987, pp. 111–15.

Gane, M., '*Baudrillard: Selected Writings* by M. Poster', *Sociological Review*, vol. 37, no. 3, 1989, pp. 572–74.

Gane, M., 'Ironies of Postmodernism: Fate of Baudrillard's Fatalism', *Economy and Society*, vol. 19. no. 3, August 1990, pp. 314–31.

Gane, M., *Baudrillard: Critical and Fatal Theory*, London: Routledge, 1991.

Gane, M., *Baudrillard's Bestiary: Baudrillard and Culture*, London: Routledge, 1991.

Gane, M., 'French Anti-Feminism: The Case of Jean Baudrillard', *Modern and Contemporary France*, no. 44, January, 1991, pp. 19–25.

Gane, M., 'Seduction by Jean Baudrillard', *Theory, Culture and Society*, vol. 19, no. 2, May 1992, pp. 183–84.

Gane, M. (ed.) *Baudrillard Live: Selected Interviews*, London: Routledge, 1993.

Gane, M., 'Introduction', in *Symbolic Exchange & Death* by Jean Baudrillard, London: Sage, 1993, pp. viii–xiv.

Gane, M., 'Bibliography of Works by Jean Baudrillard', in *Symbolic Exchange & Death* by Jean Baudrillard, London: Sage, 1993, pp. 243–47.

Gane, M., 'Radical Theory: Baudrillard and Vulnerability', *Theory, Culture & Society*, vol. 12, 1995, pp. 109–23.

Gane, M. '*Baudrillard and Signs* by Gary Genosko', *The Sociological Review*, 1995, pp. 392–94.

Geier, M., 'Symbolic Exchange and Death by Jean Baudrillard', Argument, vol. 25, May 1983, pp. 444–45.

Genosko, G., 'Adventures in the Dromosphere', Borderlines, no. 17, 1989–90, pp. 34–36.

Genosko, G., 'The Bar of Theory', Borderlines, no. 20/21, Winter 1990–91, pp. 59–61.

Genosko, G., 'Virtual War', Borderlines, no. 24–25, 1992, pp. 51–52.

Genosko, G., 'The Struggle for an Affirmative Weakness: De Certeau, Lyotard, and Baudrillard', Current Perspectives in Social Theory, vol. 12, 1992, pp. 179–94.

Genosko, G., 'Bar Games: Baudrillard's Encounters with Sign', PhD thesis, University of Toronto, 1993.

Genosko, G., 'The paradoxical effects of macluhanisme: Cazeneuve, Baudrillard and Barthes', Economy and Society, vol. 23, no. 4, 1994, pp. 400–32.

Genosko, G., Baudrillard and Signs: Signification Ablaze, London: Routledge, 1994.

Giradin, J.C., 'Towards a Politics of Signs: Reading Baudrillard', Telos, no. 20, 1974, pp. 127–37. (Originally published in Les Temps Modernes, no. 329, 1973, pp. 1026–43).

Glover, D., 'Symbolic Exchange and Death by Jean Baudrillard', Radical Philosophy, no. 73, 1995, pp. 45–46.

Gottdiener, M., 'The System of Objects and the Commodification of Everyday Life: The Early Work of Baudrillard', in Postmodern Semiotics: Material Culture and the Forms of Postmodern Life, Oxford, 1995, pp. 34–53.

Gueldry, M., 'America: Jean Baudrillard', French Review, vol. 66, no. 2, 1992, pp. 351–52.

Gught, D.V., 'The Other, By Himself by Jean Baudrillard', Cahiers Internationaux de Sociologie, no. 83, July 1987, p. 428.

Guillaume, M., 'Une Approche ironique de figures transpolitiques', Critique, vol. 40, no. 442, 1984, pp. 198–213.

Hamilton, P., 'Baudrillard: One Man Think Tank', The Sunday Times, 11 December, 1994, pp. 18–19.

Hayles, K.N., 'In Response to Jean Baudrillard: The Borders of Madness', Science-Fiction Studies, vol. 18, 1991, pp. 321–29.

Hayward, P., 'Implosive Critiques – A Consideration of Jean Baudrillard's In the Shadow of the Silent Majorities', Screen, vol. 25, no. 4–5, 1984, pp. 128–33.

Heartney, E., 'Reluctant Prophet (Jean Baudrillard)', Art News, vol. 86, no. 7, 1987, p. 18.

Hebdige, D., 'Banalarama, or can pop save us all?', New Statesman & Society, vol. 1, December, 1988, pp. 29–32.

Hefner, R., 'Baudrillard's Noble Anthropology: The Image of Symbolic Exchange in Political Economy', Substance, no. 17, 1977, pp. 105–13.

Helmling, S., 'A Postmodern Jeremiah: Selected Writings by Baudrillard', Kenyon Review, vol. 12, no. 1, 1990, pp. 204–7.

Hoberman, J., 'Review of America', Journal of Aesthetics and Art Criticism, no. 47, 1989, p. 199.

Hoberman, J., 'Lost in America: Jean Baudrillard, Extraterrestrial', Voice Literary Supplement, March 1989, pp. 15–16.

Hoffie, P., 'The Second Coming of Jean Baudrillard', Art Monthly Australia, no. 70, June 1994, pp. 13–14.

Horrocks, C., and Jevtic, Z., *Baudrillard for Beginners*, Cambridge: Icon, 1996.

Howe, S., 'Where Dreams Come True: *America* by Jean Baudrillard', *New Statesman and Society*, vol. 1, no. 24, 1988, p. 39.

Hughes, R., 'The Patron Saint of Neo-Pop', *New York Review of Books*, vol. 36, no. 9, 1 June 1989, pp. 29–32.

Hussey, M., '*Suite Vénitienne Please Follow Me* by Calle and Baudrillard', *America Book Review*, vol. 11, no. 2, May–June 1989, p. 17 and 20.

Irigaray, L., 'La Femme n'est rien et c'est là sa puissance', *Histoires d'elles*, no. 21, March 1980, p. 3.

Jaccard, R., 'Baudrillard arpenteur du néant', *Le Monde*, 28 September 1990.

Jaccard, R., 'La splendeur du vide', *Le Monde*, 13 January, 1995, p. 9.

Jaccard, R., 'Le simulacra du réel', *Le Monde*, 6 October, 1995, p. 9.

Jacob, A., '*La Gauche divine*', *L'Homme et la Société*, no. 75–76, 1985, pp. 266–67.

Joseph, D., 'Critical Images of Marx's Materialism', *Critique of Anthropology*, vol. 4, no. 13–14, 1979, pp. 197–201.

Kellner, D., 'Baudrillard, Semiurgy and Death', *Theory, Culture and Society*, vol. 4, 1987, pp. 125–46.

Kellner, D., 'Boundaries and Borderlines: Reflections on Baudrillard and Critical Theory', *Current Perspectives in Social Theory*, vol. 9, no. 19, 1989, pp. 5–22.

Kellner, D., *Jean Baudrillard: From Marxism to Postmodernism and Beyond*, Cambridge: Polity, 1989.

Kellner, D. (ed.) *Baudrillard: A Critical Reader*, Oxford: Basil Blackwell, 1994.

Kester, G., 'The Rise and Fall? of Baudrillard', *New Art Examiner*, November 1987, pp. 20–23.

Knee, P., '*Fatal Strategies* by Baudrillard', *Laval Théologique et Philosophique*, vol. 41, no. 1, 1985, pp. 132–33.

Krips, H., 'Jean Baudrillard: – *From Marxism to Postmodernism and Beyond* by D. Kellner', *Philosophy of the Social Sciences*, vol. 23, no. 3, 1993, pp. 390–95.

Kroker, A., 'The Disembodied Eye: Ideology and Power in the Age of Nihilism', *Canadian Journal of Political and Social Theory*, vol. 7, no. 1–2, 1983, pp. 194–234.

Kroker, A., 'Magritte/Baudrillard/Augustine: The Arc of a Dead Power', *Canadian Journal of Political and Social Theory*, vol. 8, no. 1–2, 1984, pp. 53–69.

Kroker, A., 'Baudrillard's Marx', *Theory, Culture and Society*, vol. 2, no. 3, 1985, pp. 69–83.

Kroker, A., 'Panic Value: Bacon, Colville, Baudrillard and the Aesthetics of Deprivation', *Life after Postmodernism: Essays on Value and Culture*, ed. J. Fekete, London: Macmillan, 1988.

Kroker, A., 'Panic Baudrillard', *Communication*, vol. 10, no. 3–4, 1988, pp. 259–70.

Kroker, A., '"Why Should We Talk When We Communicate So Well?", Baudrillard's Enchanted Simulation', in *The Possessed Individual: Technology and Postmodernism*, ed. A. Kroker, London: Macmillan, 1992, pp. 51–81.

Kroker, A. and Levin, C., 'Baudrillard's Challenge', *Canadian Journal of Political and Social Theory*, vol. 8, no. 1–2, 1984, pp. 5–16.

Kroker, A. and Levin, C., 'Cynical Power: The Fetishism of the Sign', in *Ideology and Power: in the Age of Lenin in Ruins*, ed. A. and M. Kroker, Montreal: Culture Texts, 1991, pp. 123–38.

Lash, S., 'Dead Symbols: An Introduction', *Theory, Culture & Society*, vol. 12, no. 4, November, 1995, pp. 71–78.

Lazano, J., 'Baudrillard – From Critical Theory to Ironic Theory, or From Resistance to Hyperconformity', *Cuadernos del Norte*, vol. 5, no. 26, 1984, pp. 14–16.

Lazarus, N., '*Baudrillard: From Marxism to Postmodernism and Beyond* by D. Kellner', *The Sociological Review*, vol. 39, no. 1, 1991, pp. 168–72.

Lazarus, N., '*Baudrillard's Bestiary: Baudrillard and Culture* by M. Gane', *Sociological Review*, vol. 42, no. 1, 1994, pp. 120–22.

Lechte, J., 'Jean Baudrillard', in *Fifty Key Contemporary Thinkers: From Structuralism to Postmodernity*, London: Routledge, 1994, pp. 233–37.

Lee, M.E., '*Baudrillard: Critical and Fatal Theory* by M. Gane', *Social Science Quarterly*, vol. 74, no. 1, 1993, p. 239.

Lee, R., 'In the Shadow of reason: from Weber's elective affinity to Baudrillard's fatalism', *Economy and Society*, vol. 23, no. 4, 1994, pp. 387–99.

Lemert, C.C., '*Baudrillard: Selected Writings*, ed. M. Poster', *Contemporary Sociology – A Journal of Reviews*, vol. 18, no. 4, 1989, pp. 639–40.

Lester, J., '*Baudrillard: Selected Writings*, ed. M. Poster', *Political Studies*, vol. 37, no. 4, 1989, pp. 674–75.

Levin, C., 'De la Séduction', *Telos*, no. 45, 1980, pp. 198–202.

Levin, C., 'Baudrillard: Critical Theory and Psychoanalysis', *Canadian Journal of Political and Social Theory*, vol. 8, nos 1–2, 1984, pp. 35–52 and in *Ideology and Power: in the age of Lenin in Ruins*, ed. A. and M. Kroker, Montreal: Culture Texts, 1991, pp. 170–87.

Levin, C., 'Introduction to Baudrillard', in *The Structural Allegory: Reconstructive Encounters with French Thought* ed. J. Fekete, Minneapolis: University of Minnesota Press, 1984, pp. 46–53.

Levin, C., *Jean Baudrillard: a study in cultural metaphysics*, Hemel Hempstead: Prentice-Hall, 1996.

Linker, K., 'From Imitation, to the Copy to Just Effect: On Reading Baudrillard', *Artforum*, vol. 22, no. 8, 1984 pp. 44–47.

Lotringer, S., 'Dropping out of History', *Impulse*, Spring/Summer 1983, pp. 10–13.

Luke, T.W., 'Jean Baudrillard's Political Economy of the Sign', *Art Papers*, vol. 10, no. 1, 1986, pp. 22–25.

Luke, T.W., 'Power and Politics in Hyperreality – The Critical Project of Jean Baudrillard', *Social Science Journal*, vol. 28, no. 3, 1991, pp. 347–67.

McCann, G., 'Real Hype', *Radical Philosophy*, no. 56, Autumn 1990, pp. 58–59.

MacDonald, A., 'Seduction by Jean Baudrillard', *Queens Quarterly*, vol. 99, no. 2, 1992 pp. 466–68.

Maras, S., 'Baudrillard and Deleuze: Reviewing the Postmodern Scene', *Continuum*, vol. 2, no. 2, 1989, pp. 163–91.

Marcus, J., '*America* by Jean Baudrillard', *New York Times Book Review*, February 1989, p. 19.

Maschino, M.T., 'Les Temps des commentateurs', *Quinzaine Littéraire*, no. 581, 1991, p. 22.

Matamoro, B.A., 'A Critique of *Political Economy of the Sign* by Baudrillard', *Cuadernos Hispanoamericanos*, vol. 1983, no. 394, 1983, pp. 239–40.

Mathy, J.P., 'Escape from History: How Can One Be European?', in *Extrême-Occident: French Intellectuals and America*, University of Chicago Press, 1993, pp. 224–34.

Mauhler, M.G., 'Jean Baudrillard and Television', *Filofski Vestnik*, vol. 14, no. 1, 1993.

Melaver, M., 'Heterology and the Postmodern – Bataille, Baudrillard and Lyotard by J. Pefanis', *Poetics Today*, vol. 12, no. 4, 1991, pp. 817–18.

Melber, A., 'Baudrillard: Critical and Fatal Theory by Mike Gane', *Sociology – The Journal of the British Sociological Association*, vol. 28, no. 2, 1994, pp. 614–17.

Mellancamp, P., 'Seeing is Believing – Baudrillard and Blau', *Theatre Journal*, vol. 37, no. 2, 1985, pp. 141–54.

Merrin, W., 'Uncritical Criticism? Norris, Baudrillard and the Gulf War', *Economy and Society*, 23, 1994, pp. 433–58.

Miller, J., 'Baudrillard and his Discontents', *Artscribe International*, no. 63, May 1987, pp. 48–51.

Miller, D.J., '*For a Critique of the Political Economy of the Sign* by Jean Baudrillard', *Humanities and Society*, vol. 11, no. 1, 1987, pp. 118–20.

Moore, S., 'Baudrillard – A Different Drummer?', in *Male Order: Unwrapping Masculinity*, ed. R. Chapman, London: Lawrence & Wishart, 1988, pp. 180–85.

Morris, M., 'Asleep at the Wheel', *New Statesman*, vol. 113, 26 June, 1986, pp. 28–9.

Morris, M., 'Chapter 10', in *The Pirate's Fiancée*, London: Verso, 1988.

Mourrain, J., 'The Homogenization of *America*', *Canadian Journal of Political and Social Theory*, vol. 14, no. 1–3, 1990, pp. 120–25.

Murphy, J.W., '*Baudrillard: From Marxism to Postmodernism and Beyond* by D. Kellner', *American Journal of Sociology*, vol. 96, no. 2, 1990, pp. 482–83.

Nacci, M., 'Quando il moderno non è piu di moda. *L'America* di Jean Baudrillard', *Intersezioni*, vol. 7, no. 2, pp. 379–86.

Nordquist, J., 'Social Theory: A Bibliographic Series, no. 24 – Jean Baudrillard: A Bibliography', *Reference and Research*, Santa Cruz, CA, 1991.

Norris, C., 'Lost in the Funhouse: Baudrillard and the Politics of Postmodernism', in *Postmodernism and Society*, ed. R. Boyne and A. Rattansi, Basingstoke: Macmillan, 1990, pp. 119–53. (Also in *Textual Practice*, vol. 3, no. 3, 1989, pp. 360–87.)

Norris, C., 'Baudrillard and the War that Never Happened and "Postscript"', in *Uncritical Theory: Postmodernism, Intellectuals and the Gulf War*, London: Lawrence & Wishart, 1992, pp. 11–31 and 192–96.

Norris, C., 'Consensus Reality and Manufactured Truth – Baudrillard and the War that Never Happened', *Southern Humanities Review*, vol. 26, no. 1, 1992, pp. 43–66.

Norton, J., '*America*: Jean Baudrillard', book review, *Discourse: Journal for Theoretical Studies in Media and Culture*, vol. 14, no. 3, Summer 1992, pp. 167–74. (A brief earlier version of this appeared in *Sulfur*, no. 27.)

O'Reilly J., 'The Vanishing of Jean Baudrillard', PhD thesis, University of Warwick, 1992.

O'Reilly, J., 'Turn On, Tune In And Put Your Feet Up For The Evening', *Radical Philosophy*, 68, 1994, p. 57.

O'Reilly, J., 'The Transparency of Evil by Jean Baudrillard', *Radical Philosophy*, no. 68, 1994, p. 57.

O'Reilly, J., 'Baudrillard Live', *Radical Philosophy*, no. 68, 1994, p. 57.

Panoff, M., 'Bibliographie: *Le Miroir de la production*', *Revue Française de Sociologie*, vol. 17, no. 1, 1976, pp. 117–19.

Patton, P., 'Introduction', in *The Gulf War Did Not Take Place* by Jean Baudrillard, Sydney: Power Publications, 1995, pp. 1–21.

Pefanis, J., *Heterology and the Postmodern. Bataille, Baudrillard and Lyotard*, Durham, NC and London: Duke University Press, 1991.

Philo, C., 'Baudrillard's Bestiary: *Baudrillard and Culture* by M. Gane', *Environment and Planning D: Society and Space*, vol. 10, pp. 483–85.

Poirier, R., 'America deserta', *London Review of Books*, 16 February 1989, pp. 2–4.

Poster, M., 'Translator's Introduction', in *The Mirror of Production* by Jean Baudrillard, Telos, 1975, pp. 1–15.

Poster, M., 'Semiology and Critical Theory: From Marx to Baudrillard', *Boundary*, vol. 2, no. 8, 1979.

Poster, M., 'Technology and Culture in Habermas and Baudrillard', *Contemporary Literature*, vol. 22, no. 4, 1981, pp. 456–76.

Poster, M., 'Introduction', in *Jean Baudrillard: Selected Writings*, Cambridge: Polity, 1988, pp. 1–9.

Poster, M., 'Baudrillard and TV Ads: the Language of the Economy', in *The Mode of Information: Poststructuralism and Social Context*, Cambridge: Polity, 1990, pp. 43–68.

Prévos, A., '*America* by Jean Baudrillard', *Contemporary French Civilization*, vol. 11, no. 2, 1987, pp. 258–60.

Pyke, S., 'Photograph of Jean Baudrillard', in *Philosophers*, Manchester: Cornerhouse, 1993, unpaginated.

Ratcliff, C., 'The Work of Roy Lichtenstein in the Age of Walter Benjamin's and Jean Baudrillard's Popularity', *Art in America*, vol. 77, no. 2, 1989, pp. 110–23 and p. 177.

Ree, J., 'Old Mole has Another Orgy: *The Transparency of Evil: Essays on Extreme Phenomena*', *New Statesman and Society*, 30 April 1993, p. 46.

Rejinders, F., Bloem, M. and Groot, P., 'De oorsprong van Europa de verschining van Amerika, en de verdwijning van de indian over Baudrillard en siderall Amerika', *Museum Journal*, vol. 33, no. 5–6, 1988.

Revill, D., 'Report: Jean Baudrillard', *Paragraph*, vol. 13, no. 3, 1990, pp. 263–300.

Robbins, M., 'Philosopher's Art Escapes the Duty of Reality', *The Australian*, 22 April 1994, p. 6.

Robbins, M., 'Baudrillard's Barren View of Reality', *The Australian*, 27 April 1994, p. 21.

Robins, K., 'The War, the Screen, the Crazy Dog and Poor Mankind', *Media, Culture and Society*, vol. 15, no. 2, 1993, pp. 321–27.

Roderick, R., 'Beyond a Boundary – Baudrillard and New Critical Theory', *Current Perspectives in Social Theory*, vol. 9, 1989, pp. 3–4.

Rodriguez, H., '*The Mirror of Production* – Baudrillard', *Palabra y el Hombre*, no. 48, 1983, pp. 94–96.

Rojek, C., 'Baudrillard and Leisure', *Leisure Studies*, no. 9, 1990, pp. 7–20.

Rojek, C. and Turner, B.S. (eds), *Forget Baudrillard?*, London: Routledge, 1993.

Romangé, T., '*Cool Memories* by Baudrillard', *Europe Revue Littéraire Mensuelle*, vol. 65, no. 703, 1987, pp. 210–11.

Ross, A., 'Baudrillard's Bad Attitude', in *Seduction and Theory*, ed. D. Hunter, Champaign: University of Illinois Press, 1989, pp. 214–25.

Rotman, B., 'Who is Baudrillard', *The Guardian*, 21 September 1988.

Rotman, B., 'After the Orgy is Over: *The Transparency of Evil* by Jean Baudrillard', *Times Literary Supplement*, no. 4739, 1994, p. 22.

Rubenstein, D., 'The Mirror of Reproduction – Baudrillard and Reagan's America', *Political Theory*, vol. 17, no. 4, 1989, pp. 582–606.

Ruddick, N., 'Ballard/Crash/Baudrillard', *Science Fiction Studies*, vol. 19, November 1992, pp. 354–60.

Sandywell, B., 'Forget Baudrillard', *Theory, Culture & Society*, vol. 12, no. 4, November, 1995, pp. 125–52.

Santamaria, V., 'Jean Baudrillard: Critique of a Critique', *Critique of Anthropology*, vol. 4, no. 13–14, 1979, pp. 179–95.

Sarup, M., 'Baudrillard and some cultural practices', in *An Introductory Guide to Poststructuralism and Postmodernism*, Hemel Hempstead: Harvester Wheatsheaf, 1993, pp. 161–77.

Sim, S., 'The Text Must Scoff at Meaning': Baudrillard and the Politics of Simulation and Hyperreality, in *Beyond Aesthetics: Confrontations with Poststructuralism and Postmodernism*, Hemel Hempstead: Harvester/ Wheatsheaf, 1992, pp. 118–33.

Singer, B., 'Baudrillard's Seduction', in *Ideology and Power: in the Age of Lenin in Ruins*, ed. A. and M. Kroker, Montreal: Culture Texts, 1991, pp. 139–51.

Smart, B., 'On the Disorder of Things: Sociology, Postmodernity and the "End of The Social"', contains a section entitled 'The End of the Social: Baudrillard on Sociology', *Sociology*, vol. 24, no. 3, August, 1990, pp. 397–416.

Smart, B., 'Seduction by Jean Baudrillard', *Contemporay Sociology – An International Journal of Reviews*, vol. 20, no. 3, 1991, p. 461.

Smith, E.V., 'Baudrillard: From Marxism to Postmodernism and Beyond by D. Kellner', *Sociological Inquiry*, vol. 61, no. 3, 1991, pp. 401–2.

Smith, P.J., 'Goytisolo, Juan and Baudrillard, Jean – *The Mirror of Production* and the *Death of Symbolic Exchange*', *Revista de Estudios Hispanics*, vol. 23, no. 2, 1989, pp. 37–61.

Smith, R.G., 'Baudrillard's Geographical Imagination: An Enquiry into the Space between Marxism and Poststructuralism', PhD thesis, Department of Geography, University of Bristol, England, 1995, pp. 1–343.

Smith, R.G., 'Bibliography of the Writings of Jean Baudrillard', in Baudrillard's Geographical Imagination: An Enquiry into the Space between Marxism and Poststructuralism, PhD thesis, Department of Geography, University of Bristol, England, 1995, pp. 289–304.

Smith, R.G., 'The Illusion of the End or Events on Strike by Jean Baudrillard', *Environment and Planning A*, vol. 27, no. 6, June, 1995, pp. 1018–20.

Smith, R.G., 'The End of Geography and Radical Politics in Baudrillard's Philosophy', *Environment and Planning D: Society & Space*, vol. 15, no. 3, June, 1997, pp. 305–20.

Smith, R.G., 'The Gulf War Did Not Take Place by Jean Baudrillard', *Environment and Planning A*, vol. 29, no. 5, May, 1997, pp. 946–49.

Smith, R.G., 'Cool Memories II by Jean Baudrillard', *Environment and Planning A*, vol. 29, no. 6, June, 1997, pp. 1130–31.

Sobchack, V., 'Baudrillard's Obscenity', *Science Fiction Studies*, vol. 18, November 1991, pp. 327–29.

Soja, E.W., 'Postmodern Geographies and the Critique of Historicism' (contains section entitled 'A Little Bit of Baudrillard'), in *Postmodern Contentions: Epochs, Politics, Space* ed. J.P. Jones III, W. Natter and T.R. Schotzki, Bloomington: Indiana University Press, 1992, pp. 119–20. (An extended version appears in *Thirdspace: Journeys to Los Angeles and Other Real-and-Imagined Places*, London: Blackwell, 1996, pp. 239–44.)

Sorenson, J., 'The Transparency of Evil by Jean Baudrillard', *Canadian Journal of Sociology*, vol. 20, no. 1, 1995, pp. 127–28.

Stearns, W. and Chaloupka, W. (eds), *Jean Baudrillard: The Disappearance of Art and Politics*, London: Macmillan, 1992.

Stivale, C.J., 'La Gauche Divine by Jean Baudrillard', *French Review*, vol. 60, no. 5, 1987, pp. 742–44.

Stivale, C.J., 'Baudrillard: Critical and Fatal Theory by M. Gane', *Criticism – A Quarterly for Literature and the Arts*, vol. 35, no. 2, 1993, pp. 295–98.

Swingewood, A., '*Selected Writings* by Baudrillard', *British Journal of Sociology*, vol. 41, no. 2, 1990, p. 295.

Tacconi, F., '*America* by Jean Baudrillard', *Domus*, no. 684, 1987.

Tacussel, P., 'Une Pensée crépusculaire: Jean Baudrillard', *Revue d'Esthétique*, no. 16, 1989, pp. 161–63.

Taraki, L., 'The Gulf War Did Not Take Place by Jean Baudrillard', *Contemporary Sociology – A Journal of Reviews*, vol. 26, no. 2, 1997, pp. 138–41.

Tarter, J., 'Baudrillard and the Problematics of Post-New Left Media Theory', *American Journal of Semiotics*, vol. 8, no. 4, 1991, pp. 155–71.

Taurek, B.H.F., 'Ethics beyond Morality – Sartre, Levinas, Baudrillard', *Deutsche Zeitschrift für Philosophie*, vol. 39, no. 11, 1991, pp. 1212–30.

Tester, K., 'The Illusion of the End by Jean Baudrillard', *Sociology – The Journal of the British Sociological Association*, vol. 29, no. 4, 1995, pp. 747–48.

Thackara, J., 'Jogging *Cool Memories*', *Listener*, 1 December, 1988, pp. 45–6.

Tristani, J.L., 'Jean Baudrillard, *Le système des objets*', *Cahiers Internationaux de Sociologie*, vol. 47, July–December, 1969, pp. 177–81.

Turner, B.S., 'A Note on Nostalgia', *Theory, Culture and Society*, vol. 4, 1987, pp. 147–56.

Valente, J., 'Hall of Mirrors: Baudrillard on Marx', *Diacritics*, vol. 15, no. 2, Summer 1985, pp. 54–65.

Vandergueht, D., 'The Other as Seen by Himself–Baudrillard', *Cahiers Internationaux de Sociologie*, vol. 83, July 1987, p. 428.

Vidich, A.J., 'Baudrillard's *America*: Lost in the Ultimate Simulacrum', review article, *Theory, Culture and Society*, vol. 8., no. 2, May 1991, pp. 135–44.

Vine, R., 'The "Ecstasy" of Jean Baudrillard', *New Criterion*, no. 7–9, 1989, pp. 39–48.

Wakefield, N., *Postmodernism: The Twilight of the Real*, London: Pluto, 1990.

Ward, S., 'In the shadow of the deconstructed metanarratives: Baudrillard, Latour and the end of realist epistemology', *History of the Human Sciences*, vol. 7, no. 4, pp. 73–94.

Watt, S., 'Baudrillard's *America* (and Ours?): Image, Virus, Catastrophe', in

Modernity and Mass Culture, ed. James Naremore and Patrick Bratlinger, Bloomington: Indiana University Press, 1991, pp. 135–57.

Wernick, A., 'Sign and Commodity: Aspects of the Cultural Dynamic of Advanced Capitalism', *Canadian Journal of Political and Social Theory*, vol. 8, no. 1–2, 1984, pp. 17–34, and in *Ideology and Power: in the Age of Lenin in Ruins*, ed. A. and M. Kroker, Montreal: Culture Texts, 1991, pp. 152–69.

Wernick, A., 'Post-Marx: Theological Themes in Baudrillard's *America*', in *Shadow of Spirit*, ed. Philippa Berry, New York: Routledge, 1992.

Whitehouse, I., '*Selected Writings* by Baudrillard', *Modern Languages Review*, vol. 85, October 1990, p. 989.

Wieviorka, M., 'La Société système selon Jean Baudrillard', *La Quinzaine Littéraire*, no. 55, 16–31 March, 1990, p. 25.

Wieviorka, M., '*The Transparency of Evil – Essays on the Phenomena of Extremes*', *La Quinzaine Littéraire*, no. 55, 16–31 March, 1990, p. 26.

Wilcox, L., 'Baudrillard, Delillo's *White Noise*, and the End of Heroic Narrative', *Contemporary Literature*, vol. 32, no. 3, 1991, pp. 346–65.

Zurbrugg, N., 'Baudrillard's *Amérique*, and the "Abyss of Modernity"', *Art and Text*, no. 29, 1988, pp. 40–63.

Zurbrugg, N., 'Baudrillard, Modernism and Postmodernism', *Economy and Society*, vol. 22, no. 4, November 1993, pp. 482–500.

Zurbrugg, N., "Apocalyptic'? 'Negative'? 'Pessimistic'?: Baudrillard, Virilio, and techno-culture', in *Photography Post Photography*, ed. Stuart Koop, Melbourne: Centre for Contemporary Photography, 1995, pp. 72–90.

Zurbrugg, N., 'Baudrillard and the Ambiguities of Radical Illusion', *Performance Research*, vol. 1, no. 3, 1996, pp. 1–5.

INDEX

Lightning Source UK Ltd.
Milton Keynes UK
13 January 2011